Noble Women of the North

NOBLE WOMEN
OF THE NORTH

compiled and edited by

SYLVIA G. L. DANNETT

New York • THOMAS YOSELOFF • London

© 1959 by Sagamore Press, Inc.
Library of Congress Catalogue Card Number: 58-9556

Thomas Yoseloff, *Publisher*
11 East 36th Street
New York 16, N. Y.

Thomas Yoseloff Ltd.
123 New Bond Street
London W. 1, England

Acknowledgmnts

In order to obtain material for a project such as this, the aid, the service, and the advice of many people are necessary and it is to them that I wish to express my heartfelt gratitude. Without their co-operation this book could never have been adequately completed.

Nancy Babcock, Reference Librarian, City Library, Manchester, New Hampshire.

Dorothy C. Baker, Reference Assistant, Boston Medical Library, Boston, Massachusetts.

Elizabeth Baughman, Reference Librarian, Chicago Historical Society, Chicago, Illinois.

Dorothy W. Bridgwater, Assistant Reference Librarian, Yale University, New Haven, Connecticut.

Herber O. Brigham, Librarian, Newport Historical Society, Newport, Rhode Island.

Frank R. Chase, Assistant Reference Section, Peoria Public Library, Peoria, Illinois.

W. C. Chen, Librarian, Kalamazoo College, Mandelle Memorial Library, Kalamazoo, Michigan.

Henry J. Dubester, Chief, General Reference and Bibliography Division, Library of Congress, Washington, D.C.

Anthony T. Greski, Mayor, City of Burlington, New Jersey.

Margaret Hackett, Reference Librarian, Library of the Boston Atheneum, Boston, Massachusetts.

Mary Jo Hatfield, Librarian, *The Peoria Journal Star*, Peoria, Illinois.

William Heidt, Jr., Curator, The DeWitt Historical Society of Tompkins County, Ithaca, New York.

Herbert H. Herwitt, Chief, Reference Department, Chicago Public Library, Chicago, Illinois.

5

Dr. James J. Heslin, New York Historical Society, New York, New York.

Elizabeth Hilderbrand, Head, Reference Section, Peoria Public Library, Peoria, Illinois.

Edna Huntington, Librarian, Long Island Historical Society, Brooklyn, New York.

Iowa, State Historical Department of, Des Moines, Iowa.

Iowa, State Historical Society of, Iowa City, Iowa.

Elsie M. Jones, Curator, Delaware County Historical Society, Chester, Pennsylvania.

Geneva Kebler, Research Assistant, Michigan Historical Commission, Lansing, Michigan.

Alisa Klagsbrun, Library of The Jewish Theological Seminary of America, New York, New York.

George MacBeath, Curator, Department of Canadian History, New Brunswick Museum, St. John, New Brunswick, Canada.

Frances C. Mason, Assistant, Reference Department, Public Library, Flint, Michigan.

David C. Mearns, Manuscript Division, Library of Congress, Washington, D.C.

Isidore S. Meyer, American Jewish Historical Society, New York, New York.

Max S. Miller, Publisher, *The Kansas Record*, Russell, Kansas.

Clarence M. Mitchell, Librarian, Alfred University Library, Alfred, New York.

Virginia Murphy, Reference Librarian, University of Houston, Houston, Texas.

Mrs. Edgar Nathan, Jr., Member, Jewish Historical Society of New York.

E. B. Nettleton, Guilford Public Library, Guilford, Connecticut.

New York Academy of Medicine, Fifth Avenue, New York, New York.

New York Public Library, American History Room, New York, New York.

Clement D. O'Rourke, Librarian, *Milwaukee Sentinel*, Milwaukee, Wisconsin.

William J. Petersen, Superintendent, State Historical Society of Iowa, Iowa City, Iowa.

Portchester Public Library, Portchester, New York.

Dr. C. Percy Powell, Manuscript Division, Library of Congress, Washington, D.C.

Delia H. Pugh, President, Burlington County Historical Society, Burlington, New Jersey.

Stephen T. Riley, Librarian, Massachusetts Historical Society, Boston, Massachusetts.

Rutherford D. Rogers, Chief, Reference Department, New York Public Library, New York, New York.

Charles Roos, Head, Document Section, National Library of Medicine, Washington, D.C.

Josephine W. Sale, M. D. N. Reference Librarian, Hartford Public Library, Hartford, Connecticut.

Scarsdale Public Library, Scarsdale, New York.

Congressman Fred Schwengel, Davenport, Iowa, admirer of Annie Turner Wittemyer and responsible for recovery of many of her original letters and passes.

Elleine H. Stones, Chief, Burton Historical Collection, Detroit Public Library, Detroit, Michigan.

Louise W. Turpin, Chief, History Division, Brooklyn Public Library, Brooklyn, New York.

Mary L. Ulmer, Historical Room Librarian, Houston Public Library, Houston, Texas.

Tordis O. Vatshug, Acting Head, Document Section, National Library of Medicine, Washington, D.C.

Clyde C. Walton, Illinois State Historical Society, Springfield, Illinois.

Marjorie Waterman, Chief, Reading Room, Connecticut Historical Society, Hartford, Connecticut.

Maxwell Whiteman, Assistant to the director, American Jewish Archives, Cincinnati, Ohio.

White Plains Public Library, White Plains, New York.

Glendon D. Willey, Acting Personnel Officer, Treasury Department Fiscal Service, Washington, D.C.

R. G. Wood, Chief Archivist, War Records Branch, National Archives, Washington, D.C.

Further acknowledgments for information concerning hospitals and nursing:

Cecile Covell, Assistant Director of Nursing at Columbia Presbyterian Hospital, New York, New York, at the time I was there. Also Miss Boehm and all the Floor Nurses of the Neurological Institute, Columbia Presbyterian Hospital, Seventh Floor, 1944-1946, Louise Binder, R.N.; Geraldine Bishop, R.N.; Ellen Clune, R.N.; Agnes Manacek, R.N.; Minnie Marx, R.N.; Teresa Murray, R.N.

Annie Laurie Crawford, R.N., Assistant Executive Secretary, American Nurses Association, New York City.

Dr. A. L. Garbat, Lenox Hill Hospital, New York, New York.

Ruth W. Hubbard, General Director, The Visiting Nurse Society of Philadelphia, Pennsylvania.

Emily K. Johnson, Public Relations Associate, Eastern Area, National Student Recruitment Program, New York Infirmary for Women and Children, New York, New York.

Dr. Carl Smith, New York Hospital, New York, New York.

Dr. Byron Stookey, Columbia Presbyterian Hospital, New York, New York.

H. Yvonne Ward, Assistant Executive Secretary, American Nurses Association.

And particular thanks to Valda Hancock Wagner, portrait artist, for her editorial criticism and interest.

For
EMANUEL DANNETT
my husband

Foreword

The subject of Women of the Civil War is a vast one. Long neglected by historians save for an occasional biography of such well-known women as Clara Barton, Mary Bickerdyke, and Louisa Alcott, there was an enormous amount of material to be sifted through in order to keep the book from assuming gargantuan proportions. Extensive research has uncovered not a few, but hundreds of patriotic, brave women whose deeds honored their country. They served on battlefields in the East, the West, the Southwest, and with Sherman's Army in the South.

Because the department of the East included the nation's capital where many dramatic scenes occurred, I decided to confine material in this book to that area. Where women of the West served in the East or came to Washington, Virginia, or Pennsylvania for some particular purpose, their narratives too have been included.

It required stern self-discipline to select from the thousands of heartbreaking letters, the hundreds of stirring diary entries, only those that fitted into the self-imposed restrictions—those whose names have been omitted will have to share in the reflected glory of their sisters in mercy.

SYLVIA G. L. DANNETT

Contents

Illustrations

Dramatis Personae

From the East

DR. ELIZABETH BLACKWELL, first woman doctor—head of New York Infirmary, New York, New York.

SOPHRONIA E. BUCKLIN, Auburn, New York—schoolteacher.

DOROTHEA LYNDE DIX, Hampden, Maine—social reformer.

SARAH EMMA EDMONDS (FRANKLIN THOMPSON), Flint, Michigan—Canadian-born; served with Departments of West and East.

HARRIET FOOTE HAWLEY, Guilford, Connecticut—wife of the future Governor and Senator of Connecticut.

ANNA HOLSTEIN, Philadelphia, Pennsylvania—housewife; served with her husband, WILLIAM HOLSTEIN, with the Army of the Potomac.

CHARLOTTE E. McKAY, Wakefield, Massachusetts—widow.

JOSEPHINE PHILIPS, New York, New York—"Hospital Visitor" at Jews' Hospital (Mt. Sinai), New York, New York.

MARY PHINNEY VON OLNHAUSEN, Manchester, New Hampshire —one-time designer of print goods in Manchester Print Works; widow.

LOUISA LEE SCHUYLER, New York and Dobbs Ferry, New York—socially prominent. Great granddaughter of Alexander Hamilton.

ADELAIDE W. SMITH, Brooklyn, New York.

ABBY HOWLAND WOOLSEY, CAROLINE CAISSON WOOLSEY (CARRY), ELIZA WOOLSEY (MRS. JOSEPH HOWLAND), GEORGEANNA M. WOOLSEY (GEORGY), HARRIET ROOSEVELT

21

Woolsey (Hatty), Jane Stuart Woolsey, Mary Woolsey (Mrs. Robert Howland—poetess), New York, New
York—socially prominent sisters; cousins of the tenth president of Yale College.

Jane Newton Woolsey, New York, New York—mother of the
Woolsey sisters.

Katharine P. Wormeley, Providence, Rhode Island—British-
born; social figure.

From the West

Jane C. Hoge, Chicago, Illinois—socially prominent housewife
and mother—graduate of Young Ladies' College of Philadelphia—accomplished musician—became a great humanitarian
and "defender of the downtrodden."

Mary A. Livermore, Chicago, Illinois—housewife and mother;
lecturer; formerly schoolteacher in Boston, Massachusetts.

Belle Reynolds, Peoria, Illinois—young housewife.

Julia Susan Wheelock, Kalamazoo, Michigan—schoolteacher.

Annie Turner Wittemyer, Keokuk, Iowa—widow—schoolteacher.

Some Men Of The North

Dr. Henry W. Bellows—President, United States Sanitary
Commission.

Dr. Willard Bliss—United States volunteer from Michigan.

Ambrose Burnside—military leader.

Simon Cameron; Secretary of War—appointed Dorothea Dix
as Superintendent of Women Nurses.

Admiral David Farragut—military leader.

Ulysses S. Grant—military leader.

Dr. William A. Hammond—Surgeon General of the Medical
Department.

JOSEPH HOOKER—military leader.

PHILIP KEARNY—military leader.

ABRAHAM LINCOLN—President of the United States.

GEORGE B. McCLELLAN—military leader.

FREDERICK LAW OLMSTED—General Secretary, United States Sanitary Commission.

DR. JOSEPH PARRISH—husband of Lydia—with Philadelphia Branch of the United States Sanitary Commission.

ADMIRAL DAVID DIXON PORTER—military leader.

WILLIAM T. SHERMAN—military leader.

EDWIN M. STANTON—Secretary of War.

CHARLES WILLIAM WOOLSEY—brother of the Woolsey sisters.

Time: 1861-1865

We often hear the remark that these are days that try men's souls. I think they try women's souls, too. I shall remember you and all the noble women of the North when this land is at peace.

ABRAHAM LINCOLN (*to Nurse Harriet M. Scott on his visit to Armory Square Hospital in Washington, 1865*)

Noble Women of the North

1   The Beginning of It All

THE SIEGE OF FORT SUMTER IN CHARLESTON BAY HARBOR, SOUTH Carolina, was begun two months before Lincoln was inaugurated as President. The Rebel batteries in the neighborhood of Charleston had been built and armed in the last three months of what the Woolseys called the "imbecile administration of Mr. Buchanan and his traitorous Cabinet." Major Robert Anderson and his men at the Fort, left without food or ammunition, were surrounded and besieged by Brigadier General Beauregard and his Confederate soldiers. Reinforcements were needed at the Fort, but to send them implied invasion of the South—and war.

On April 11, 1861, Anderson refused an order to surrender to General Beauregard—on April 12, the besieged Commander of Sumter received notice that Beauregard would attack the Fort. After thirty-four hours of continuous bombardment, Anderson was compelled to surrender. The last hope for peace was abandoned, and the United States became embroiled in a bloody and costly war that was to last four years.

WHAT AWFUL TIMES WE HAVE FALLEN UPON
Abby Howland Woolsey

When the members of the Woolsey family outgrew toys, they were introduced to politics. And when the Civil War broke out, the entire Woolsey family promptly enlisted. Their home at 8

29

*Brevoort Place, New York City, became a headquarters for all
the family friends and the little strong mahogany table that
their uncle had made for Charley was brought down to the parlor, bandage-roller was attached, and "for months bandage-
rolling was the family fancywork, and other festivities really
ceased."*

*The seven Woolsey girls were the daughters of Charles Wil-
liam and Jane Newton Woolsey, and first cousins once removed
of President Woolsey of Yale.* Their heritage was rich in pio-
neer spirit: several of their ancestors were founders of the country and pilgrims on the* Mayflower *and* Anne. *Their father was
drowned just before the birth of their only brother, Charles
William, and the eight children were brought up by their wid-
owed mother. Another woman might have been daunted at the
great responsibility but Jane Newton Woolsey met it with courage. Eliza was to write later, "I thank God for such a mother
and such a father and for the goodly heritage that came to us
through them."*

*Reared by a mother who hated slavery, although her ancestors
for generations had been Virginia slaveholders, the Woolseys
"walked with her in the straight path of abolitionism and would
have none of the Democratic party."*

*In 1856, when the Frémont campaigners with misguided zeal
and loud enthusiasm proposed to sing the "Pathfinder" into the
White House, the Woolseys with the many young men who
flocked to their standard sang, hour after hour, the patriotic
doggerel of the campaign song book. Many a song went hot
from No. 8 Brevoort Place, the New York home, to the campaign printing office, and was shouted at political meetings "for
an end that a merciful Providence averted."*

*In describing her family, one sister said that they had all "cut
[their] political teeth on* The New York Tribune, *and were in*

* Tenth president of Yale College.

the right frame of mind to keep step with the steady march to the inevitable through the Kansas perplexities, the John Brown raid, and the election of Mr. Lincoln, to the firing of the first gun by the Rebels upon the national flag at Fort Sumter."

It is not surprising to find, therefore, that the seven girls and their brother, imbued with this strong feeling of patriotism, entered into the service of their country at the very outset of the War. Four of the girls enlisted as nurses and served on hospital transports with the Army of the Potomac, in field hospitals at the front, and in army hospitals in Washington, D.C., and Rhode Island. Jane Newton Woolsey did her share of service, flitting back and forth among her brood from New York to Washington to Fishkill, where daughter Eliza Woolsey Howland had her home. Charles William entered the 164th New York Regiment, and was immediately assigned as aide-de-camp at army headquarters.

Through journals, through newspaper articles, and through family letters we get a graphic picture of the effect of the outbreak of the war on the life of a patriotic, philanthropic American family and on their home town, New York City.

In this letter Abby writes her sister in Fishkill of the situation in New York City after the shocking firing on Fort Sumter.

8 Brevoort Place, New York,
April 14, 1861.

What awful times wc have fallen upon! The sound last night of the newsboys crying till after midnight with hoarse voice, "Bombardment of Fort Sumter," was appalling. Cousin William Aspinwall was seen at a late hour going into the Brevoort House—no doubt to give what little comfort he could to Mrs. Anderson. This storm, which has been raging a day or two at the South, and has just reached us, has scattered the fleet sent to reinforce and provision Fort Sumter, and the vessels can neither rendezvous nor co-operate with Major Anderson who is there without food, without help, and without instructions. Is Providence against us too?

The city is like a foreign one now; the flag floats from every public building and nearly every shop displays some patriotic emblem. Jane amused herself in shopping yesterday, by saying to everyone: "You have no flag out yet! Are you getting one ready?" etc.

Shopkeepers said in every instance: "No—well—we mean to have one: we are having one prepared," etc. She met Mr. Charles Johnson, of Norwich, who had been down to see the Massachusetts contingent off—a splendid set of men—hardy farmers, sailors from Marblehead, some in military hats, some in fatigue caps, some few in slouched felts—all with the army over-coat. C. J. had a talk with some of them in their New England vernacular, which he described as very funny, ". . . thought there might be some fightin', but by golly! There's one thing we want to do—a lot of us—just pitch into an equal number of South Carolinas." C. J. says a few gentlemen in Norwich came in to the Norwich Bank to his father and authorized him to offer Governor Buckingham $137,000 as a private subscription. This is beside the $100,000 offered by the other bank, the Thames.

Yesterday Mother and I went round to see Mary Carey, who was out, but seeing policemen about the door of the Brevoort House, colors flying, and a general look of expectancy on the faces of people in opposite windows, we hung round and finally asked what was going on? "Why, nothing, Ma'am, only Major Anderson has just arriv'." Sure enough, he had driven up rapidly, reported himself at General Scott's headquarters, and then driven round to the hotel. In five minutes the crowd on foot had got wind of it and came surging up Eighth Street with the Jefferson Guard, or something of the sort—a mounted regiment—

who wished to give the Major a marching salute. Band playing, colors flying, men's voices cheering lustily, and everywhere hats tossed up and handkerchiefs waving—it was an enthusiastic and delightful tribute! We clung to an iron railing inside an adjoining courtyard and, safe from the crush of the crowd, waved our welcome with the rest and saw Major Anderson come out, bow with military precision several times, and then retire. He looked small, slender, old, wrinkled, and grey, and was subdued and solemn in manner. Charley Johnson was on hand, of course—he is up to everything—and later in the day pressed his way in with some ladies, shook hands impressively and prayed, "God bless you, Sir!" "I trust he will!" said Major Anderson, and expressed himself honored by the interest felt in him. Our Charley went round in the evening, found Mr. Aspinwall in close conversation with the Major in the parlor, but not liking to intrude, looked his fill at him through the crack of the door.

Yesterday was "one of the days" in 10th Street—a steady stream of people all day. While Mother and I went out for a few calls and had our little adventure, as above described, Jane took a short constitutional. C. Johnson, whom she met, gave her a flag, and as she walked up Broadway a large omnibus with six horses passed, gaily decked with flags and filled with gentlemen—some delegation—going to wait on Major Anderson as they supposed. Jane said she could not help giving her flag a little twirl—not daring to look to the right or left—and instantly the whole load of men broke out into vociferous cheers. They tell us that quantities of Union cockades were worn in the streets yesterday, and I should not be surprised if they should become universally popular. Just at dusk Will Winthrop came in to say good-bye. To our immense surprise, he said he and Theodore joined the Seventh Regiment a week ago—he as a

private in the ranks and Theodore in the artillery in charge of
a howitzer—and they were all to leave this afternoon for Washington. It seemed to bring war nearer home to us. Mother was
quite concerned, but I cannot but feel that the Seventh Regiment is only wanted there for the moral influence. It will act
as guard of honor to the Capitol and come home in a fortnight.
However, the demand for troops in Washington is very urgent.
They are telegraphing here for all the regular officers. Even
Colonel Ripley, the Denny's cousin, who arrived on government
business yesterday on his way to Springfield, was overtaken by
a telegram as he took his seat in the New Haven train and
ordered back by night train to Washington. Other men received similar dispatches, and the idea is that Washington may
be attacked at once now that Virginia is gone out, and the fear
is that if done this week it may be taken. Troops are hurrying
on. The Rhode Island contingent passed down at nine this
morning, the Seventh goes at three—that will be a grand scene!
We shall be somewhere on Broadway to see them pass. Georgy
has been busy all the morning cutting up beef sandwiches and
tying them up in white papers as rations. Each man tonight
must take his supply with him for twenty-four hours, and Theodore Winthrop, who was in last night, suggested that we should
put up "something for him and Billy in a newspaper." The
Seventh is likely to have more than it needs in that way; it is
being greatly pampered; but it all helps to swell the ardor of
those who stay behind, I suppose. The more troops who can
be sent off to Washington, the less chance for fighting. The
immensity of our preparations may overawe the South. Last
night we had rather jolly times, joking and telling war anecdotes,
and worked ourselves up into a very merry cheerful spirit. It is
well that we can sometimes seize on the comic points of the
affair or we should be overwhelmed by the dreadful probabilities.

THE SOUTHERN PRESS BLAZED WITH HATRED OF THE NORTH

Mary A. Livermore

Mary Livermore was endowed with an almost phenomenal capacity for work. She was her own housekeeper, directed her servants, gave personal supervision to the education and training of her children, and entertained her husband's patrons and friends "as circumstances demanded," in addition to her position of co-editor of her husband's weekly newspaper.

This energetic, ambitious daughter of Timothy Rice and Zebiah Vose Ashton, was the fourth in a family of six children— two boys and four girls. She was born on December 19, 1820, on Salem Street at the north end of Boston, which was then a city of not more than forty thousand. The Rice home was "eminently and severely religious," and it is possible that this early training gave Mary a self-discipline that was to help her in her future work. As soon as the Rice children were able to walk they were taken to church, where their father made certain that strict attention was paid to the services. If Mary was so much as caught nodding, her father's "red bandanna handkerchief came flirting down the pew so skillfully that it gave me a little slap in the face, waking me like the blast of a trumpet."

At the age of fourteen, Mary graduated from the Hancock School for Boys and Girls and received one of the six medals annually awarded to girls for good scholarship and good behavior. After this, her future "seemed to hang in the balance." It was here that the independence and initiative Mary was to display later first asserted itself. Too impatient to await her father's "slow decision concerning the next step" in her training, Mary took a job with a dressmaker in the neighborhood. At the end of her apprenticeship she presented her mother with a dress purchased with her earnings.

At last it was decided that Mary should enter the Female Seminary at Charlestown (later included within the limits of Boston), to pursue a regular course of study. Mary wrote of this later: "It was the happiest moment I had ever known when I found myself inducted into the studious life of the seminary." She accomplished in two years "the course that was laid out for four," and was elected to the Board of Instruction as teacher of Latin, French, and Italian.

The death of a favorite sister left Mary brokenhearted. She decided to accept an invitation to teach the children of a family in Virginia "to get away from surroundings which continually recalled the tragedy through which I had passed." Despite her father's disapproval—he believed a daughter's place was with her parents—Mary began her "preparations for the journey and three years' absence immediately and with clandestine haste." Up to the last moment she expected her father to prevent her departure. Instead, he kissed her tenderly, reminding her not to forget she had a father's house always open to her.

Mary was brought face to face with slavery at the Henderson plantation in Virginia. She witnessed outrages "inflicted on the poor blacks" which she called "deeds of barbarism," and commented on the "brutalizing effect of slavery on the owners, even those who had the finest character." Mary returned to the North a radical Abolitionist, and identified herself with movements that opposed all forms of oppression.

On May 7, 1845, Mary Rice married the Reverend Daniel Parker Livermore, who had been her "teacher and guide in matters of religion." In 1857, the Livermores moved to Chicago, Illinois, where Mr. Livermore became proprietor and editor of The New Covenant, the Universalist paper of the Northwest, and a small publishing house and book store connected with it. Mary became her husband's associate editor, and at the con-

vention in the Chicago Wigwam in 1860, where Abraham Lincoln was nominated for the presidency, she was the only woman reporter present.

When the Civil War "burst in fury on the land" Mary Livermore was in her native state and gives a vivid picture of the effect of the War on Boston.

The opening of the War of the Rebellion found me in Boston, my native city. My own home had been in Chicago for years, but my aged father was thought to be dying, and the stern speech of the telegram had summoned me to his bedside. It was a time of . . . unconcealed anxiety. The Southern press blazed with hatred of the North, and with fierce contempt for her patience and her avowed desire for peace. Northern men and women were driven from Southern homes, leaving behind all their possessions, and thankful to escape with life. . . .

Monday dawned, April 15. Who that saw that day will ever forget . . . the voice of Abraham Lincoln calling for seventy-five thousand volunteers for three months! They were for the protection of Washington and the property of the government. All who were in arms against the country were commanded to return home in twenty days, and Congress was summoned to meet on the 4th of July.

This proclamation was like the first peal of a surcharged thunder-cloud, clearing the murky air. The South received it as a declaration of war, the North as a confession that civil war had begun; and the whole North arose as one man. . . .

Everywhere the drum and fife thrilled the air with their stirring call. Recruiting offices were opened in every city, town, and village. . . . Hastily formed companies marched to camps of rendezvous, the sunlight flashing from gun-barrel and bayonet, and the streets echoing the measured tread of soldiers. Flags floated from the roofs of houses, were flung to the breeze from chambers of commerce and boards of trade, spanned the surging streets, decorated the private parlor, glorified the schoolroom, festooned the church walls and pulpit, and blossomed everywhere. All normal habits of life were suspended, and business and pleasure alike were forgotten. . . .

When, on the morning of Tuesday, volunteers began to arrive in Boston, Faneuil Hall, the old Cradle of Liberty, was opened for their accommodation. As they marched from the railroad stations, they were escorted by crowds cheering. . . . Merchants and clerks rushed out from stores, bareheaded, saluting them as they passed. Windows were flung up; and women leaned out into the rain, waving flags and handkerchiefs. Horsecars and omnibuses halted for the passage of the soldiers, and cheer upon cheer leaped forth from the thronged doors and windows. The multitudes that followed after, and surged along on either side, and ran before in dense and palpitating masses, rent the air with prolonged acclamations.

As the men filed into Faneuil Hall, in solid columns, the enthusiasm knew no bounds. Men, women, and children seethed in a fervid excitement. . . . I saw the dear banner of my country, rising higher and higher to the top of the flagstaff, fling out fold after fold to the damp air, and float proudly over the hallowed edifice. Oh, the roar that rang out from ten thousand throats! Old men, with white hair and tearful faces, lifted their hats to the national ensign, and reverently saluted it. Young men greeted it with fierce and wild hurrahs. . . .

I had never seen anything like this before. I had never dreamed that New England, slow to wrath, could be fired with so warlike a spirit. Never before had the national flag signified anything to me. But as I saw it now, kissing the skies, all that it symbolized as representative of government and emblematic of national majesty became clear to my mental vision.

By six o'clock on that afternoon of Tuesday, April 16, three regiments were ready to start for Washington, and new companies were being raised in all parts of the state. On the afternoon of the next day the Sixth Massachusetts, a full regiment one thousand strong, started from Boston by rail, leaving the Fourth Massachusetts to follow.

An immense concourse of people gathered in the neighborhood of the Boston and Albany railroad station to witness their departure. The great crowd was evidently under the influence of deep feeling, but it was repressed, and the demonstrations were not noisy. In all hands were evening editions of the daily papers; and as the record of the disloyal behavior of Maryland and Virginia was read aloud, the comments were emphatic in disapproval. With the arrival of the uniformed troops, the excitement burst out into a frenzy of shouts, cheers, and ringing acclamation. Tears ran down not only the cheeks of women, but those of men; but there was no faltering. A clergyman mounted an extemporized platform, to offer prayer, where he could be seen and heard by all, and a solemn hush fell on the excited multitude. . . . His voice rang out to the remotest auditor. The long train backed down where the soldiers were scattered among mothers, wives, sweethearts, and friends uttering last words of farewell.

"Fall into line!" was the unfamiliar order that rang out, clear and distinct, with a tone of authority. The blue-coated soldiers released themselves tenderly from the clinging arms of affection, kissed again, and again, and again, the faces upturned to theirs, white with the agony of parting, formed in long lines, company by company, and were marched into the cars. The two locomotives, drawing the long train slowly out of the station, whistled a shrill "good-bye"—every engine in the neighborhood shrieked back an answering farewell—from the crowded streets, the densely packed station, the roofs of houses, the thronged windows, and the solid mass of human beings lining both sides of the track, farther than the eye could see, there rang out a roar of good wishes, and parting word, accompanied with tears and sobs, and the waving of hats and handkerchiefs—and the Sixth Massachusetts was on its way to Washington. Ah, how little they, or we, foresaw the reception awaiting them in the streets of Baltimore!

NEW YORK IS ALL ON ONE SIDE NOW

Jane Stuart Woolsey

Jane Stuart Woolsey gives her impressions of early scenes in Washington and New York in the first weeks of the war.

8 Brevoort Place, New York,
April, 1861.

The three great local incidents this week have been the arrival of Major Anderson, the leaving of the 7th Regiment, and the great mass meeting today in Union Square, or rather whose centre was Union Square, for the huge sea of men overflowed the quadrangle of streets where the speakers' stands were, and surged down Broadway, up Broadway, through Fourteenth Street and along Fourth Avenue far beyond the Everett House. We were in a balcony at the corner of Union Square and Broadway and saw the concourse, though we could not distinguish the words of any speaker. We could only tell when the "points" were made by the thousands of hats lifted and swung in the air and by the roar of the cheering. Every house fronting the square, and up and down the side streets, was decorated with flags and festoons, and the Sumter flag, on its splintered staff, hung over the stand where the gentlemen of the Sumter command were.

The Puritan Church had a great banner afloat on its tower. Trinity set the example to the churches yesterday, when a magnificent flag was raised on its tall spire with a salvo of artillery. The sight was a grand one today, and in some of its features peculiar. As the tide rolled up under our balcony we could see scarcely a man who was not earnest-looking, grave, and resolved, and all seemed of the best classes, from well-dressed gentlemen down to hard-working, hard-fisted draymen and hod-carriers, but no lower. There was not a single intoxicated man as far as we could see, or a single one trying to make any disturbance or dissent. You will see by the reports of the meeting who were the officers, speakers, etc., and judge how all colors of opinion were represented and were unanimous. New York, at any rate, is all on one side now—all ready to forget lesser differences, like the household into which grief has entered. Almost every individual, man, woman, and child, carried the sacred colors in some shape or other, and the ladies at the windows had knots of ribbon, tricolored bouquets, and flags without number. There was not a policeman to be seen from our outlook, though no doubt there were some about the square, but the crowd kept itself in order and perfect good nature, and whenever the flag appeared at the head of any procession or deputation it fell back instantly and respectfully to let it pass through. The resolutions, Committee for Patriotic Fund, etc., you will see in the papers.

I have given the first place to the meeting because it was the most recent, but yesterday was a more exciting and saddening day than this. Beside Meredith Howland, Captain Schuyler Hamilton, Howland Robbins, and other friends and acquaintances in the "Seventh," our two cousins Theodore and William Winthrop went. All these are privates except Merry, who is on the staff—Paymaster. The Winthrops came in their accoutrements at one o'clock to get their twenty-four hours' rations (sandwiches which Georgy had been making all morning), and we filled their cases and liquor flasks, with great satisfaction that we were able to do even such a little thing for them. We gave them a hearty "feed," buckled knapsack straps for them, and sent them off with as cheerful faces as we could command. They were in excellent spirits, on the surface at any rate, and promised to come back again in glory in a little while. We in our turn promised to go down to them if they needed us. Poor fellows! It was heart-sickening to think of any such necessity. Then we went down to a balcony near Prince street in Broadway, and saw them off. The whole street was densely crowded, as today, and the shops and houses decorated—only there were three miles of flags and people. After long waiting we began to see in the distance the glimmer of the bayonets. Then the immense throng divided and pressed back upon the sidewalks, and the regiment came—first the Captain of Police with one aid, then the Artillery corps, then company after company, in solid march, with fixed faces, many of them so familiar, so pleasant, and now almost sacred. The greeting of the people was a thing to see! The cheers were almost like a cannonade. People were leaning forward, shouting, waving handkerchiefs, crying, praying aloud, and one block took up the voice from the other and continued the long, long cry of sympathy and blessing through the entire route. Some friends of the soldiers who marched all the way with them to the Jersey cars said the voice never ceased, never diminished, till they reached the end of that first triumphal stage of their journey. It was a triumph though a farewell. At Ball and Black's Major Anderson was in the balcony with Cousin John's and Cousin William Aspinwall's families, and each company halted and cheered him as it passed. Except for this, they looked neither right nor left, but marched as if at that moment they were marching into the thick of battle. They were not long in passing, and the crowd closed in upon them like a parted sea. We watched the bayonets as far and long as we could see them, and the last we saw was a late warm beam of sunshine touching the colors as they disappeared.

Great anxiety is felt tonight about their arrival in Washington and what they may meet there. Many gentlemen here think the forces in the District quite inadequate and blame anybody and everybody for not hurrying on more troops. A gentleman was here late this afternoon looking for Cousin William Aspinwall. They were hunting him up everywhere where there was any chance of his being found, to make instant arrangements for steam vessels to take reinforcements tomorrow. Several regiments are ready, only waiting orders and means of transit. Uncle Edward came to the meeting today—very grave indeed—and I don't doubt very efficient and open-handed as usual, in anything that needed his help. He has ordered a great flag for the "barrack." Joe has set one flying from his house-top. He (J. H.) has joined a cavalry company in Fishkill who are drilling for a Home Guard or a "reserve." Charley has joined a similar company (foot) in town. He is uneasy and wants to "do something." Uncle Edward says: "Stay at home, my boy, till you're wanted, and if the worst comes to the worst, I'll shoulder a musket myself!"

Major Anderson was the hero of Cousin Anna's party last night. Only Charley represented us; we didn't feel "up to it." C. said it was a very handsome party, as usual with their entertainments, and that a portrait of Major Anderson was hung in the picture gallery, wreathed with laurel, and all the *Baltic's* flags decorated the hall and supper room. Thirty of the expected guests had marched at four o'clock with the 7th. Major Anderson is very grave, almost sad, in expression and manner, as a man may well be who has been through such scenes and looks with a wise eye into such a future; but if anything could cheer a man's soul it would be such enthusiasm and almost love as are lavished on him here. He says "they had not had a biscuit to divide among them for nearly two days, and were almost suffocated." They say he talks very little about it all; only gives facts in a few modest words. He is "overwhelmed" with the sight of the enthusiasm and unanimity of the North; "the South has no idea of it at all." He says that he "felt very much aggrieved at being attacked at such disadvantage"; that "for four weeks he only received *one* message from government, and was almost broken down with suspense, anxiety, and ignorance of what was required of him." He went to all the stands today at the mass-meeting, and was received with a fury of enthusiasm everywhere. Yesterday he was obliged to leave the balcony at Ball and Black's, the excitement and applause were so overpowering; and he goes about with tears in his eyes all the time. . . .

I have been writing while the others have gone to the Philharmonic concert. They have come back and had a splendid scene at the close—singing of "The Star-Spangled Banner," solo, and chorus by the Liederkranz and the whole huge audience, standing, to the hundred stringed and wind instruments of the orchestra, while a great silken banner was slowly unrolled from the ceiling to the floor. Then followed rounds of vociferous applause, and three times three for everything good, especially for Major Anderson, and the 7th.

The Massachusetts contingent passed through on Thursday, and then we got the news of the cowardly assault in Baltimore.* The poor fellows tasted war very soon. Tonight the city is full of drum-beating, noise, and shouting, and they are crying horrible extras, full of malicious falsehoods (we hope). G. G., we hear, is going from home to his Mother's and back again, all the evening, contradicting them. There should be authentic

---

* The Sixth Massachusetts, crossing Baltimore to the Washington depot, were set upon by a furious mob of roughs and pelted with stones and brickbats. Two soldiers were killed and eight wounded, and the troops forming in solid square with fixed bayonets at last forced their way through the crowds.

news by this time of the progress of the 7th, but people will not believe these horrible rumors, and refuse to believe anything.

There is the most extraordinary mixture of feeling with everyone—so much resistless enthusiasm and yet so much sadness for the very cause that brings it out. It seems certainly like a miracle, this fresh and universal inspiration of patriotism surmounting the sorrow, like a fire kindled by God's own hand from His own altar—and this alone ought to inspire us with hope of the future.

And later Jane wrote to a friend in Paris:

We all have views now, men, women, and little boys,
       Children with drums
  Strapped round them by the fond paternal ass,
  Peripatetics with a blade of grass
       Betwixt their thumbs,

from the modestly patriotic citizen who wears a postage stamp on his hat to the woman who walks on Broadway in that fearful object of contemplation, a "Union bonnet," composed of alternate layers of red, white, and blue, with streaming ribbons "of the first." We all have our views of the war question and our plans of the coming campaign. An acquaintance the other day took her little child on some charitable errand through a dingy alley into a dirty, noisy, squalid tenement house. "Mamma," said he, "isn't this South Carolina?"

Inside the parlor windows the atmosphere has been very fluffy, since Sumter, with lint-making and the tearing of endless lengths of flannel and cotton bandages and cutting out of innumerable garments. How long it is since Sumter! I suppose it is because so much intense emotion has been crowded into the last two or three weeks that the "time before Sumter" seems to belong to some dim antiquity. It seems as if we never were alive till now; never had a country till now. How could we ever have laughed at Fourth-of-Julys? Outside the parlor windows the city is gay and brilliant with excited crowds, the incessant movement and music of marching regiments and all the thousands of flags, big and little, which suddenly came fluttering out of every window and door and leaped from every church tower, housetop, staff, and ship-mast. It seemed as if everyone had in mind to try and make some amends to it for those late grievous and bitter insults. You have heard how the enthusiasm has been deepening and widening from that time.

A friend asked an Ohio man the other day how the West was taking it. "The West" he said, "the West is all one great Eagle-scream!" A New England man told us that at Concord the bells were rung and the President's call was read aloud on the village common. On the day but one after that reading, the Concord Regiment was marching into Fanueil Hall. Somebody in Washington asked a Massachusetts soldier: "How many more men of your state are coming?" "All of us," was the answer. One of the wounded Lowell men crawled into a machine shop in Baltimore. An "anti-Gorilla" * citizen, seeing how young he was, asked, "What brought you here fighting, so far away from your home, my poor boy?" "It was the stars and stripes," the dying voice said. Hundreds of such stories are told. Everybody knows one. You read many of them in the papers. In our own little circle of friends one mother has sent away an idolized son; another, two; another, four. One boy, just getting over diphtheria, jumps out of bed and buckles his knapsack on. One throws up his passage to Europe and takes up his "Enfield." One sweet young wife is packing a regulation valise for her husband today, and doesn't let him see her cry. Another young wife is looking fearfully for news from Harper's Ferry, where her husband is ordered. He told me a month ago, *before Sumter,* that no Northman could

* That was the newspaper's way of spelling "Guerrilla."

be found to fight against the South. One or two of our soldier friends are surgeons or officers, but most of them are in the ranks, and think no work too hard or too mean, so it is for The Flag. Captain Schuyler Hamilton was an aid of General Scott's in Mexico, and saw service there, but he shouldered his musket and marched as a private with the 7th. They wanted an officer when he got down there, and took him out of the ranks, but it was all the same to him; and so on, indefinitely. . . .

We women regretfully "sit at home at ease" and only appease ourselves by doing the little we can with sewing machines and patent bandage-rollers. Georgy, Miss Sarah Woolsey * and half a dozen other friends earnestly wish to join the Nurse Corps, but are under the required age. The rules are stringent, no doubt wisely so, and society just now presents the unprecedented spectacle of many women trying to make it believed that they are over thirty!

The Vermont boys passed through this morning, with the "strength of the hills" in their marching and the green sprigs in their button-holes. the other day I saw some companies they told me were from Maine. They looked like it—sun-browned swingers of great axes, horn-handed "breakers of the glebe," used to wintering in the woods and getting frostbitten and having their feet chopped off and conveying huge fleets of logs down spring-tide rivers in the snow and in the floods.—The sound of the drum is never out of our ears.

Never fancy that we are fearful or gloomy. We think we feel thoroughly that war is dreadful, especially war with the excitement off and the chill on, but there are so many worse things than gun-shot wounds! And among the worst is a hateful and hollow peace with such a crew as the "Montgomery mutineers." There was a dark time just after the Baltimore murders, when communication with Washington was cut off and the

* A cousin.

people in power seemed to be doing nothing to re-establish it.
It cleared up, however, in a few days, and now we don't feel
that the "social fabric"—I believe that is what it is called—is
"falling to pieces" at all, but that it is getting gloriously mended.
So, "Republicanism will wash"—is washed already in the water
and the fire of this fresh baptism, "clothed in white samite,
mystic, wonderful," and has a new name, which is *Patriotism.* . . .

WHAT PART DO I PLAY IN THIS GREAT DRAMA?

Sarah Emma Edmonds

*Sarah Emma Edmonds rendered a dual service during the
Civil War, as nurse and spy, and played a dual role, first as a
man and then as a woman.*

*A Canadian by birth, the incredible Emma did not have to
take part in the great conflict, but with a great loyalty for her
adopted country and a religious fervor that is consistently evident in her own book, she thanked God that she was permitted
"in this hour of my adopted country's need" to express a little
of the gratitude that she felt for the people of the United States.
In addition to possessing this noble motive she no doubt
couldn't resist what promised, and certainly turned out to be,
a highly adventurous experience fraught with great danger and
responsibility.*

*If trousers were suitable for a job as book agent, they were
certainly preferable to a calico skirt on the battlefield and, in
the role of Franklin Thompson, Emma Edmonds marched and
fought and lived in an army of men for more than two years
without having her true sex discovered.*

Sarah Emma Edmonds was born in 1841, in Salisbury, New

Brunswick, Canada. *There were already three girls in the Edmonds family and just one boy. Since Farmer Edmonds had wanted only male progeny to begin with he considered the advent of Sarah Emma a cruel act of Providence. The girl was made aware of her father's antagonism and developed an aversion toward men. However she sought the companionship of her brother. Emma manifested boyish traits at an early age. She tamed colts, went hunting, swam, and rode horseback, while rebelling all the while against the "restraits that were imposed on the women of her day."*

Emma Edmonds was independent as well as energetic, and while still in her teens became a partner of Miss Henrietta Perrige in a millinery store in Moncton. At this point her father, who appears to have been an extreme Victorian, arranged for "his still unwanted daughter's marriage" to a man that she clearly detested. One night, when she should have been checking the contents of her hope chest, Emma Edmonds, disguised as a boy, climbed out her bedroom window and escaped. This escapade is said to have been inspired by the first novel she ever read, Fanny Campbell, the Female Sailor, *in which the heroine disguises herself as a boy to rescue her lover from pirates.*

Emma Edmonds must have had tongue firmly in cheek when she wrote in her reminiscences* that her purpose in coming to the United States had been to study for the foreign missionary service. In any event, she next turned up as Franklin Thompson a book agent for a Connecticut publishing house, and finally went west to represent the firm in Flint, Michigan, where she was looked upon by her friends in the community as a "good looking, likable, successful young man, who made money, dressed well, drove his own horse and buggy, and had many 'lady friends.'"

---

* Later Emma was to admit to inaccuracies in her early published reminiscences.

When the Civil War broke out, Emma Edmonds, then twenty years old, went to Washington to become a nurse. Since she was playing the role of a young man she had no difficulty "in joining up."

Early in the spring of 1861, I was returning from the far West and as I sat waiting for the train which was to bear me to my adopted home in New England, and was meditating upon the events which had transpired during the past few months, the record of which was destined to blacken the fair pages of American history, I was aroused from my reverie by a voice in the street crying *"New York Herald*—Fall of Fort Sumter—President's Proclamation—call for seventy-five thousand men!" This announcement startled me, while my imagination portrayed the coming struggle in all its fearful magnitude. War, civil war, with all its horrors seemed inevitable, and even then was ready to burst like a volcano upon the most happy and prosperous nation the sun ever shone upon. The contemplation of this sad picture filled my eyes with tears and my heart with sorrow.

It is true, I was not an American—I was not obliged to remain here during this terrible strife—I could return to my native land where my parents would welcome me to the home of my childhood, and my sisters would rejoice at my coming. But these were not the thoughts which occupied my mind. It was not my intention, or desire, to seek my own personal ease and comfort while so much sorrow and distress filled the land. But the great question to be decided was, what can I do? What part am *I* to act in this great drama? I was not able to decide for myself—so I carried this question to the Throne of Grace, and found a satisfactory answer there.

Ten days after the President's proclamation was issued, I was ready to start for Washington,* having been employed by the

* Emma was actually mustered in on May 25, 1861.

Government, and furnished with all the necessary equipments.
I was not merely to go to Washington and remain there until
a battle had been fought and the wounded brought in, and
then in some comfortable hospital sit quietly and fan the
patients, after the Surgeon had dressed their wounds; but I was
to go to the front and participate in all the excitement of the
battle scenes, or in other words, be a *Field Nurse.*

The great West was stirred to its center, and began to look
like a vast military camp. Recruiting offices were filled with men
eager to enroll their names as defenders of their country—and
women were busily engaged in preparing all the comforts that
love and patriotism could suggest for those who were so soon
to go forth to victory or to death, while the clash of arms and
strains of martial music almost drowned the hum of industry,
and war became the theme of every tongue.

About this time I witnessed the departure of the first Western troops which started for Washington. The regiments were
drawn up in line—fully equipped for their journey—with their
bright bayonets flashing in the morning sunlight. It was on the
principal street of a pleasant little village of about a thousand
inhabitants, where there was scarcely a family who had not a
father, husband, son, or brother in that little band of soldiers
who stood there ready to bid them farewell, perhaps for years—
perhaps forever. A farewell address was delivered by the village
Pastor, and a New Testament presented to each soldier, with
the following inscription: "Put your trust in God—and keep
your powder dry." Then came the leave-taking—but it is too
painful to dwell upon—the last fond word was spoken, the last
embrace given, then came the order, "march"—and amid the
cheers of the citizens—with banners proudly floating, and the
bands playing "The Star Spangled Banner," they moved forward on their way to the Capital. On looking back now upon
the scenes of that morning, notwithstanding I have looked upon

others much more thrilling since then, yet I cannot recall that
hour without feelings of deep emotion. While I stood there
and beheld those manly forms convulsed with emotion, and
heard the sobs of those whom they were leaving behind, I
could only thank God that I was free and could go forward and
work, and was not obliged to stay at home and weep. A few
hours more, and I, too, was on my way to Washington.

When I reached Baltimore I found the city in an uproar—
mobs were gathered in the streets and the utmost excitement
prevailed: and as the crowded cars moved through the city toward the depot, the infuriated mob threw showers of stones,
brickbats, and other missiles, breaking the windows and wounding some of the soldiers. Some of the men could not forbear firing into the crowd—notwithstanding their orders to the contrary
—however, it had a good effect, for the mob soon dispersed;
they probably had not forgotten the Sixth Massachusetts and
the Pennsylvania troops which had passed through a short
time before. The cars soon reached the depot, and started immediately for Washington—where we arrived in due time—
weary, and in great need of food and sleep.

2 The Call for Women

WITH THE FIRING OF THE FIRST GUN AT SUMTER THE POSITION OF women in America underwent a radical change. Old prejudices and restrictions against them were soon to be swept aside to meet the great exigencies of war. Votaries of the feminist ideas of Susan B. Anthony, Lucretia Mott, and other leaders of the woman's suffrage movement, who had been fighting for their political and legal, and professional independence, now found a new and welcome outlet for expressing their patriotic zeal.

At home, women became busily engaged in preparing all the comforts for the boys in blue. Around the evening lamp one member of the family read aloud the latest news from the seat of war, as old and young prepared lint, others knit stockings, some capped with a rim of our national colors, and others cut out and put together that monstrosity, the havelock, that easy mark for the enemy's riflemen. Then to piano accompaniment the young people might give a rattling chorus of *John Brown's Body, Tenting Tonight*, or some other war songs. Many sewing bees were instituted, and in home kitchens many a delicacy was prepared. In early December, Christmas boxes were made up of all kinds of dainties to send to the army. Obliging patriotic shopkeepers would succumb to winsome smiles, and duly add to the holiday contributions.

The pupils of the Wesleyan Female College at Cincinnati knitted a hundred pairs of socks. Appended to the package were these words: "Assure our brave men that gratitude to them mingles with our desire to serve our country." A Mrs. Frazer of

Duxbury, Massachusetts, knitted continuously, and might be said literally to have taken up the thread of history, as eighty-five years before she had knitted stockings for the soldiers of the Revolution. Mary Henderson of Indiana, an aged blind woman, in November, 1861, knitted a dozen pairs of socks out of yarn she twisted herself on her old-time spinning wheel.

Innumerable relief societies sprang up, many under religious auspices: the Christian Commission that sent agents to various field hospitals, and the Hebrew Ladies' Soldiers' Aid Society that sewed garments, wrapped bandages, and packed food cartons at home. There were relief organizations in Boston, Cincinnati, Chicago, and Philadelphia, and before long almost every city was able to boast of a relief organization of its own.

Private hospitals offered their services and facilities to the army. St. Luke's and the Jews' Hospital in New York volunteered to provide complete care for the wounded, including medical aid, supplies, food, and entertainment. Young ladies of the community sat at the bedsides of the soldiers and read to them. Wealthy women called for ambulatory cases in their carriages and took them for drives in Central Park.

But while women were needed on the home front to organize and administer relief societies, it became more and more apparent that they were needed in the field. In her new capacity as field worker, lecturer and, above all, hospital nurse, woman achieved a modicum of independence.

Ten days after Fort Sumter fell, quiet, determined, forty-year-old Dr. Elizabeth Blackwell, the first woman in the world to be given a degree as doctor of medicine, felt that something had to be done about America's deplorable nursing situation. In the spring of 1861, the United States Army still had no general hospital. There were only military and post hospitals, the largest containing forty beds. There was no trained, efficient medical staff. There were no female nurses at all, and the male nurses, generally convalescent soldiers, had little or no instruction and often required nursing themselves. There was no sick-diet kitchen, no prompt supply of medicines and no means of humanely transporting the sick and wounded. The military and medical systems were created entirely in the very midst of the war.

In the municipal hospitals, such as Bellevue in New York and Old Blockley in Philadelphia, patients were cared for by convalescents or poorly paid and generally incompetent attendants who were often vicious and ignorant. Prisoners and paupers, former inmates of the almshouses, and charwomen unable to get other work took the low wages offered to nurse the sick. In New York, some of the nursing care at Bellevue was given by prostitutes who, in the notorious Five Points Police Court, were given the option of going to prison or to hospital service for ten days. Stealing and cheating and drunkenness were prevalent among female as well as male "nurses." Many a drunken nurse would be found sleeping under the bed of a dead patient after having consumed the liquor provided as a stimulant for the very sick. Dr. Blackwell had interned at Old Blockley Almshouse and Hospital in Philadelphia amidst the fetid atmosphere of hospital wards, the foul smells from unwashed bodies, and unsanitary conditions, and she recognized at once that drastic changes had to be made. Florence Nightingale had set a magnificent example of what could be done by women through the nursing care she gave the soldiers during the Crimean War. Like Florence Nightingale, Elizabeth Blackwell believed that only good women, properly trained, should be nurses. With this in mind, she called a meeting of the leading women of New York and several men as well, to plan for some kind of nursing care to meet the emergency. At this meeting, held at her own New York Infirmary for Women and Children, which she and her sister Emily had founded seven

years earlier, a Central Relief Committee was organized and a
letter was drafted calling for a mass meeting at Cooper Union.
This dramatic, epoch-making document was signed by ninety-
two of the ladies. The Reverend Dr. Bellows assisted in framing
the constitution for the association.

On the morning of April 25, 1861, the streets around Cooper
Union were lined with hansoms and the family coaches of
Astors, Roosevelts, Schuylers, Woolseys, and other First Families. Hoop-skirted dames and damsels wearing fashionable man-
tles and enchanting spring bonnets made their way eagerly into
the building on Cooper Square in Manhattan. Nearly three
thousand belles of society gathered together that morning to
deliberate "on measures for the consolation and comfort of the
gallant men who are about to risk their lives." Every seat in
the great Hall was occupied as Vice-President Hamlin took the
chair and announced the intention of the ladies to form an organization which they proposed to call the "Central Relief Association." It was to aid the wounded and sick in the coming
war. Dr. Blackwell made a stirring plea to the women to organize and take an actual part in the war effort. The meeting
was afterwards addressed by the Reverend Dr. Bellows, Surgeon
Coffin, one of the heros of Fort Sumter, the Reverend Dr.
Bethune, and the Reverend Dr. Hitchcock, in addition to Drs.
Stevens, Wood, and several other equally prominent medical
men. A board of twenty-four managers was then chosen and
plans were adopted to centralize and direct their efforts. The
proposed Relief Association was enthusiastically endorsed by
all present, and Louisa Lee Schuyler was elected its first president.

The call for women had been sounded.

Two problems were faced immediately—the need to look after
the comforts of the soldiers and the need to train nurses. Dr.

Blackwell outlined the required qualifications for a nurse, and offered to train a group at her New York Infirmary.

The New York association became the leading group in the East.

Within thirty days after President Lincoln's request for 75,-ooo men the Women's Central Relief Association of New York had chosen, from hundreds of candidates interviewed by Dr. Blackwell herself, one hundred competent women to be trained as nurses for three months by physicians and surgeons of New York, at Bellevue Hospital.

Other women were trained by serving short terms of apprenticeship in available hospitals throughout the country. In Washington, D.C., hotels and mansions were converted into hospitals; eventually, in other cities near the lines of battle, even divinity schools and churches were similarly converted to house the sick and wounded soldiers.

There were others in the early days who nurtured a plan to organize women as war nurses. Church groups, private charity groups, and prominent individuals, too, sent nurses to the front. On the third Sunday in April, 1861, at Plymouth Church in Brooklyn, New York, Henry Ward Beecher read a call for women as volunteers to work in New York "for the good of the soldiers" and as volunteer nurses. The Honorable Henry Raymond of *The New York Times* organized a band of ladies to go to Washington to serve in the hospitals; and others too numerous to mention here established groups of their own. The nobility of Mr. Raymond's motives is open to question, since he was subsequently accused of having a cozy little romance with the woman he put in charge of the contingent of potential Florence Nightingales.

The Michigan Soldiers' Relief Association of Washington, D.C., is claimed to have been the first of its kind put in operation in the field on the Atlantic Slope, and the last to leave it.

It began its humane work in the autumn of 1861, continuing successfully until September, 1866. It proved a source of great relief to Michigan soldiers serving in the Army of the Potomac.

Each relief group proposed to follow the volunteers of its neighborhood with benefactions. Chaos resulted. Women ransacked their storerooms and preserve closets for canned fruits and pots of jam and marmalade, which they packed with clothing, books, stationery, etc. Baggage cars were soon flooded with fermenting sweets and broken pots of jelly. Badly canned meats had to be thrown away. Packages were lost. Constant movement of troops made it impossible for express agents to forward boxes to special regiments. The plan failed.

At length it was obvious that a central national relief organization was necessary. The Woman's Central Relief Association of New York joined the physicians and surgeons of the hospitals of that city and the Medical Association for Furnishing Hospital Supplies in a joint appeal to President Lincoln for a national official commission.

On June 9, 1861, the Secretary of War issued an order creating the body which became known as the United States Sanitary Commission, a forerunner of the American Red Cross. Later, other relief bodies merged with the national organization. Eight prominent men were appointed to the Commission. The Reverend Dr. Henry W. Bellows became its president and Frederick L. Olmsted the general secretary.

The Woman's Central Relief Association now became a branch of the Sanitary Commission, and under Louisa Lee Schuyler's leadership the relief organizations throughout the country were co-ordinated, bringing all into one harmonious, magnificent system.

The work of the newly organized United States Sanitary Commission was based on the Federal principle. Its ministrations were not limited by state boundaries and the soldiers were recognized as members of the Union, not as representatives of individual states.

Among its many duties, the Commission investigated conditions in army hospitals and camps; supplied nurses and matrons to hospitals and army transports under its supervision; studied problems of sanitation and general hygiene; supplied food, clothing, and medicine to the troops; invented hospital cars for humane transportation of the wounded; and maintained a Hospital directory through which information could be obtained concerning the invalids in the 233 general hospitals of the army and concerning men reported as "missing" or "fate unknown."

As women volunteered in increasing numbers, tongues began to wag and heads to shake. Not everyone welcomed the idea of girls going to war. Many male and female voices shouted it was "no place for women." In respectable communities, overly virtuous creatures looked upon hospitals as houses of death. The medical profession secretly and openly trembled, and there were many who believed the situation was getting out of hand. There had to be, the high moguls decided, a Superintendent of Nurses who would control this growing army of women, a suitable supervisor who would see that the members of the fair sex did not forget propriety in their newfound freedom, and that above all they would remember at all times that they were inferior to all male citizenry, particularly in hospitals.

Someone absolutely reliable was needed for the job. Elizabeth Blackwell was the logical choice, but the medical profession said "No." They still could not forgive her for invading their masculine profession, and with all their might threw their support behind Dorothea Dix, the sixty-year-old spinster and social reformer. Secretary of War Simon Cameron appointed her Superintendent of Nurses. The male rights of the medical profession seemed safe in her hands.

No one openly disputed—at least not too openly—the right of the woman who had revolutionized lunacy laws to be in charge of the care of sick and wounded soldiers, but there were undercurrents of dissatisfaction. The Dix Plan for Nurses was not popular with the young girls, particularly the more comely ones. "No women under thirty need apply to serve in goverment hospitals," the manifesto declared. "All nurses are required to be plain-looking women. Their dresses must be brown or black with no adornments. No hoop skirts."

Dorothea had cast her die and a wail of female voices rose in anguish. Hoops were fashionable. How could any girl so much as walk without one? The Superintendent stood firm. She stood on her record, too, and it was a good one. At fourteen she had become a schoolteacher; at twenty-two she had written her first book; and when turning forty, she had embarked on a crusade on behalf of the maltreated insane, through which she won an international reputation.

But even the best of women, as well as of men, have their weaknesses. Dorothea could be very petty and arbitrary, placing too much stress on age and looks. She was opinionated and capricious. She played favorites. On the other hand, she had great compassion for suffering humanity, and a sense of responsibility. From the start she had to contend with a disorganized Medical Department. Dorothea did not approve of sending her "girls" to the tented field hospitals, particularly those girls who proved to be younger and less plain. However, when the nurses pleaded with her later on in the war to allow them to go to the front lines where the conditions among the wounded grew increasingly appalling, she gave her consent. In her defense it might be said that Dorothea felt that adjustment to the primitive conditions in the hospitals in this pre-antiseptic era might prove too difficult for young girls.

No stipulation was made by the Government for women

nurses to work in post and field hospitals. No provision was made for their pay. In many instances, the Superintendent of Nurses was to pay the women herself, out of her own pocket, and there is no knowing whether or not she was ever reimbursed by the Government.

The curtain rose on the first act of the great human drama. Before the terrible defeat at Gettysburg, the American women had answered their country's call. Uninformed, untrained, and unwanted by the medical staff, selfless in their desire to help the suffering men, these valiant women cheered the soldiers in the darkest days of the war, read to them, mothered them, wrote letters home to wives and mothers and sweethearts. They served on fields of carnage, working by candlelight or by the faint glow of an army lantern, making their way through mud and dust, wading through blood and gore while enemy shells fell about them, until every wounded man was moved from the battlefield.

Throughout the four years of the conflict, an army of women continued to increase their ranks as they marched to fight their battle against sickness and death, clamoring for passes to the front, lying about their ages, cutting the red tape that entangled the Medical Department. They resorted to every means within their power to obtain a position in one of the military hospitals.

The women faced the dangers of infectious diseases as well as of war. No serums protected them from typhoid, diphtheria, pneumonia, and smallpox. Tuberculosis and malaria could be as destructive as the Minié bullets. In the pre-antiseptic era when the same washbasin was used for all, each sponge hid a menace. Gangrene and dysentery were often fatal. Lockjaw resulted from a slight wound or minor operation.

From their homes, from factories, from schools, serving maids and ladies, schoolteachers and schoolgirls, wives and daughters of enlisted men, Catholic Sisters and Protestant religious groups responded with enthusiasm to serve in hospitals all over the country. In the makeshift hospitals hastily improvised in unsuitable buildings, the women embarked upon their new field of duty and it was not long before army nurses began following the regiments to the front to appear on every battlefield from Bull Run to Appomattox.

NO YOUNG LADIES SHOULD BE SENT

Dorothea Lynde Dix

In the following extracts from a letter to Louisa Lee Schuyler at the office of the Woman's Central Relief Association of New York, Dorothea Dix discusses the possible training of the women nurses.

Washington, D.C.
April 29, 1861.

In regard to nurses, they should by no means come on now. If a conflict ensues, let the leading surgeons of New York direct and decide the course which should be adopted. Meantime, no better course can be taken, either of unselfishness should services be required or for future usefulness to the cause of humanity, than for some suitable organized instruction in nursing duties to be given.

No young ladies should be sent at all but women who can afford to give their services and time and meet part of their expenses or the whole, who will associate themselves by twos to be ready for duty at any hour of day or night—those who are sober, earnest, self-sacrificing, and self-sustained; who can bear the presence of suffering and exercise entire self-control, of speech and manner; who can be calm, gentle, quiet, active, and steadfast in duty, also who are willing to take and to execute the directions of the surgeons of the divisions in which they are stationed.

These are some of the many requirements of those who would propose themselves as nurses for the sick and wounded.

As soon as possible I will write to you as you suggest, making a call, but nothing need delay suitable women of strong hearts and willing spirit from making themselves fully acquainted under surgical direction with their prospective duties.

Dorothea Dix had a sense of humor, too. When an applicant appeared for an interview in the cycling costume of the period— full pants buttoning over the tops of her shoes, skirt falling slightly below the knees, and a jacket with tight sleeves, the chief read the girl's credentials and then looked her up and down in silence until the girl blushed. Then Dorothea rose to her full five feet and said:

The dress you wear is abominable, and I do not wish any of my nurses to dress in this manner. But you came highly recommended and I have long known of your work. . . . But I didn't know you wore such dress. However, you can wear it if you choose. . . .

GOODNESS ME! A NURSE!

Georgeanna M. Woolsey

As part of their excellent work, the Woman's Relief Association organized a nursing staff for the army, selecting one hundred women and sending them to the various hospitals in New York City for such drill as could be secured in a few weeks through the co-operation of the attending staff. The United States Sani-

tary Commission undertook to secure recognition for these women from the War Department with the pay of privates, and they were sent on to the army hospitals on requisition from Miss Dix and others, as needed. Georgeanna Woolsey and her sister Eliza Howland were among the first trainees.

It was hard work getting myself acceptable and accepted what with people at home saying "Goodness me! a nurse! All nonsense! Such a fly-away!" and what with the requisites insisted upon by the grave committees, I came near losing my opportunity.

First one must be just so old, and no older; have eyes and a nose and mouth expressing just such traits, and no others; must be willing to scrub floors, if necessary, etc., etc. Finally, however, by dint of taking the flowers out of my bonnet and the flounce off my dress; and by toning down, or toning up, according to the emergency, I succeeded in getting myself looked upon with mitigated disapprobation, and was at last sat upon by the committee and passed over to the Examining Board. The Board was good to me. It had to decide upon my physical qualifications; and so, having asked me who my grandfather was, and whether I had had the measles, it blandly put my name down, leaving a blank, inadvertently, where the age should have been, and I was launched, with about twenty other neophytes, into a career of philanthropy more or less confused.

Then began serious business. Armed with a blue ticket,* I presented myself with the others at the door of a hospital and was admitted for instruction. "Follow me," said our guide, and we followed in procession. "This will be your ward; you will remain here under so and so, and learn what you can; and this yours; and this, *yours*." That was *mine!* I shall never forget the hopeless state of my mind at this exact point. To be left stand-

* A pass, signed by Christine Griffin, secretary of the Woman's Association.

ing in the middle of a long ward, full of beds, full of sick men—
it was appalling! I seized another nurse, and refused to be
abandoned. So they took pity, and we two remained, to use our
eyes and time to the advantage of the Army of the Potomac
which was-to-be.

We took off our bonnets and went to work. Such a month
as we had of it, walking round from room to room, learning
what we could—really learning something in the end, till finally,
what with writing down everything we saw, and making elaborate sketches of all kinds of bandages and the ways of applying
them, and what with bandaging everybody we met, for practice,
we at last made our "reverses" without a wrinkle; and at the
end of the month were competent to any very small emergency
or very simple fracture. . . .

I remember it gave me a little shock that first day in the ward
to hear the young "house" say peremptorily: "Nurse, basin!"
I presented the basin promptly, and as promptly tumbled over
in a faint at seeing a probe used for the first time. I came out
from this ignominy to find that my associate nurse was dashing
my face with water from a tumbler in which she dipped her
fingers before offering it to me to drink from.

Before the summons from the army, though, came sickness
among our soldiers passing through the great cities. Measles
and typhoid fever began almost immediately. New wards in hospitals had to be opened, and the beds were filled faster than
we could make them. Such nice fellows, too, from the country
villages as were brought in.

My first patient of the war was a Duryea's Zouave, not a country boy though, but one of those poor desolate creatures,
so many of whom the army has sheltered, giving them the first
home they have ever known. My Zouave was dying when he
enlisted; he had no friends, no place to live in, no place to die
in, so he told me, and came into the army for the sake of finding

one. "I felt the sickness coming on, and I knew if I was a soldier they would put me into a hospital, and *then* I could die there."

Poor soul! He was young and refined in look and manner, and so comforted by little attentions, so appreciative of them;— and never to have had anything of the kind given him through all his lonely life!

Now, in these few last days of it there was a satisfaction in doing everything for him, in being as good to him as possible. In bringing him all that a gentleman's son might have had. So, with his poor tired head on my arm, I fed him with jellies and ices, and in little ways tried to comfort him. We owed him all the blessing we could bring into these last few moments of a dreary life.

My Zouave died, and they buried him in his fine new clothes —the best he had ever had—and put him to sleep in his own bed; now at last, *his own*, that no one would dispute with him; no one grudge him possession of forever.

8 Brevoort Place,
New York, Sunday, 1861.

In anticipation of a possible march on Tuesday I have got myself ready and hold myself under orders for any moment. As for some sort of a hospital costume, if we chance to need one, I have two grey cottonish cross-grained skirts, and a Zouave jacket giving free motion to the arms—so the skirts can be, one of them, always in the wash; and a white Zouave will take the place of the waist when that is in the tub. Four white aprons with waists and large pockets; two stick-out and washable petticoats to take the place of a hoop, and a nice long flannel dressing-gown, which one may put on in a hurry and fly out in, if the city is bombarded or "anything else." Then for quiet and civil costume, I have only one dress made of black grenadine, like Mary's, and a black Neapolitan straw with green ribbon will make it all very nice. I shall make up a trunk of towels, and old scraps of linen and cotton, soap, cologne, oil-silk, sponges, etc., and have it stored away in the hotel in Washington for use, if necessary. Any towels or old sheets you may have to dispose of we shall probably find useful if we are able to do anything for the sick. I have also under consideration a small camp cooking affair, about two feet square, with lamp and all complete, which I shall probably get—cheap and very useful in an emergency—could cook up little things for ourselves at any rate. If we find that we shall be allowed to march with the regiment, or rather *ride*, we could easily have grey flannel skirts and shirts made in Washington. So I don't see that we may not be very comfortable and useful, and consequently happy, even in following the war.

I SET OUT TO REACH MISS DIX'S RESIDENCE

Sophronia E. Bucklin

Sophronia Bucklin, a vivacious young schoolteacher from Auburn, New York, applied for a commission as nurse in the Union Army, and managed not only to get herself accepted in spite of her youth by the Superintendent of Nurses, but to become a great favorite with her as well. Sophronia's meetings with Dorothea Dix are among the most entertaining of her graphically recorded Civil War experiences, which started with an appointment to Judiciary Square Hospital in Washington.

From the day on which the boom of the first cannon rolled over the startled waters in Charleston harbor, it was my constant study how I could with credit to myself get into the military service of the Union.

"It is no place for women" was the cry on every hand. . . . Still the steady streams of youthful valor flowed into the red shambles of war, and were sacrificed at the streaming altars. . . .

I met the Board of Managers of the Soldiers' Aid Society (of Auburn), stated my errand, and as they had a pass for one nurse, I was nominated, recommended, and voted upon, receiving the appointment, subject to the approval of Miss D. L. Dix, Superintendent of Women Nurses in the military hospitals of the Union.

In due time, under the cover of "Official Business," my appointment was confirmed, and accompanied by circulars, which served to define clearly the requisites for service.

I was *not* of the requisite age, but no special inquiries on that subject rendering it necessary for me to testify to my years, I resolved not to be kept from the great work because no wrinkles seamed my face, and no vestige of grey hair nestled among my locks. I could, and did, bring all other testimonials, and within eight days, with the regulation supply of clothing in a small trunk, and Miss Dix's letter of instructions in my pockets, I was journeying alone from the city of Auburn to the beleaguered Capital. . . .

It was a novel thing to journey on a military ticket—car passengers stared as though a Government nurse were a nondescript, and public curiosity a cardinal virtue. Thanks to the kindness of Miss Dix, to whom I was to report on my arrival in Washington, my journey was planned, and no accident of note occurred to break its perfect working.

A few thoughts were given to the report that the railroad track was not in order from New York to Baltimore, but the cars moved on with no break in their usual time. At Baltimore, failing to meet Col. Belger, to whom I was referred by Miss Dix, relieved of the necessity of venturing out into the blank darkness of the depot in that midnight hour, I retained my seat in the cars, and waited for them to move.

The lonely night ride was wearisome in the extreme. Finally we entered the great cavernous depot at Washington. It was dark as though the smoke from a thousand grim-throated furnaces had settled upon its walls, and thousands of soldiers shook there the dust from their feet, brought from every State in the Union.

I stood alone in the city of strangers, vainly waiting for the appearance of Col. Belger, whom the conductor had promised to find, and accompany hither. Every carriage had disappeared, and still I waited for Col. Belger's coming before seeking conveyance to the house of Miss Dix.

There was not a seat, or tank of water, or civilized convenience of any kind whatever, and tired, thirsty and hungry, after two days and nights of travel, I stood wretchedly surveying the situation. . . . I began to realize that a soldier's life was anything but pastime.

I accosted a dirty ragged little girl, who was passing through the depot, and asked her if she could procure me some water. With a prolonged stolid look into my face, she hurried away without a word, soon however returning with a battered tin tumbler filled with dirty-looking water. Although so filthy as to be revolting, I took a swallow to quench my feverish thirst, and used the remainder, by pouring it on my handkerchief, to wash the dust of travel from my hands and face. . . .

I took the street cars, and went out to seek her residence [Miss Dix's].

Dust was flying thickly through the murky air of Washington. Officers were riding at the topmost speed, up and down the avenues, and a train of supply wagons, with from four to six mules attached, stood solidly packed together for two miles in length.

Everything was bustle and excitement—the bright new uniforms of the officers—the glitter of military trappings were all new sights to my wondering eyes. It had not entered my heart that the army had reached such gigantic proportions, and consumed such marvellous supplies.

But what most interested me, in the great moving panorama of war, was the sight of wounded men, lying on blood-stained stretchers, under fly tents, being borne in at every hand where a sheltering roof made it possible to establish a hospital. The Capitol, Patent Office, city churches, and even private dwellings were turned from their legitimate usage into hospitals.

These sights, which especially recalled to mind the errand on which I had come, made all the courage in my soul recoil at one dread bound.

At Fifteenth street I left the car and set out on foot to reach Miss Dix's residence. Up and down the street I passed, and repassed, unable to find the number designated by my orders, as they had been read. Prompted by feelings of despair, I made inquiries, and found that the numbers did not range so high, and that I was misdirected. On producing her letter the mistake was rectified, and I was very soon at Miss Dix's door.

There I was kindly received by her housekeeper, who said, pityingly, "Why, you poor child, I have seen you running up and down here all the morning."

Miss Dix was absent on the battlefield . . . directing and organizing the force of women nurses who received orders from her hands. My appointment, however, awaited me, and also a letter of introduction to Dr. Charles Page, the surgeon in charge of Judiciary Square Hospital, to which I was assigned for duty.

At Judiciary Square Hospital I was shown to my quarters, and kindly welcomed by Miss Clark, the woman nurse from whom I was to take my instructions.

Urging me to occupy one of the two beds which were in the room, and remarking upon my tired worn look, she left me with an injunction to try hard to rest, while she must hasten away to the bedside of a dying man in our ward.

I had never been so near death before . . . I could not sleep . . . sounds of woe resounded about me, mingled now and then with hilarious laughter. I wondered if ever in this bare room, with only the length of an unpainted board for the partition walls between wards, halls, nurses' quarters, and all other officers, I should ever sleep again. A shuffling past my door started me to my feet. . . . Miss Clark returned with the information that the man was dead, and carried to the dead-house; . . .

The porter's call of "Dinner for the ladies—turn out for dinner—all things are ready—turn in to dinner," was a welcome cry, for I had eaten nothing substantial for two days.

There was no duty for me that day, and after dinner was over, I went with Miss Clark to the dead-house to see the man who died in the morning.

Could I ever suppress the shuddering that passed over me, as I entered the low wooden house, in which on rude benches lay the cold white corpses of three men?

A cloth saturated with blood lay over a bench, and I was so wrought upon by the sadness of the scene, that I only desired to hasten away from the dreadful place.

I clung to Miss Clark with the tenacity of long-established friendship in these first experiences of hospital service.

At the usual time we were called to a supper, consisting of the same dark, dirty bread, with dried apple-sauce, and tea which was black with strength. An introductory visit to the wards in which my labors were to commence so soon ended the long, strange day. I looked upon the narrow iron bedsteads furnished with bed of straw, one straw pillow, two sheets, one blanket and counterpane, three rows of which ran the length of the long room, forming narrow passageways through which we walked. . . .

It was no small matter for me to apply the wet towel to the faces of bronzed and bearded men; it was no slight task to comb out the tangled hair and part it over foreheads which seemed hot with the flash of cannon. . . .

Forty-six wounded men lay helpless on the iron bedsteads in our ward at Judiciary Square Hospital, and from out the hall enough more had gone into the convalescents' room, to swell the entire number under our care to eighty. Each of the fourteen wards, which projected in wings from the long central building, held also its full quota.

Amongst the wounded were many hopelessly shattered, who would henceforth drag useless members through life, and some who would miss forever the good stout limbs which lay in the trenches. . . .

Our duties here were to distribute food to the patients, when brought up from the kitchen; wash the faces and hands, and comb the heads of the wounded; see that their bedding and clothing was kept clean and whole, bring pocket handkerchiefs, prepare and give the various drinks and stimulants at such times as they were ordered by the surgeons.

Surgeons and officers were very kind to us, but they gave stringent orders which we were sometimes almost willing to disobey. . . .

Women's help had not been counted on. . . . Women nurses were not allowed to go into the kitchen for articles of any kind; consequently the patients were many times obliged to go without the countless little comforts which a sick fancy craves. We devised many ways to relieve their wants, begging tea, sugar, and other luxuries of loyal ladies—of Miss Dix, of State agents, and of Sanitary and Christian Commissions, and when these failed us, the boys took the hard-earned pay of soldiers, and sent out for the articles themselves. We would prepare tea for them by slipping a basin of water into the stove in the ward, and by dropping the tea into it when boiling.

It was then taken to our quarters, and carried thence in a bowl, having all the appearance of official ordering, if a surgeon or the officer of the day chanced to pass through the ward. The men had for their food whatever the surgeon chose to order for them while on his daily rounds.

It was Miss Dix's wish that we should learn to dress wounds, but we were peremptorily ordered from the ward, when that process was in operation. One day I was sent out with an abrupt, "Nurse, we can dispense with your services now," and, retiring to our room, I stretched myself upon my little iron bedstead to ease my weary feet and limbs.

While in this position, as I lay thinking of my work, a strange woman in black came in with noiseless steps, and appeared before me. She put various questions to me, with an authority which I was too startled to dispute. She gave me instructions in regard to duty, lectured me roundly on this seeming neglect, and when my lips opened to plead my defence, an admonitory "hush" from the strange figure closed them again.

I was altogether too young for a nurse, she said. Then came visions of disgrace—of the shame which would overcome me, if Miss Dix should send me home. . . . When an order came, summoning me to appear before Miss Dix at seven o'clock on the following morning, I discovered that my strange visitor was no other than the Superintendent of Women Nurses.

I found her busy with letters, and, after watching her in uneasy nervousness, as she dashed off two or three, I gathered courage enough to say, "Miss Dix, I should like to return as soon as possible to my duties."

She replied, "You can go, dear." At the same time she opened a drawer in her table and took therefrom a five-dollar bill, which she handed me, saying, "This is not pay—only a little present from me."

I took it in confusion, and, as she bade me a kind, "Good morning," I hastened back to the hospital.

COME DOWN AND BE INTRODUCED TO DR. BLACKWELL

Georgeanna M. Woolsey

After Georgy had finished her month's training she and her sister Eliza decided to go to war with Eliza's husband Joe, and made plans to leave for Washington.

June, 1861.

I am ready and glad to go anywhere and any time with you and dear Joe. You will probably go with him to Washington at any rate. You and I could be companions for each other at the hotel as long as the regiment camps near the city, and, judging from the way the other regiments have been disposed of, that is likely to be the arrangement for them for some time. We should be able to see them every day and perhaps go even farther South. Since Joe has taken the sick under his care we PERHAPS shall be able to be a part of the regiment as other women have been, and may keep together in this way, doing what we can. . . .

Two of our bands of nurses have been sent on from the Hospital already, and with a letter of introduction from our Association (which is accepted by the government). I shall probably be able to go where I please as far south as Hospitals have been established; and so we may be able perhaps to keep up with the Sixteenth. If you can, don't you think you had better come down and be introduced to Dr. Elizabeth Blackwell and others, and go for a few days to one of the hospitals opened to us, so that you may be able to give references from our association if necessary? It may save you some delay and be useful to you in other ways. I am ready, or shall be at the shortest notice to do as you say. I cannot tell you how we all feel about this. We shall try and not feel at all, only our hearts are with you and Joe always. . . .

MARY BROKE THE NEWS OF MY GOING TO THE SERVANTS
Eliza Woolsey Howland

Eliza had definitely abandoned any idea of staying behind in Fishkill without her husband. He advised her to go to her mother's for a while until he had a chance to look over the scene in Washington. She wrote to him before she left for New York.

I write chiefly to remind you of the stand of colors which Tiffany is making and promises for Wednesday. You may want to have them presented to the regiment the day they pass through New York, and, if so, will have to arrange the affair with the Colonel. I do not wish to appear in the matter, but you can present them in my name, or, if you like, perhaps Charley will be willing to, but don't have any fuss or parade about it, and DON'T let the men tramp through the city A LA McChesney till they are exhausted. The colors will remain at Tiffany's till the Colonel sends for them or notifies me.

Mary and Robert and the children are still here and all well.

Mary broke the news of my going to the servants, who were very sorry for me and for themselves. In the course of next week I shall wind up my affairs—pay my debts, etc., and go to Mother's. I shall go down on Wednesday when the regiment passes through New York, at all events for the day and night, unless I hear to the contrary from you.

The 16th New York left Albany for Washington. At Washington Square, before embarking for the South, the regiment was presented with a stand of colors, state and national, made by Tiffany & Co., Eliza's gift.

Colonel Davies then delivered the state flag to the color sergeant, who bore it to the line. Waving the national flag before the regiment, he asked each company if they would defend it. A prolonged "yes" rang from one end of the line to the other, followed by deafening cheers and waving of caps.

Washington, July 8, 1861.

I should have begun by dating my letter Ebbitt House,* we having been established here since Saturday, spending the first three days of our visit, or probation, at the "National," in the fifth story, a prey to several inconveniences, but refreshingly near processions. Joe sent his man down to meet us, and came himself after evening drill. He looks brown and well; is dashing around on horseback all day from camp to the War Department, and back again to camp, where he must spend seven hours

* The Ebbitt House in Washington was a rambling, untidy place on F Street, which became a sort of Army Headquarters, filled with officers and men connected with the service. We (G. and E.) were given a large parlor on the second floor, where cot beds were set up for us, and we began a sort of half army life, with bundles of hospital supplies stacked in all the corners and extemporized arrangements for comfort. We were close by Willards and in the midst of all that was going on, and just opposite the headquarters of the Sanitary Commission. Charley, having seen us established, hurried home. . . .

a day drilling. Then all the cracks are filled up with our society out there. We go out every day in time for evening drill, and stay till it is time to shut up for the night, having a nice time in the door of Joe's tent "in the cool of the day," and this sort of thing we fondly thought was going to last an indefinite length of time, till yesterday, when Joe surprised us by the news that they were ordered into Virginia, and would leave on Tuesday or Wednesday. The Colonel has been made an acting Brigadier General, and he and Joe were eight hours in the saddle yesterday, flying round selecting three regiments to form the Brigade with the Sixteenth. Joe has been in today on the same business, being entrusted to decide upon them and take whichever he thought best; and has chosen the Eighteenth, Twenty-first, and Thirty-first—all from New York. So on Wednesday I suppose they will move over the bridge, and then we shall deliver our letters of introduction and plunge into occupation of some kind.

Washington is the stillest place for a city I have ever been in; nobody knows anything, or has anything to say. Everything is guesswork. A few doleful little boys call the evening papers round the doors of the hotel, but in a tone that fixes a gloom upon you. I hate the *Eve-en-ing Star* already, and our only news comes via New York. The *Tribune, Times,* and *Herald* have a great deal of information about what goes on here, and it generally proves true. . . . One longs now and then for a real living and lying "Extra" boy, with his mouth full of fearful statements, all disproved by his paper which you imprudently buy. We went, of course, to the opening of Congress and also to hear President Lincoln's message, read on the fifth.

Charley has been about visiting the camps at Alexandria, Georgetown, and Arlington, but for all this a pass is necessary, which can only be procured through General Mansfield on introduction by someone known to him. If Lenox knows anyone at home who knows the General it would save him half a day to

get his letter before coming on. Charley got his through Colonel
Davies who is a relative of the General's. I hope Lenox will
come on, but it is too bad that he will not see Joe.

Here comes a regiment down *this* street. About 15,000 men
have gone over into Virginia since we came on. Joe goes up in
rank with his Colonel as his aide—is now Captain and Assistant
Adjutant General—and the Brigade will be in McDowell's Division. . . . The regiment has marched past—the Massachusetts
Eleventh just from Harrisburg, all in beautiful order, gray uniforms and large clean havelocks. New England doesn't do anything by halves. . . . And here goes another company, guarding
thirteen well-filled baggage wagons and followed by its regiment.
We have only to flourish our handkerchiefs and the dear fellows
will kiss their hands, twirl their hats, and manifest affection for
the entire woman population of the North. They are the Fourth
Maine, and are going over into Virginia. I must put up my letter
and watch them marching along. Our love to the Doctor and
the boys.

3 It Is a Miracle That the Patients Survived

THE WOMEN WHO FIRST WORKED IN THE HOSPITALS IN AND NEAR Washington City and later in the field had to adapt themselves to the inadequacies of the makeshift hospitals, until 1862, when Lincoln requested Dr. Willard Bliss, a volunteer from a Michigan regiment, to organize a system of general hospitals in and about the Capital. Many of the advanced reforms in the so-called "Banner" hospitals, such as the special diet kitchen, were introduced by the women nurses and Sanitary Commission agents in the course of the War.

But the women had more than makeshift hospitals and lack of organization to contend with. Their greatest difficulty in the beginning, and in many instances throughout the War, was dealing with the Medical Department, a creaking antiquated institution that had demonstrated a complete lack of preparedness at the outbreak of each of the earlier wars. The Civil War was no exception.

The hierarchy in the Medical Department consisted of a Surgeon General, an Assistant Surgeon General, and a number of post surgeons. Many of the doctors were contract surgeons who served a limited period of time. These contract surgeons were criticized by the Medical Department, the Sanitary Commission, and the women. They were accused of many things, from malpractice to eating up the Sanitary Commission goodies intended for the patients. All reports, returns, and communications concerned with army medical matters were to be made to the Surgeon General's office, and all orders relating to army

79

medical matters were to be issued from there. Before long, each
hospital had a Surgeon in Charge and four Acting Assistant
Surgeons, so-called because they had been civilian physicians
and now served as noncommissioned officers under contract.
A matron looked after the linen room and kitchen—her presence
barely tolerated by the male staff. But the presence of female
nurses was to serve as a constant source of irritation to many of
the men, who went to great lengths to make their lives as unpleasant as possible.

The office of the Surgeon in Charge in Washington was soon
working overtime. Surgeons were detailed to visit the temporary
hospitals each morning, but the number of hospitals and patients increased so rapidly it took all day to make the rounds.
As a result, there was a great deal of added suffering.

Young doctors, many unskilled and without sufficient training, flocked to the army from medical schools and hospitals.
They were frequently called upon to perform operations in the
field hospitals with no preparation other than a quick course in
military surgery at the outbreak of the War. A small pocket text,
A Handbook of Operative Surgery, had been hurried to press
and was in such demand that it went into twenty editions. The
book was carefully illustrated and briefly explained the most
common type of operations. A series of essays and handbooks
in a condensed form contained the conclusions of the highest
medical authorities with regard to those medical and surgical
questions likely to present themselves to military surgeons.
There were strict rules concerning amputations, for example:
"In army practice on the field, amputations when necessary
ought to be primary . . . therefore amputate with as little delay
as possible."

Women to whom "operating theater" had been an almost
unknown term were called upon to hand saw and needles to
these surgeons. Afterward, it was their duty to bathe the wounds

and change the dressings. In emergencies, of which there were many, the nurses set fractures and made anterior splints without advice. The survival of the patients under horrifying conditions is miraculous.

THE TOP OF THE PATENT OFFICE BECAME A HOSPITAL

Eliza Woolsey Howland

Eliza writes her husband, Joe, about her new job as an Army Nurse in Washington with sister Georgeanna.

Where do you think I am writing? In the Patent Office (Hospital) where we heard the other day that a large number of sick men had been brought from the 19th Indiana regiment. We found them in a dirty and forlorn condition and have come to do what we can. The whole regiment, nearly, is down with sickness, from great exposure when they first arrived, they say. The assistant surgeon of the regiment and the matron are here all the time, and a number of Washington women come in to help every day.

One of the first extemporized hospitals of the war was in the top story of the Patent Office, where the 19th Indiana regiment was brought, nearly every man of them. The great, unfinished lumber room was set aside for their use, and rough tables—I can't call them beds—were knocked together from pieces of the scaffolding. These beds were so high that it was impossible to reach them, and we had to make them up with brooms, sweeping off the mattresses, and jerking the sheets as smooth as we could. About six men could be accommodated on one table. These ran the whole length of the long room, while on the stacks of marble slabs, which were some day to be the floor, we spread mattresses, and put the sickest men. As the number increased, camp beds were set up between the glass cases in the outer room, and we alternated—typhoid fever, cog wheels and patent churns—typhoid fever, balloons and mouse traps (how *many* ways of catching mice there are!)—typhoid fever, locomotives, water wheels, clocks—and a general nightmare of machinery.

Here, for weeks, went on a sort of hospital picnic. We scrambled through with what we had to do. The floors were covered with lime dust, shavings, nails, and carpenters' scraps. We had the rubbish taken up with shovels, and stacked in barrels at one end of the ward. The men were crowded in upon us; the whole regiment soaked with malignant, malarial fever, from exposure, night after night, to drenching rains, without tents. There was so much of this murderous, blundering, want of prevision and provision, in the first few months of the war—and is *now*, for that matter.

Gradually, out of the confusion came some system and order. Climbing up to the top of the Patent Office with each loaf of bread was found not to be an amusing occupation, and an arrangement of pulleys was made out of one of the windows, and any time through the day, barrels of water, baskets of vegetables, and great pieces of army beef might be seen crawling slowly up the marble face of the building.

Here, for weeks, we worked among these men, cooking for them, feeding them, washing them, sliding them along on their tables, while we climbed up on something and made up their beds with brooms, putting the same powders down their throats with the same spoon, all up and down what seemed half a mile of uneven floor;—coaxing back to life some of the most unpromising—watching the youngest and best die.

I remember rushing about from apothecary to apothecary, in

the lower part of the city, one Sunday afternoon, to get, in a great hurry, mustard, to help bring life into a poor Irishman, who called me Betty in his delirium, and, to our surprise, got well, went home, and at once married the Betty we had saved him for.

By-and-by the regiment got through with the fever, improvements came into the long ward, cots took the place of the tables, and matting covered the little hills of the floor. The hospital for the 19th Indiana became the "U.S. General Hospital at the Patent Office," and the "volunteers for emergencies" took up their saucepans and retired.

HOSPITALS IN CAMP

Sarah Emma Edmonds

At the end of May, Sarah Emma Edmonds, known to all as Franklin Thompson, arrived in Washington to serve as a "male" nurse with the Michigan Infantry.

Soon after reaching Washington I commenced visiting the temporary hospitals which were prepared to receive the soldiers who arrived there sick. The troops came pouring in very fast, and the weather being extremely warm, all the general hospitals were soon filled, and it seemed impossible to prepare suitable or comfortable accommodations for all who required medical attention.

There are many things in connection with this war that we are disposed to find fault with, and we think the blame rests upon such and such individuals—but after investigating the matter, we find that they are all owing to a combination of circumstances entirely beyond the control of those individuals—and it requires time to bring about the desired results. This has been my experience with regard to the hospital department. After walking through the streets for hours on a sultry southern day in search of one of those temporary hospitals, I would find a number of men there delirious with fever—others had been sunstruck and carried there—but no physician to be found in attendance. Then, I would naturally come to the conclusion that the surgeons were all slack concerning their duty—but upon going to the office of the surgeon in charge of that department, would find that a certain number of surgeons were detailed every morning to visit those hospitals, and were faithfully performing their duty; but that the numbers of hospitals and patients were increasing so fast that it required all day to make the tour. Consequently the last ones visited were obliged to wait and suffer—without any blame attaching to the surgeons.

Then another great evil was to be remedied—there were thousands of sick men to be taken care of—but for these the Government had made no provision as regards more delicate kinds of food—nothing but hard bread, coffee, and pork, for sick and well, alike. The Sanitary Commission had not yet come into operation and the consequence was our poor sick soldiers suffered unspeakably from want of proper nourishment. . . . Typhoid fever began to make its appearance in camp, as the burning sun of June came pouring down upon us, and the hospitals were soon crowded with its victims. It was then that my labors began in earnest, and as I went from tent to tent, ministering to the wants of those delirious, helpless men, how thankful I was that it was my privilege to take some small part in so great a work. . . .

I shall notice, briefly, the manner in which the hospitals are conducted in camp. There are large tents furnished for hospital purposes, which will accommodate from twenty to twenty-five men. These tents are usually put up in the most pleasant and shady part of the camp; the inside is nicely leveled and board floors laid if boards can be procured; if not, rubber blankets are laid down instead. Sometimes there are straw ticks and cot bedsteads furnished, but not in sufficient quantity to supply all the hospitals. Along each side of the tent the sick are laid, on blankets or cots, leaving room to pass between the beds. In the center of the tent stands a temporary board table, on which are kept books, medicines, et cetera. The hospital corps consists of a surgeon, an assistant surgeon, a hospital steward, a wardmaster, four nurses, two cooks, and a man of all work to carry water, cut wood, and make himself generally useful. The immediate care of the sick devolves upon those four nurses, who are generally detailed from the ranks, each one being on duty six hours without intermission. The surgeons visit the patients twice every day, oftener if required; the prescriptions are filled by the hospital steward, and the medicine is administered by the nurses. The nurses are usually very kind to the sick, and when off duty in the hospital, spend much of their time in digging drains around the tents, planting evergreens, and putting up awnings, all of which add much to the coolness and comfort of the hospital. Draining the grounds is a very important part of hospital duty, for when those terrible thunderstorms come, which are so frequent in the south, it is impossible to keep the tent floors from being flooded, unless there are drains all around the tents. Great excitement prevails in camp during those tempests—the rain comes down in torrents, while the wind blows a hurricane—lifting the tents from the ground, and throwing everything into wild confusion. I have seen a dozen men stand for hours around one hospital, holding down the ropes and tent poles to prevent the sick from being exposed to the raging elements.

Jane Stuart Woolsey

Jane Stuart Woolsey was the fourth sister to serve her country during the Civil War. She worked as a superintendent of Fairfax Seminary Hospital in Alexandria from November, 1862, until the end of the war.

First Days.

On a blue-and-gold day in the edge of November, . . . two ladies, with their luggage, were carefully packed into an ambulance . . . at the door of a great city hotel. They were setting out—for a lonely outpost hospital to which they had been invited by the officer in charge, as supervisors of the nursing and cooking department.

Through the unclean paste of the city streets; over a long bridge and a turbid river, hindered by endless wagon trains, halted by German sentinels who read the passes upside down; along roads in which the heavy wheels turned back the soft soil as a plough turns the loam in the fields; through little sparkling streams that rushed across the carriage-way; by miles and miles of treeless, open, desolate country—fields on fields full of deep red dwarf oaks and low, thick, yellow shrubbery—in the smoky sunshine and sweet, spicy air; at last, climbing by long slopes a pleasant height, they came to the grove skirting the Hospital grounds, and wound up to the brick rear court of a large quadrangle of buildings.

The officer in charge came out to meet them, and took them over to their lodgings in the parsonage, a few yards from the central offices. They were so fortunate as to be assigned quarters in the house with the Chaplain and his family, and were shown into a large octagon-sided room, with bare, clean floor, two camp beds, with bed-sacks stuffed with straw, two little tables with regulation tin basins, and in the wide fireplace a huge black cylinder of sheet-iron, giving out a dull roar, and growing red here and there in spots.

Out of the windows lay the sweetest country. Just under them were the remnants of a garden—lilac, syringa, and straggling bushes on which two or three late, pale roses fluttered and hung. These stood up to their knees in the long, rough grass, and the grass covered the rolling ground down to the feathery edge of trees and the deep-cut, yellow crossroads. Beyond the road the red fields reached far away, and beyond the fields curving and shining, moved the river. A streak of mist, and a steeple here and there, showed where the nearest town grovelled along the river's edge; and on the left, looking through miles of airy purple, hung in the smoke of the city and the autumn vapor a wonderful white dome, not yet lifting aloft, nor having the right to lift the finished figure of Liberty. Months and years made every gleam and shadow, every color and line of the landscape dear and familiar to the two who looked out upon it delighted, on the first day of their new life.

The Hospital was a divinity school in the old days, but very early in the wartime professors and pupils fled southward, in such unseemly haste to declare for the rebellion that doors were left ajar, women's gowns hanging in the cupboards, books lying open, face downward, on the tables. One of the first cares of the Surgeon in Charge was to have all these books collected, carefully boxed, and sent to the nearest provost marshal for safekeeping. The deserted buildings first fell into the hands of brigade and division commanders, were occupied as headquarters for a few months, and were then set apart for general hospital uses.

HOW MUCH UNFEELING THE WOMEN NURSES ENDURED

Georgeanna M. Woolsey

No one knows, who did not watch the thing from the beginning, how much opposition, how much ill-will, how much unfeeling want of thought, these women nurses endured. Hardly a surgeon of whom I can think, received or treated them with even common courtesy. Government had decided that women should be employed, and the army surgeons—unable, therefore, to close the hospitals against them—determined to make their lives so unbearable that they should be forced in self-defence to leave. It seemed a matter of cool calculation, just how much ill-mannered opposition would be requisite to break up the system.

Some of the bravest women I have ever known were among this first company of army nurses. They saw at once the position of affairs, the attitude assumed by the surgeons, and the wall against which they were expected to break and scatter; and they set themselves to undermine the whole thing.

None of them were "strong-minded." Some of them were women of the truest refinement and culture; and day after day they quietly and patiently worked, doing, by order of the surgeon, things which not one of those gentlemen would have dared to ask of a woman whose male relative stood able and ready to defend her and report him. I have seen small white hands scrubbing floors, washing windows, and performing all menial offices. I have known women, delicately cared for at home, half fed in hospitals, hard worked day and night, and given, when sleep must be had, a wretched closet just large enough for a camp bed to stand in. I have known surgeons who purposely and ingeniously arranged these inconveniences with the avowed intention of driving away all women from their hospitals.

These annoyances could not have been endured by the nurses but for the knowledge that they were pioneers, who were, if possible, to gain standing ground for others—who must create the position they wished to occupy. This, and the infinite satisfaction of seeing from day to day sick and dying men comforted in their weary and dark hours, comforted as they never would have been but for these brave women, was enough to carry them through all and even more than they endured.

At last, the wall against which they were to break began to totter; the surgeons were most unwilling to see it fall, but the knowledge that the faithful, gentle care of the women nurses had saved the lives of many of their patients, and that a small rate of mortality, or remarkable recoveries in their hospitals, reflected credit immediately upon *themselves*, decided them to give way, here and there, and to make only a show of resistance. They could not do without the women nurses; they knew it, and the women knew that they knew it, and so there came to be a tacit understanding about it.

When the war began, among the many subjects on which our minds presented an entire blank was that sublime, unfathomed mystery—"Professional Etiquette." Out of the army, in practice which calls itself "civil," the etiquette of the profession is a cold spectre, whose presence is felt everywhere, if not seen; but in the Medical Department of the Army, it was an absolute Bogie, which stood continually in one's path, which showed its narrow, ugly face in camps and in hospitals, in offices and in wards; which put its cold paw on private benevolence, whenever benevolence was fool enough to permit it; which kept shirts from ragged men, and broth from hungry ones; an evil Regular Army Bogie, which in full knowledge of empty kitchens and "exhausted funds," quietly asserted that it had need of nothing, and politely bowed Philanthropy out into the cold.

All this I was profoundly ignorant of for the first few months

of the war, and so innocently began my rounds with my little
jelly pots and socks knit at home for the boys—when, suddenly,
I met the Bogie:—and what a queer thing he was! It was a hot
summer morning, not a breath of air coming in at the open
windows—the hospital full of sick men, and the nurses all busy,
so I sat by a soldier and fanned him through the long tedious
hours. Poor man, he was dying, and so grateful to me, so afraid
I should tire myself. I could have fanned him all day for the
pleasure it was to help him, but the Bogie came in, and gave
me a look of icy inquiry. My hand ought to have been paralyzed
at once, but somehow or other, it kept moving on with the fan
in it, while I stupidly returned the Bogie's stare.

Finding that I still lived, he quietly made his plan, left the
room without saying a word, and in ten minutes afterward developed his tactics. He was a small Bogie—knowing what he
wanted to do, but not quite brave enough to do it alone; so he
got Miss Dix, who was on hand, to help him, and together they
brought all the weight of professional indignation to bear upon
me. I "must leave immediately." Who was I, that I should
bring myself and my presumptuous fan, without direct commission from the surgeon-general, into the hospital? Not only must
I leave at once, but I must *never return*.

This was rather a blow, it must be confessed. The moment
for action had arrived—I rapidly reviewed my position, notified
myself that I was the Benevolent Public, and decided that the
sick soldiers were, in some sort, the property of the B.P. Then I
divulged *my* tactics. I informed the Bogies (how well that rhymes
with Fogies) that I had ordered my carriage to return at such
an hour, that the sun was hot, that I had no intention whatever
of walking out in it, and that, in short, I had decided to remain.
What there was in these simple facts, very quietly announced,
to exorcise the demon, I am unable to say, but the gratifying
result was that half an hour afterward Professional Etiquette

made a most salutary repast off its own remarks; that I spent the remainder of the day where I was; that both the Bogies, singly, called the next morning to say, "Please, sir, it wasn't *me*, sir—'twas the other boy, sir"; and from that time the wards were all before me.

When Georgy wrote home about her run-in with Miss Dix her family urged her not to be disturbed by the Superintendent of Nurses, and Jane wrote a consoling few words to Georgy and Eliza.

Your rebuff by Miss Dix has been the subject of great indignation, but we all devoutly hope you will not mind it in the least. . . . Whatever you do, go in and win. Outflank the Dix by any and every means in your power, remembering that prison visitors and hospital visitors and people who really desire to do good have taken no notice of obstacles except to vanquish them, and as soon as one avenue was closed have turned with perfect persistence to another. We shall be disappointed if you do not establish some sort of relations with the hospitals, at least enough to give you free access, and to make a reliable channel for such things as we can send. . . .

Having established their own position and made it clear that they had no intention of being bluffed off, they were accepted by the surgeons and Miss Dix at their own valuation. From that moment things ran smoothly for the Woolsey girls. All hospitals were open to them, and their relations with Dorothea Dix became cordial and friendly as the following notes show.

My dear Miss Woolsey: I am thankful you are going to the hospital. Express to the good nurses my kind regards and purpose of seeing them as soon as I am able. Thanks for the lovely flowers. With cordial regards to Mrs. H. I have very little strength; excuse brevity and abruptness. I must have some consultation with you as soon as I am BETTER, concerning the position of the nurses. I fear they are overtasked.

Very cordially yours,

D. L. Dix.

My dear Miss Woolsey: Will you give a little attention to the hospitals at Alexandria through next week for me if convenient? Any requisition on my stores will always be promptly met. . . .

Yours most cordially,

D. L. Dix.

THE SURGEON TOLD ME HE HAD NO ROOM FOR ME

Mary Phinney von Olnhausen

The personality of Mary Phinney, Baroness von Olnhausen, that emerges from her letters and extracts from her autobiography, is of a woman who devoted her life to helping others— on her own terms. The reports of her experiences as a Civil War nurse are neither fascinating nor exciting, but the frank, blunt way in which she tells the inside story of the hospitals in which she worked helps to round out the medical picture of the two wars in which she participated. When Mary criticizes, she pulls no punches, and is the first to admit to her own displays of bad temper while at Mansion House Hospital in Alexandria in 1861 or, later, a hospital in Chateau Thierry in 1870.

At the outbreak of the Civil War Mary Phinney von Olnhausen appealed immediately to Miss Dix, who promised to place her at once, but who delayed so long that Mary had just begun to doubt her when the summons came to start for Washington.

Mary was decidedly unwelcome when she landed at Mansion House Hospital in Alexandria. Although she was escorted there by Miss Dix herself, no red carpet was laid out for her. In fact, the doctors left the door wide open, hoping Mary would quickly use it to leave. The poor woman sent out an SOS to the Superintendent of Nurses, who said, "Stay on at all costs—in the name of Susan B. Anthony and the female world," or words to that effect. Sex to Dorothea probably meant nothing more than gender.

Mary hung on. She had courage as well as tenacity and it took plenty of both with the entire staff against her, with no room of her own and the floor for her bed.

Miss Dix told me on the journey that the surgeon in charge was determined to give her no foothold in any hospital where he reigned, and that I was to take no notice of anything that might occur, and was to make no complaint whatever might happen. She was a stern woman of few words.

There seemed to be much confusion about the Mansion House—which before the war was a famous hotel—and every part of it was crowded. She left me in the office and went in search of Dr. S. The sight of the wounded continuously carried through on stretchers, or led in as they arrived from the boats that lay at the foot of the street on which the hospital stood (this was just after that awful Cedar Mountain battle—August 9)—seemed more than I could bear, and I thought Miss Dix would never come. At last she appeared, with Dr. S., who eyed me keenly and, it seemed to me, very savagely, and gave me in charge of an orderly to show me to the surgical ward, as it was called. It consisted of many small rooms, with a broad pass between them. Such a sorrowful sight; the men had just been taken off the battlefield, some of them had been lying three or four days almost without clothing, their wounds never dressed, so dirty and wretched. Someone gave me my charges as to what I was to do; it seemed such a hopeless task to do anything to help them that I wanted to throw myself down and give it up. Miss Dix left me, and soon the doctors came and ordered me to follow them while they examined and dressed the wounds. They seemed to me then, and afterwards I found they were, the most brutal men I ever saw.

So I began my work, I might say night and day. The surgeon told me he had no room for me, and a nurse told me he said he would make the house so hot for me I would not stay long. When I told Miss Dix I could not remain without a room to sleep in, she, knowing the plan of driving me out, said "My child," (I was nearly as old as herself), "you will stay where I have placed you." In the meantime McClellan's army was being landed below us from the Peninsula. Night and day the rumbling of heavy cannon, the marching of soldiers, the groaning of the sick and wounded were constantly heard; and yet in all that time I never once looked from the windows, I was so busy with the men.

One of the rooms of the ward was the operating room, and the passing in and out of those who were to be operated upon, and the coming and going of surgeons added so much to the general confusion. I doubt if at any time during the war there was ever such confusion as at this time. The insufficient help, the unskillful surgeons, and a general want of organization were very distressing; but I was too busy and too tired for want of proper sleep to half realize it. Though I slept at the bedsides of the men or in a corner of the rooms, I was afraid to complain lest I be discharged. I was horribly ignorant, of course, and could only try to make the men comfortable; but the staff doctors were very friendly and occasionally helped me, and someone occasionally showed me about bandaging, so by degrees I began to do better. The worst doctor had been discharged, much to my joy, but the other one, despite his drinking habits, stayed on. After the morning visit it was no use calling upon him for anything, and I had to rely on the officer of the day if I needed help. I know now that many a life could have been saved if there had been a competent surgeon in the ward.

At this time the ward was full of very sick men and sometimes two would be dying at the same time, and both begging me to stay with them, so I got little sleep or rest. Moreover, I had no room of my own. Occasionally a nurse would extend the hospitality of the floor in hers, and I would have a straw bed dragged in on which to get a few hours' sleep. This, with a hurried bath and fresh clothes, was my only rest for weeks. It was no use to complain. The surgeon simply stormed at me and said there was no room; while Miss Dix would say, "You can bear it a while, my child; I have placed you here and you must stay." I was at that time her only nurse in the Mansion House. Later she succeeded in getting rid of all the others and replacing them with her own.

THE SURGEON IN CHARGE TOOK MY STOVE AWAY

Sophronia E. Bucklin

While Dr. W. A. Hammond, surgeon with the One Hundred Twenty-sixth New York Volunteers, was in charge of her hospital, Sophronia was happy, but when a Dr. Burmeister returned to take charge, she became victim to the harsh resentment with which many of the doctors treated the army nurses.

The return of Dr. Burmeister was the beginning of a series of trials for me, as there were nurses among us who were ever ready to harass those who tried to do their whole duty.

Miss Dix sent a box of grapes to me requesting me to divide them with the nurses tenting with me, for the benefit of the patients. I did so, but soon discovered that the grapes were left untouched for days, and were not appropriated for the purpose for which they were intended. Because they were ready to find fault with these things I was daily reported to ears quite ready to take in slanderous tales.

Miss Dix appeared in the hospital one day, when affairs were near their consummation . . . and asked one of the nurses, who manifested no little enmity toward me, "Will you state the reason why you cannot tent with Miss Bucklin?" She remained silent, and Miss Dix continued. "If Miss Bucklin *does* cook for her men, the process cannot discommode you—for the stove is under the fly and out of your way, while she has a box and cupboard to keep her materials in. Surgeon Hammond is highly pleased with her labors. You are both good nurses, but I would not be justified in sending Miss Bucklin away because you do not wish to tent with her."

Then turning to me, she said, "Why don't you talk to your tentmates?" I replied, "Because I was told by Dr. Hammond to keep silence, as I was reported to him every day." I then rehearsed the story of my trials. . . .

The nurse's face grew scarlet with passion, and she broke forth, "I never was sent away from three hospitals." "Stop!" interrupted Miss Dix, "you shall not talk in that way. Miss Bucklin was relieved from two hospitals for simply doing her duty, as she seems to be doing now. I understand all of that."

Miss Dix could get no specific accusation against me, and she left me to the mercy of my tormentors, apparently in the full conviction that I was strong enough to take care of myself.

I had been advised by a few friends to resign, but I chose rather to remain, under all the unpleasant circumstances, than to risk being sent home while the end of the war seemed yet far off. I had little terror of being relieved now. I understood that men and women could be easily annoyed for simply attending to their duties, and I was sufficiently hardened for such contingencies.

I saw the enraged nurse go to the quarters of the surgeon in charge, and in a short time thereafter, he came over, and abruptly asked, "Where the devil did you get this stove?"

"Dr. Hammond procured it for me of the Sanitary Commission," I replied. "Well," he continued, "I want another stove, and I'll send for this." I protested—but in vain, the stove was taken.

I went immediately to the Christian Commission, and obtained a larger and better one, and prepared food as before, when able to obtain it. I was now reported as cooking for other wards than my own. The woman who had charge of the extra diet kitchen, and with whom the surgeon in charge boarded, came in one day and asked what I was going to have for my boys, adding, that she would keep back the Government supplies, if I thought I could beg enough to feed them.

I only replied, "My boys are entitled to their rations, and you must not withhold them."

Soon I received another call from the surgeon in charge, and he interrogated me in regard to extra cooking again. I replied, as before, that I only prepared food for my own patients. "Any way," he said, "I will take *this* stove, and that will stop the devilish work."

An order soon came for it, and I was left without the means of cooking for the wounded. One of the nurses went to the extra diet kitchen to board, another went to the Christian Commission, our cook was sent to his own regiment, and I was left alone. In this dilemma I decided to go to Washington and purchase a stove and furniture and see what virtue there would be in actual possession, and to go without Dr. Burmeister's knowledge.

I soon afterwards learned that Messrs. Burmeister and Dalton had been relieved from their positions, and that the hospital was then in charge of men whose executive powers, or their wills, were more favorable to the condition of the wounded.

I HAVE KNOWN TENDERHEARTED CONTRACT SURGEONS

Jane Stuart Woolsey

Contract surgeons were more or less victims of a system which made them an anomalous civil element in a military establishment, with but little military restriction and no military incentive in the shape of promotion. They had no position, small pay, and mere nominal rank. They were a temporary expedient in the first place—and who shall say what better one could have been devised for the emergency?—but the emergency went by, and the expedient was stretched into a corps of fifteen hundred men to whose hands were committed the wards of almost all General Hospitals. They served their little term, made their little experiments, and disappeared. The class was bad; it was under no bonds to be anything else; the exceptions were many and most honorable. I have known a "contract surgeon" for three months —six months—to refuse to attend a dying man, or attempt to ease his mortal agony because the patient was "no good anyhow" and the surgeon "had company." I have known one to operate on the slightly injured member and let the shattered one go, and on being "relieved" for drunkenness, begin in a neighboring hospital a fresh career of cutting off the wrong leg; and one who recommended a man for field duty with two inches of the bone of his right arm gone, and explained it by saying he was sure he wouldn't have sent him up if he had only known it.

But I have also known contract surgeons faithful, sagacious, tenderhearted, carrying their professional skill and their professional honor into the meanest contraband hut at any hour of the day or night, spending day and night with their soldier patients, watching them, devising every manner of expedient for their relief, humoring their fancies, telling them cheerful stories, tending them like brothers and sons.

WORMS HAD GROWN ON THE LIVING FLESH
Sophronia E. Bucklin

Sophronia's introduction to surgery as it was conducted in the field hospitals.

About the amputating tent lay large piles of human flesh—legs, arms, feet, and hands. They were strewn promiscuously about—often a single one lying under our very feet, white and bloody—the stiffened members seeming to be clutching ofttimes at our clothing.

A few tents were up, for shelter, and, as fast as they were vacated by transportation to Washington, they were filled up from the numbers who were lying upon the ground, waiting to have their wounds dressed. A general and hurried care was exercised for their many and pressing wants—it was all we could under the circumstances afford them.

Death met us on every hand. It was a time of intense excitement. Scenes of fresh horror rose up before us each day. Tales of suffering were told, which elsewhere would have well-nigh frozen the blood with horror. We grew callous to the sight of blood, and great gashed lips opened under our untrembling hands. . . .

A soldier came to me one day, when I was on the field, requesting me to dress his wound, which was in his side. He had been struck by a piece of shell, and the cavity was deep and wide enough to insert a pint bowl. This cavity was absolutely filled with worms; not the little slender maggots from which a woman's hand is wont to shrink in nervous terror, but great blackheaded worms, which had grown on the living flesh, and surfeiting of the banquet some of them crawled into his hair, and over his torn clothing.

While I was endeavoring to clear them from the wound, one of the surgeons came around, and paused to watch me at work. "That is too hard for you; I will assist you some," he said, and taking the can of chloroform—which always accompanied us on our rounds, the contents serving our purpose instead of fire in causing the strips of adhesive plaster to remain over the wounds —he poured the entire contents of the can into the mass of creeping life, which for a moment fought the contest with the fiery fluid and then straightened out.

Turning to an attendant, the surgeon ordered the wounded man to be stripped of his torn and bloody uniform, and a clean shirt and drawers to be put on him instead. "Then," he said to me, "you can dress the wound as you see fit."

I took a full pint of the dead worms from his side, thoroughly washed out the wound, and filled it with soft lint, wet in cold water, then bandaged him about the waist. I never saw him again—the transport being about to leave, all who had been attended to were put on board, and this soldier among the rest. . . .

Often they would long for a drink of clear, cold water, and lie on the hard ground, straining the filthy river water through closely set teeth.

So tortured were we all, in fact, by this thirst, which could not be allayed, that even now, when I lift to my lips a drink of pure, cold water, I cannot swallow it without thanking God for the priceless gift.

In the midst of our labors Miss Ballard (another nurse) was taken ill. . . . Her ward was composed of the worst cases in the hospital, the greatest number of severely wounded I ever saw together—most of them amputations—and their groans night and day were almost past endurance, for many of them were fighting the fever in their delirium. The ward fell to my care after she was taken ill.

The time for our departure came on in the course of military events. We were startled by the division surgeon, one evening, as we retired to our quarters, with the information that we might hold ourselves in readiness to leave at any hour during the night. We sat up, shaking with the cold, not daring to go to bed, until the surgeon again appeared and bade us retire, as he would call us early enough to arise and dress ourselves.

We sought our beds, and had scarcely got warm under the blankets when the steward called out to us, "Get up—you must get up—we are going to take the tent down."

We arose and dressed . . . the next cry was, "PACK YOUR THINGS AS SOON AS POSSIBLE—THE REBS ARE COMING!" . . . When about to be turned into the darkness of the chilly night, the order was countermanded, and we sat waiting for the morning twilight.

AMPUTATIONS HAD BEEN HASTILY GONE OVER

Eliza Harris

Mrs. Harris wrote infrequently to the Ladies' Aid Society in Philadelphia, but when she did her letters were shocking tales of suffering.

We filled two ambulances with bread and butter, prepared stewed fruit, eggnog, lemons, oranges, cheese, shirts, drawers, stockings, and handkerchiefs, and went out to meet a train of ambulances bearing the wounded from United States Ford. Reaching Stoneman's Station, where we expected to meet the train, we learned we were a half hour too late, but could overtake them; so we pressed forward, and found ourselves in the rear of a long procession of one hundred and two ambulances. The road being narrow, steep, and most difficult, we could not pass, and so were obliged to follow, feeling every jolt and jar for our poor suffering ones, whose wounds had just reached that point when the slightest motion is agony.

When this sad procession halted near the hospital of the Sixth Army Corps, we prepared to minister to the sufferers. Some gentlemen of the Christian Commission were there to assist us. No pen can describe the scene. Most of these sufferers had been wounded on the 3d instant.

Amputations and dressings had been hurriedly gone over, and then much neglected, necessarily so, for the Rebel surgeons had more than enough to occupy them in the care of their own wounded. You know we left most of our wounded on the right in their hands.

By day and by night I see their poor mutilated limbs, red with inflammation, bones protruding, worms rioting as they were held over the sides of the ambulance to catch the cooling breeze! Those anguished faces—what untold suffering they bespoke! Many a lip quivered, and eyes filled with tears, when approached with words of sympathy; and not a few told how they had prayed for death to end their sufferings, as they were dashed from side to side, often rolling, in their helplessness, over each other, as they were driven those twenty weary miles.

THAT OPERATING TABLE!

Belle Reynolds

Belle Reynolds describes the dreadful suffering of the wounded after the Battle of Pittsburgh Landing, or Shiloh, where she had gone to be near her husband, and help nurse the soldiers.

At nine o'clock we left the boat. . . . We climbed the steep hill opposite the Landing, picked our way through the corrals of horses, past the long lines of trenches which were to receive the dead, and came to an old cabin, where the wounded were being brought. Outside lay the bodies of more than a hundred, brought in for recognition and burial—a sight so ghastly that it haunts me now. We passed on, and entered the house, which contained three rooms. In one were some fifty wounded; in another (smaller) the surgeons were amputating. The ladies left me there, and went to the tents, which were also filled. The sight of a woman seemed to cheer the poor fellows, for many a "God bless you!" greeted me before I had done them a single act of kindness. The first call was for water; and none could be obtained nearer than the river. I stepped to the door, and called for volunteers to go with me to the river for water. Fifteen offered their services. Captain Norton furnished each with a pail, which they filled, and supplied the wants of the poor sufferers. After bathing and bandaging their burning wounds, I gave each some jelly, and distributed among them the little bread we had brought with us; but the supply was small for hungry men, and I found a sutler's stand, and emptied the contents of my purse for gingerbread—singular food for sick men, but very acceptable. . . .

And that operating table! These scenes come up before me now with all the vividness of reality . . . one by one, they would take from different parts of the hospital a poor fellow, lay him out on those bloody boards, and administer chloroform; but before insensibility, the operation would begin, and in the midst of shrieks, curses, and wild laughs, the surgeon would wield over his wretched victim the glittering knife and saw; and soon the severed and ghastly limb, white as snow and spattered with blood, would fall upon the floor—one more added to the terrible pile.

Until three o'clock I had no idle moments; then, having done all in my power to minister to so much wretchedness, I found my long-taxed nerves could endure no more. One of the surgeons brought me a spoonful of brandy, which revived me. Feeling that my labors were at an end, I prepared to leave, and had just turned to go in the direction of the boat, when a hand was laid upon my shoulder. The shock was so sudden I nearly fainted. There stood my husband! I hardly knew him—blackened with powder, begrimed with dust, his clothes in disorder, and his face pale. We thought it must have been years since we parted. It was no time for many words; he told me I must go. There was a silent pressure of hands. I passed on to the boat. . . .

At night I lived over the horrors of the field hospital and the amputating table. If I but closed my eyes, I saw such horrible sights that I would spring from my bed; and not until fairly awakened could I be convinced of my remoteness from the sickening scene. Those groans were in my ears; I saw again the quivering limbs, the spouting arteries, and the pinched and ghastly faces of the sufferers.

4 Closer to the Scenes of Battle

FROM THE MILITARY HOSPITALS IN AND AROUND WASHINGTON, THE army nurses soon moved closer to the scene of battle.

The first serious engagement with the enemy, the First Battle of Bull Run, July, 1861, resulted in a Confederate victory. "Raw troops, fresh from the counting room, farm, and workshop," commanded by officers who had never smelled gunpowder, marched into Virginia to attack the Rebels with as much gaiety as if they were off on a military picnic. Not one of them doubted that this battle would make short shrift of the Rebels, and put an end to the Rebellion. The Union soldiers plundered as they marched, "riotous with fun and frolic," accompanied by Congressmen, reporters, civilians—all who could get passes from the Federal government—in carriage, omnibuses, and on horseback, as confident as the soldiers that they would witness an easy victory.

After marching thirteen hours without pause, tired, hungry, and "agonized with thirst," the Northern soldiers suddenly met ten thousand fresh Confederate troops led by Generals Joe Johnston and P. T. Beauregard. Not having anticipated such opposition, they became panic-stricken, turned around, and fled back to Washington in complete disorder—"men in regiments and men in groups; army wagons and sutlers' teams; riderless horses, and the thundering artillery, crushing all that came in their way," dashed across Long Bridge into the Capital during a torrential rain, cluttering the roads behind them with abandoned cannon, arms, and equipment, and leaving the dead and dying uncared for.

The initial work of the Sanitary Commission was largely that of inspection—medical men were sent to look after the sanitary conditions of soldiers' quarters in the camps and hospitals so that disease might be prevented. Its activities had been confined for the most part to distributing supplies to the sick of fresh regiments that were constantly arriving in Washington, as it was impossible for the army officers to meet these exigencies. By giving its inspectors approximately the same pay as the army surgeons received, the Commission secured the "best services of the best men." During battlefield emergencies it accepted any volunteer aid that was offered by men or women, usually with very satisfactory results.

Now, after the disastrous fight at Bull Run, however, the Sanitary Commission assumed a new role in the field. This field relief work began with supplying cold water to the fainting, parched fugitives, as they fled back across the fields of Manassas. And for the first time in American history female nurses appeared on the battlefield.

In field hospitals nurses often slept in tents with the cold, damp earth for a floor. They endured privations that called for a fortitude equal, perhaps, in many ways, to the valor and strength of the soldiers. Obliged to respond to duty at all times and in all emergencies, they could not measure their time, their sleep, nor their strength. They were under orders to serve to the fullest, until their hands were swollen and their feet blistered and their bodies ached from overstrain. They were often victims of the army "Graybacks." Typhoid fever was prevalent; bowel discharges were not disposed of and the swarming flies attacked and destroyed strong men that had escaped the disasters of the battlefield. Many nurses died from accident or enemy fire; some from disease, from overwork, and from infection. Yet all were willing to sacrifice themselves for liberty and for the Union and few turned back from their duty.

Throughout the October battles of Edward's Ferry, Drainesville, and Ball's Bluff,* the Sanitary Commission gave relief to each regiment and sent supplies to the wounded. But the full strength of their newly acquired powers was not developed nor put into practice until the following spring.

On September 5, 1861, depots of supplies were established by the Sanitary Commission at New York, Boston, Philadelphia, Washington, Cincinnati, and Wheeling. Central aid associations for the different states were already in existence. These and other centers each had hundreds of towns and villages pouring boxes of food and clothing into their depots. The boxes were all emptied and sorted, each article was marked, their sorted contents were repacked and held subject to orders from Washington. The supply work of the commission at this point was placed chiefly in the hands of the women who prepared and furnished the enormous amount of food, clothing, linens, and medical supplies that saved many lives and alleviated much suffering. The supplies were shipped to any point where they were needed or likely to be needed. Agencies were established all along the lines of active war. There were six relief agents in the Army of the Potomac alone, with wagons and horses and men to carry out their orders, with a central base of supplies to meet

* Ball's Bluff, named after a farmer named Ball, was an embankment one hundred feet high on the Virginia shore of the Potomac. The cause of the disaster in which four Union regiments ferried over the Potomac for advance toward Leesburg were driven back into the river with the loss of half their number, the names of those responsible, and the plans and purposes of those who ordered the movement were not officially made known. Congress, not satisfied with the report of General Stone, in command, called upon the War Department for the facts. Major General McClellan, who had ordered the movement, refused to furnish them. After investigation, General Stone, who had been imprisoned for six months, was restored to active duty, and acquitted of misconduct.

their calls and with means of communication between central
base and field base.

Other agents, appointed by the Commission, moved about
the country encouraging and forming aid societies. Circulars and
monthly bulletins kept people even in the far-off villages constantly informed of the wants of the Army and the disposition
of the stores and supplies the aid societies had given. The great
distributing offices were at Washington in the East.

Relief on a vast scale in all departments of the Army was the
regular daily business of the Sanitary Commission. It was reduced to such a system and operated so perfectly that before
long it became as simple to deal with troops in Texas as with
those in northern Virginia.

On the other hand, the Medical Department continued to
operate in a blundering, hit-or-miss fashion. It had no plan or
organization for the removal of the wounded from the battlefields. As early as May, 1861, the organization of an ambulance
service was proposed to General Winfield Scott. He referred the
proposal to the Surgeon General and no more was heard of it.

The United States Sanitary Commission officials were angry
about the behavior of the Medical Department and the ladies of
the Woman's Central Relief Association complained to any
higher-up who would listen. Fashionably dressed ladies in frilly
hooped skirts lobbied vigorously for improvements, for a change
in leadership. They had decided by October that they could get
no adequate improvements in the way of hospitalization and
medical care for the Army until there was a new Surgeon General at the head of an enlarged and modernized Medical Department. They had transmitted this decision to the various
Ladies' Aid Societies, and the ladies took the matter up with
army officers, physicians, and men of sound political and business experience. Ladies came out of the kitchen and drawing
room and lobbied. They spent the winter of 1861-1862 writing

voluminous letters (a common 19th century procedure), paid calls on Congressmen, Senators, and other men of influence, and bombarded the press with all kinds of publicity. In the spring of 1862, the bill to reorganize the Medical Department was passed by both Houses and signed by the President. The President then appointed William A. Hammond as Surgeon General. Everybody was happy, including Dr. Hammond, and the ladies of the Woman's Central Relief Association, New York, celebrated their victory toasting the new Medical Department over a cup of tea. Although their beverage may have been weak, Lucretia Mott's protégées were going strong!

A GREAT BATTLE WAS TO BE FOUGHT AT BULL RUN

Sarah Emma Edmonds

Marching orders received to-day—two days more, and the Army of the Potomac will be on its way to Bull Run. Two days of preparation followed their announcement. The Army of the Potomac was soon to meet the enemy for the first time—a great battle was to be fought. Oh, what excitement and enthusiasm that order produced—nothing could be heard but the wild cheering of the men, as regiment after regiment received their orders. The possibility of a defeat never seemed to enter the mind of any. All the sick in camp now were to be sent to Washington, clothes changed, knapsacks packed, letters written home, packages sent to the express office, etc. After all was done, everything in readiness, and the sick men tenderly laid in the ambulances, we passed along from one ambulance to another, speaking words of encouragement to each soldier, many a tear would start from grateful eyes, and many a feeble voice uttered an earnest "God bless you," while others would draw from their bosoms some cherished relic, and give it as a token of remembrance. . . .

The ambulances started with their freight of emaciated, suffering men. Slowly that long train wound its way toward the city, looking like a great funeral procession. . . .

The 17th of July dawned bright and clear, and everything being in readiness, the Army of the Potomac took up its line of march for Manassas. In gay spirits the army moved forward, the air resounding with the music of the regimental bands, and patriotic songs of the soldiers. No gloomy forebodings seemed to damp the spirits of the men, for a moment, but "On to Richmond" was echoed and re-echoed, as that vast army moved rapidly over the country. I felt strangely out of harmony with the wild, joyous spirit which pervaded the troops. As I rode slowly along, watching those long lines of bayonets as they gleamed and flashed in the sunlight, I thought that many, very many, of those enthusiastic men who appeared so eager to meet the enemy would never return to relate the success or defeat of that splendid army. Even if victory should perch upon their banners, and I had no doubt it would, yet many noble lives must be sacrificed ere it could be obtained.

The main column reached Fairfax toward evening and encamped for the night. Col. R.'s wife of the Second ——, Mrs. B., and myself were, I think, the only three females* who reached Fairfax that night. The day had been extremely hot, and not being accustomed to ride all day beneath a burning sun, we felt its effects very sensibly, and consequently, hailed with joy the order to encamp for the night. Notwithstanding the heat and fatigue of the day's march, the troops were in high spirits, and immediately began preparing supper. Some built fires while others went in search of, and appropriated, every available article

* This is one of the many instances in Emma Edmonds' original memoirs where she tries to conceal the fact that she was disguised as a man.

which might in any way add to the comfort of hungry and fatigued men.

The whole neighborhood was ransacked for milk, butter, eggs, poultry, etc., which were found insufficient in quantity to supply the wants of such a multitude. There might have been heard some stray shots fired in the direction of a field where a drove of cattle were quietly grazing; and soon after the odor of fresh steak was issuing from every part of the camp. I wish to state, however, that all "raids" made upon hen-coops, etc., were contrary to the orders of the General in command, for during the day I had seen men put under arrest for shooting chickens by the roadside. . . . Supper being over, pickets posted, and camp guards detailed, all became quiet for the night.

Early the next morning the reveille beat, the whole camp was soon in motion, and after a slight breakfast from our haversacks the march was resumed. The day was very hot, and we found great difficulty in obtaining water, the want of which caused the troops much suffering. Many of the men were sun-struck, and others began to drop out of the ranks from exhaustion. All such as were not able to march were put into ambulances and sent back to Washington. Toward noon, the tedium of the march began to be enlivened by sharp volleys of musketry, in the direction of the advance guard; but those alarms were only occasioned by our skirmishers, pouring a volley into everything which looked as if it might contain a masked battery, or a band of the enemy's sharpshooters.

Considerable excitement prevailed throughout the day, as we were every hour in expectation of meeting the enemy. Carefully feeling its way, however, the army moved steadily on, investigating every field, building, and ravine, for miles in front and to the right and left, until it reached Centreville, where we halted for the night.

The troops now began to feel the effects of the march, and

there was evidently a lack of that picnic hilarity which had characterized them the day before. Several regiments had been supplied with new shoes the day before leaving camp, and they found by sad experience that they were not the most comfortable things to march in, as their poor blistered feet testified; in many cases their feet were literally raw, the thick woolen stockings having chafed the skin off. Mrs. B. and I, having provided ourselves before leaving camp with a quantity of linen, bandages, lint, ointment, etc., found it very convenient now, even before a shot had been fired by the enemy.

Our surgeons began to prepare for the coming battle by appropriating several buildings and fitting them up for the wounded—among others the stone church at Centreville. . . . Late that evening as I was returning from this church, accompanied by Mr. and Mrs. B., I proposed that we should walk through the entire camp to see how the boys were employed, on this, the eve of their first battle. We found many engaged in writing by the glimmering light of the camp-fire—soldiers always carry writing materials on a march; some were reading their bibles, perhaps with more than usual interest; while others sat in groups, conversing in low earnest tones; but the great mass were stretched upon the ground, wrapped in their blankets, fast asleep, and all unconscious of the dangers of the morrow. . . .

After ascertaining the position of the enemy, Gen. McDowell ordered forward three divisions, commanded by Heintzelman, Hunter, and Tyler, Miles being left in reserve at Centreville. Sunday morning before dawn, those three divisions moved forward, presenting a magnificent spectacle, as column after column wound its way over the green hills and through the hazy valleys, with the soft moonlight falling on the long lines of shining steel. Not a drum or bugle was heard during the march, and the deep silence was only broken by the rumbling of artillery, the muffled tread of infantry, or the low hum of thousands of subdued voices.

The divisions separated where three roads branch off toward Bull Run, each taking the road leading to its respective position. Soon the morning broke bright and clear, bringing the two contending armies in plain sight of each other. The enemy was posted on heights that rose in regular slopes from the shore crowned here and there by earthworks. The woods that interfered with his cannon ranges had all been cut away, and his guns had a clean sweep of every approach. On our side the descent was more gradual, and covered with a dense forest. The roar of artillery soon announced that the battle had actually commenced.

Mrs. B. and myself took our position on the field, according to orders, in connection with Gen. Heintzelman's division, having delivered our horses to Jack for safe keeping, with strict orders to remain where he was, for we might require them at any moment. . . . Mrs. B. stood there, looking as brave as possible, with her narrow-brimmed leghorn hat, black cloth riding habit, shortened to walking length by the use of a page, a silver-mounted seven-shooter in her belt, a canteen of water swung over one shoulder and a flask of brandy over the other, and a haversack with provisions, lint, bandages, adhesive plaster, etc., hanging by her side. She was tall and slender, with dark brown hair, pale face, and blue eyes. . . .

The first man I saw killed was a gunner belonging to Col. R.'s command. A shell had burst in the midst of the battery, killing one and wounding three men and two horses. Mr. B. (the chaplain) jumped from his horse, hitched it to a tree, and ran forward to the battery; Mrs. B. and I following his example as fast as we could. I stooped over one of the wounded, who lay upon his face weltering in his blood. He was mortally wounded in the breast, and the tide of life was fast ebbing away; the stretchers were soon brought, and he was carried from the field.

Seeing the disaster from a distance, Col. R. rode up to the battery, and as he was engaged in giving orders, a solid shot came whizzing by in such close proximity to his head, that it stunned him for a moment; but soon recovering, he turned up the side of his head and shrugged his shoulders, a peculiarity of his, and in his usual nasal twang, said, "rather close quarters," and rode away, apparently, as unconcerned as if it had been a humming-bird which crossed his path. But not content with admonishing the Colonel, the same shot struck my poor little flask of brandy which lay near me on a drum-head, shattering it. . . .

Now the battle began to rage with terrible fury. Nothing could be heard save the thunder of artillery, the clash of steel, and the continuous roar of musketry. Oh, what a scene for the bright sun of a holy Sabbath morning to shine upon! Instead of the sweet influences which we associate with the Sabbath—the chiming of church bells calling us to the house of prayer, the Sabbath school, and all the solemn duties of the sanctuary, there was confusion, destruction, and death. There was no place of safety for miles around; the safest place was the post of duty. Many that day who turned their backs upon the enemy and sought refuge in the woods some two miles distant were found torn to pieces by shell, or mangled by cannon ball—a proper reward for those who, insensible to shame, duty, or patriotism, desert their cause and comrades in the trying hour of battle, and skulk away cringing under the fear of death. . . .

I was hurried off to Centerville, a distance of seven miles, for a fresh supply of brandy, lint, etc. When I returned, the field was literally strewn with wounded, dead, and dying. I saw Mrs. B. coming toward me, running her horse with all possible speed, with about fifty canteens hanging from the pommel of her saddle. To all my inquiries there was but one answer: "Don't stay to care for the wounded now; the troops are famishing with

thirst and are beginning to fall back." Mr. B. then rode up with
the same order, and we three started for a spring a mile distant,
having gathered up the empty canteens which lay strewn on the
field. This was the nearest spring; the enemy knew it, and consequently had posted sharpshooters within rifle range to prevent
the troops being supplied with water. Notwithstanding this, we
filled our canteens, while the Minié balls fell thick and fast
around us, and returned in safety to distribute the fruits of our
labor among the exhausted men.

We spent three hours in this manner, while the tide of battle rolled on more fiercely than before, until the enemy made a
desperate charge on our troops, driving them back and taking
full possession of the spring. Chaplain B.'s horse was shot
through the neck and bled to death in a few moments. Then
Mrs. B. and I dismounted and went to work again among the
wounded.

Not long afterwards Col. Cameron, brother of the Secretary
of War, came dashing along the line, shouting, "Come on boys,
the Rebels are in full retreat." The words had scarcely been uttered when he fell, pierced to the heart by a bullet. Surgeon P.
was on the ground in an instant, but nothing could be done
for him; his wound was mortal. . . .

Still the battle continues without cessation; the grape and
canister fill the air as they go screaming on their fearful errand; the sight of that field is perfectly appalling; men tossing
their arms wildly calling for help; there they lie bleeding, torn
and mangled; legs, arms, and bodies are crushed and broken as
if smitten by thunderbolts; the ground is crimson with blood;
it is terrible to witness. Burnside's brigade is being mown down
like grass by the Rebel batteries; the men are not able to stand
that terrible storm of shot and shell; they begin to waver and
fall back slowly, but just at the right moment Capt. Sykes comes
up to their relief with his command of regulars. They sweep up

the hill where Burnside's exhausted, shattered brigade still lingers, and are greeted with a shout of joy such as none but soldiers who are almost overpowered by a fierce enemy, and are reinforced by their brave comrades, can give.

Onward they go, close up to the cloud of flame and smoke rolling from the hill upon which the Rebel batteries are placed —their muskets are leveled—there is a click, click—a sheet of flame—a deep roll like that of thunder, and the Rebel gunners are seen to stagger and fall. The guns become silent, and in a few moments are abandoned. This seems to occasion great confusion in the Rebel ranks. Regiments were scattered, and officers were seen riding furiously and shouting their orders, which were heard above the roar and din of battle.

Captain Griffin's and Rickett's batteries are ordered forward to an eminence from which the Rebels have been driven. They come into position and open a most destructive fire which completely routs the enemy. The battle seems almost won and the enemy is retreating in confusion. . . .

But just as our army is confident of success, and is following up the advantage which it has gained, Rebel reinforcements arrive and turn the tide of battle. Two Rebel regiments of fresh troops are sent to make a flank movement in order to capture Griffin's and Rickett's batteries. They march through the woods, reach the top of the hill, and form a line so completely in our rear as to fire almost upon the backs of the gunners. Griffin sees them approach, but supposes them to be his supports sent by Major Barry. However looking more intently at them, he thinks they are Rebels, and turns his guns upon them. Just as he is about to give the order to fire, Major B. rides up shouting, "They are your supports, don't fire." "No, sir, they are Rebels," replied Capt. Griffin. "I tell you, sir, they are your supports," said Major B. In obedience to orders the guns were turned again, and while in the act of doing so, the supposed supports fired a volley upon the gunners. Men and horses went down in an instant. A moment more and those famous batteries were in the hands of the enemy.

The news of this disaster spread along our lines like wildfire; officers and men were alike confounded; regiment after regiment broke and ran, and almost immediately the panic commenced. Companies of cavalry were drawn up in line across the road, with drawn sabers, but all was not sufficient to stop the refluent tide of fugitives. Then came the artillery thundering along, drivers lashing their horses furiously, which greatly added to the terror of the panic-stricken thousands crowded together en masse. In this manner we reached Centerville where order was in some measure restored.

Mrs. B. and I made our way to the stone church around which we saw stacks of dead bodies piled up, and arms and legs were thrown together in heaps. But how shall I describe the scene within the church at that hour. Oh, there was suffering there which no pen can ever describe. One case I can never forget. It was that of a poor fellow whose legs were both broken above the knees, and from the knees to the thighs they were literally smashed to fragments. He was dying; but oh, what a death was that. He was insane, perfectly wild, and required two persons to hold him. Inflammation had set in, and was rapidly doing its work; death soon released him, and it was a relief to all present as well as to the poor sufferer. . . .

Our hearts and hands being fully occupied with such scenes as these, we thought of nothing else. We knew nothing of the true state of affairs outside, nor could we believe it possible when we learned that the whole army had retreated toward Washington, leaving the wounded in the hands of the enemy, and us, too, in rather an unpleasant situation. I could not believe the stern truth, and was determined to find out for myself. Consequently I went back to the heights where I had seen the troops stack their guns and throw themselves upon the ground at nightfall, but no troops were there. I thought then that they had merely changed their position, and that by going over the field I should certainly find them. I had not gone far before I saw a camp fire in the distance. Supposing that I had found a clue to the secret, I made all haste toward the fire; but as I drew near I saw but one solitary figure sitting by it, and that was the form of a female.

Upon going up to her I recognised her as one of the washerwomen of our army. . . . I soon found out that the poor creature had become insane. The excitement of battle had proved too much for her, and all my endeavors to persuade her to come with me were unavailing. I had no time to spare, for I was convinced that the army had really decamped.

Once more I started in the direction of Centerville. I had not gone more than a few rods before I heard the clatter of horses' hoofs. I stopped, and looking in the direction of the fire I had just quitted, I saw a squad of cavalry ride up to the woman who still sat there. Fortunately I had no horse to make a noise or attract attention, having left mine at the hospital with the intention of returning immediately. It was evident to my mind that those were the enemy's cavalry, and that it was necessary for me to keep out of sight if possible until they were gone. I was near a fence, against which there were great piles of brush, and as the night was becoming very dark and it was beginning to rain, I thought I could remain undetected, at least until morning. My suspicions proved to be correct. They were coming toward me, and compelling the woman to come and show them the direction I had taken; I decided to crawl under one of those brush heaps, which I did, and had scarcely done so, when up they came and stopped over against the identical pile in which I was concealed.

One of the men said "See here, old woman, are you sure that

she can tell us if we find her?" "Oh, yes, she can tell you, I know she can," was the woman's reply. They would go away a little distance and then come back again; by and by they began to accuse the woman of playing a false game; then they swore, threatened to shoot her, and she began to cry. At last they gave it up as a hopeless case and rode away taking the woman with them. . . .

The village of Centerville was not yet occupied by the Rebels, so that I might have made my escape without any further trouble; but how could I go and leave those hospitals full of dying men, without a soul to give them a drink of water? I must go into that Stone Church once more, even at the risk of being taken prisoner. I did so—and the cry of "Water, water," was heard above the groans of the dying. Chaplain B. had told them before leaving that they would soon be in the hands of the enemy—that the Army had retreated to Washington, and that there was no possibility of removing the wounded. There they lay, calmly awaiting the approach of their cruel captors, and apparently prepared to accept with resignation any fate which their cruelty might suggest. . . .

They all urged me to leave them, and not subject myself to the barbarous treatment which I would be likely to receive if I should be taken prisoner, adding, "If you do stay the Rebels will not let you do anything for us." One of the men said: "Dr. E. has only been gone a little while—he extracted three balls from my leg and arm, and that, too, with his penknife. I saw twenty-one balls which he had taken from the limbs of men in this hospital. He was determined to remain with us, but we would not consent, for we knew he would not be allowed to do any more for us after the Rebels came; and you must go too, and go very soon or they will be here."

After placing water within the reach of as many as could use their arms, and giving some to those who could not—I turned to leave them, with feelings that I cannot describe; but ere I reached the door a feeble voice called me back—it was that of a young officer from Massachusetts; he held in his hand a gold locket, and as he handed it to me he said, "Will you please to open it?" I did so, and then held it for him to take a last look at the picture which it contained. He grasped it eagerly and pressed it to his lips again and again. The picture was that of a lady of rare beauty, with an infant in her arms. She seemed scarcely more than a child herself; on the opposite side was printed her name and address. While he still gazed upon it with quivering lip, and I stood there waiting for some tender message for the loved ones, the unmistakable tramp of cavalry was heard in the street—a moment more, and I had snatched the locket from the hands of the dying man and was gone.

The streets were full of cavalry, but not near enough to discover me, as the night was exceedingly dark and the rain came down in torrents. One glance was sufficient to convince me that I could not escape by either street. The only way was to climb a fence and go across lots, which I immediately did, and came out on the Fairfax road about a mile from the village, and then started for Washington on the "double quick." I did not reach Alexandria until noon the next day—almost exhausted, and my shoes literally worn off my feet.

NEWS OF A GREAT BATTLE AT BULL RUN

Jane Newton Woolsey

During that first summer of the war, Jane Newton Woolsey in New York was concerned about her two daughters, Georgeanna and Eliza in Washington. She seriously considered joining them there, but managed to restrain the impulse until several months later.

8 Brevoort Place, New York,
Monday, July 22, 1861.

We have had an exciting night and morning. Just as we were going to bed last night we heard the distant sound of an "Extra"; it was very late; everybody in bed. We had been out to the meeting of the Evangelical Alliance at Dr. McAuley's Church. We were all undressed, but waited with anxiety till the sound approached nearer and nearer; but made up our minds not to rush down and buy one, as it might be a hoax—till at last a tremendous howl of three boys through 10th street gave us the news of a "great battle at Bull's Run. Rebels defeated! Batteries all taken!" We thanked God for this much, and went to our beds to try and sleep patiently till morning. We have now had the newspaper accounts as far as they go, but long for further and later. Your two letters of Saturday, Georgy, we have also this morning; many thanks for both; rejoiced to hear good news from Joe so direct, and that you are both well and *busy*. It is better so. I feel this morning as if I could fly right off to Washington, and can scarcely resist the impulse to start at once. Would you like to see me? . . .

The girls are packing a box for your distribution at the hospitals—Jane rolling a fresh lot of bandages. Poor Kate, our housemaid, looks quite distressed to-day, thinking her brother may have been foremost in the ranks, as the paper stated "the First Massachusetts led in the advance, and had suffered much." Dr. Tyng made an inspiring address last night to a densely crowded audience. He said he was greatly surprised to see such an assemblage when he had supposed the city deserted, and thought such an audience was a sufficient appeal without a word from him, as showing the deep interest manifested in this "righteous" cause—"I say *righteous*, for I firmly believe if there ever was a righteous, holy war, direct from the hand of God, this is one." . . . There were some very interesting letters read from the different chaplains, and some from the men themselves of different regiments. Dr. Hoge has resigned, and left his charge to Dr. Spring, on account of his attachment to the South! and his desire to be there at this time. *I* say joy go with him, but some of the people are unwilling to receive his resignation. . . . I have no news for you; we see no one, and are supposed to be out of town. It is perfectly cool and comfortable here, and we are at present better satisfied to be here. By and by we may run off for a while. God bless you both, my dear children! I wish I were close at your side. . . .

WHAT A DREADFUL COLLAPSE THE ARMY OF THE POTOMAC SUFFERED

Abby Howland Woolsey

New York,
July 27, 1861, 10 A.M.

I have just been up to the corner to see a sorry sight, the return of the 69th Regiment—oh, so shabby, so worn and weary —all sorts of hats and shirts and some with hardly any clothes at all, staggering along under their knapsacks which they should never have been allowed to carry up Broadway. The surging mass of men and women locking arms and walking with the soldiers was wonderful. It was a wild, tumultuous, promiscuous rush—not a march. Yesterday afternoon, the 8th came through. I could see from the balcony how brown they looked and sturdy, and trimmer than the 69th. The girls and Mother saw them from Brady's window. The cheers and applause they got down town, I suppose. There was not much of it up here—there was too much crying. Even policemen were in tears. What a dreadful collapse the "Grand Army" of the Potomac suffered. I don't don't think the North needed such a lesson! Perhaps they did— perhaps the people have felt as if they could march down to

Richmond whenever they chose. . . . Scott sent an inefficient general (known as a perfect windbag among brother officers) without a commissariat, without organization, without proper regimental officers, against what he knew to be a fortified camp of a hundred thousand men. The one great blunder was that the battle was fought at all. All other minor blunders—and how many there were! are included in this. . . .

Jefferson Davis is free now to do what he pleases—flushed with success. Everyone says this battle has been as good to him as an increase of a hundred thousand fighting men. . . . He will perhaps attack Washington itself. The papers speak of the danger of this—and we all feel that the city is in greater peril than it was in those April days. Under such circumstances we do not quite relish your idea of going to Alexandria. You would be cut off at once, in that town, from communication or escape. One thought that checked Mother's desire to go immediately to Washington last Monday was the idea that on reaching there she might find that women and children have been ordered to leave—for fear of an attack from Beauregard. That order may come yet. My dear sisters, I do not want to write anything depressing, but you must make up your minds after this disaster for a *long war*, an impoverished country, many reverses. So far, you have had but one thought—that of immediate success. General Scott's plan of closing in on the Rebels in Virginia and crushing them as in his fingers is blown to the winds. We are to have a protracted and somewhat equal struggle, but the North is in earnest; its fault has been *over*-eagerness. Men there always have been enough of—let them have proper officers; and as to money, Congress ought to be ashamed to haggle about direct taxation but pass the bill at once and provide ways and means. . . . I am very glad the boxes had all arrived safely. Next day you would get Aunt Emily's two barrels, and Uncle Edward's $250 in money. Buy whatever you see is needed or the surgeons and nurses want. Don't wait for red tape. If it is mattresses, cots, pillows, spirit lamps, food, sheeting, flannel, etc. to wrap wounded men in, or what not. You can have plenty of money, and it could not be better spent than in fitting up a hospital even if that *is* government work. Carry wanted me to send you some money for her, but I told her I would wait and see whether you could buy the things you needed in Washington, or whether it had better be spent here. Please let me know. We shall have enough more things to fill a barrel early next week. Shall we put in the bandage roller, or are the hospital surgeons provided? I am sorry that Mrs. Leavitt did not send you a list of the contents of *her* boxes. . . .

Don't save up things if you see them needed. It is easy to buy more slippers and mosquito net here, and it does not cost us any time or a stitch of effort to send more clothing. The Society has plenty on hand. Mrs. Parker jumped up with pleasure when we sent round the other day to see if she could let us have a few things for the trunk, and granted enough, as you saw, to fill two boxes and over. She was delighted at the idea of their being distributed where she could hear about it, and I must manage to put some scraps of your accounts together and tell her what you say. There is a fresh lot of handkerchiefs under way. Maria Gilman hemmed them on her machine.

TORCHLIGHT PROCESSION IN HONOR OF MC CLELLAN

Eliza Woolsey Howland

Joseph Howland had returned to the army after spending his week's furlough with his wife and Georgeanna at the Woolsey home in New York. Georgeanna and Eliza stayed in New York two weeks longer with their mother. On returning to Washing-

ton, they found that General Scott had just resigned as head of the Army—November 1—and General McClellan had been appointed Commander-in-Chief. They began work at once.

Ebbitt House, Washington, Nov. 11, 1861.

It is very late, but I scribble a line before going to bed to say we got over safely from camp, stopping on the way for Mr. Hopkins, who is going to Poolesville with us to-morrow. We got in at six o'clock and since then we have been in a blaze of glory, for there has been a splendid torchlight procession in honor of McClellan, with rockets and blue lights and all sorts of fine things. Of course we followed it with Chaplain Hopkins, bringing up at Mrs. Hodge's in H street, next door to McClellan's own house, where the procession halted and called out Seward and Lincoln and Cameron and McClellan himself, and there were several little speeches, the best of which was General Blenker's who said: "Citizens and soldiers, when I shtand on de battlefield with your thousands volunteers I will fight de enemy better as I shpeak your noble language." Then on tiptoe he patted McClellan on the back and I think kissed him! Seward's speech was highly vague and promiscuous.

We came home at midnight, just now, with our patriotic noses smutty from the torches.

At nine this morning we start for Poolesville and have the prospect of a fine day.

The Battle of Ball's Bluff near Poolesville had taken place while we were on "leave of absence" at home, and on our return to Washington, Major Potter, U.S. paymaster, and his wife, starting on an expedition to pay the troops up the Potomac, invited Chaplain Hopkins and ourselves to join the party, which we did with great delight, though it involved a three days' journey in our own carriage—a formidable thing at that time. It gave us an opportunity of visiting the scene of the desperate fight at the Bluff and the encampments at Poolesville and Darnestown, and of taking supplies to these distant hospitals.

From E's Journal:

The officers told us the whole story of the battle and described terrible scenes to us of cold, suffering, and death by drowning which we hope to forget. . . .

While standing on the dreadful bank where our poor wounded were dragged up (and from which we plainly saw the Rebel pickets across the river gathering in a little group), we understood fully and bitterly the wicked incompetency of whoever is responsible for this blunder. . . .

At the end of January, after much procrastination, Mother Woolsey and Hatty went on to Washington under Charley's escort for two or three weeks, which lengthened out into three months with G. and E., and proved a great delight to all accoro ing to the following by Georgeanna:

Mother, Hatty, and Charley arrived last night in the middle of the storm and mud. Mother is now writing at the table with me, while H. is gazing admiringly at a group of Irish Brigadiers at the door. Charley is out somewhere, and is to meet the rest of us in the Senate Chamber at noon. We are cosily settled and having a very nice time. The roads are almost impassable owing to melting snow and frost and incessant rain. J.'s last ride back to camp the other day was very hard. He and the General floundered about in mud "like unfathomable chewed molasses candy," and stumbled against the stumps till darkness overtook them before they reached camp. Reports are brought in of private carriages abandoned along the road, and one—Mrs. Judge Little's—was fairly dragged in two by a government team which tried to haul it out of a hole. J. says we must not think of coming out to camp.

5

On to Richmond

IN AUGUST, 1861, THE WAR DEPARTMENT ISSUED AN ORDER OFFI-
cially creating the Army of the Potomac, which was to become
one of the best-known armies throughout the world. The gallant and handsome young George Brinton McClellan became
its General in Chief. "Little Mac" found the army in a deplorable condition and set about at once reorganizing, drilling, and
instructing the troops who had been demoralized by their defeat
at Bull Run. It was an enormous task but he seemed able to
cope with it; under his direction perfect order and military
discipline was established. Even his enemies had to admit that
he had transformed a disorganized mob into an effective army.

Horace Greeley's *New York Tribune* resumed its popular "On
to Richmond" chant, and throughout the country everyone
waited now for something to happen. A great forward movement was anticipated with a quick and crushing defeat of the
enemy. But as the historian of the First Army Corps put it,
"that feverish hope was destined to receive a terrible chill." For
the Army of the Potomac did not budge. McClellan continued
his dress rehearsals and the Confederate capital remained safe
for the Confederacy.

On the home front the Aid Societies were functioning, but
people resumed a more or less normal way of life.

Finally, on March 17, the great invasion got underway and
McClelland embarked from Alexandria, Virginia, and sailed
down the Chesapeake to Fortress Monroe, where he landed some

FOUR UNION NURSES

Jane Hoge   Mary A. Bickerdyke

Mary J. Safford   Cordelia A. P. Harvey

Georgeanna M. Woolsey. (Courtesy The New-York Historical Society)

Caroline Caisson Woolsey. (Courtesy The New-York Historical Society)

Mary A. Livermore.

Sarah Emma Edmonds in hoopskirts.

Sarah Emma Edmonds in male disguise as Franklin Thompson. *(Courtesy Lucy Sterling Seelye)*

Meeting at Cooper Union Hall, April 25, 1861, to organize the Women's Central Association of Relief.

New York headquarters of the Women's Central Association of Relief at 7 & 11 Cooper Union. *(Courtesy Museum of the City of New York)*

Exterior of the Women's Central Association of Relief, which became a branch of the United States Sanitary Commission. (*Courtesy Museum of the City of New York*)

A pass for Annie T. Wittemyer, countersigned by Abraham Lincoln on October 20, 1864, reads: "Let the lady have transportation to any of the Armies, and any privileges while there, not objected to by the commanders of the Armies respectively." (*Library of Congress*)

A telegram sent by Dr. Elizabeth Blackwell to Georgeanna Woolsey in Washington directing her to meet a contingent of nurses at the railroad depot. (*Courtesy The New-York Historical Society*)

Civil War nurses in a large urban
hospital. *(Brown Brothers)*

Aboard a hospital transport, 1862. *(Culver Service)*

FLOATING HOSPITAL SERVICE

OF

THE SANITARY COMMISSION,

FOR THE CAMPAIGN IN VIRGINIA. *1862.*

TERMS OF SERVICE.

The Sanitary Commission, being itself under military authority, in order to meet its responsibilities, must require of all persons who engage in the hospital service of the army under its direction, that they place themselves, for the time being, entirely at its disposal.

Those who volunteer their services gratuitously being supposed to do so fully and in good faith, no distinction can be known between them and those who may be paid for their services, it being understood that these services, in both cases, once engaged or accepted, are to be claimed equally of right by the Commission.

ADMINISTRATION.

An agent of administration for the Commission will be appointed for each hospital vessel, who will be regarded by those on board as responsible for her fittings and supplies.

WARDS.

Each vessel will be divided into hospital wards, designed each for the accommodation of from fifty to one hundred and fifty patients. In case of convalescents, a larger number will be properly included in a ward.

SURGEONS.

A surgeon in charge will be appointed to each vessel, who will be responsible for the reception, classification, and distribution of patients in the wards. He will sign any necessary official medical reports of the vessel. Each ward will be placed under the special charge of one surgeon, and, if practicable, there will be a surgeon for each ward.

ASSISTANTS TO SURGEONS.

An assistant to the surgeon (with the title of Ward-master) is to be constantly on duty in each ward. Under instructions from the surgeon of the ward, he will superintend and be responsible for the entire treatment of the patients of the ward, during the hours in which he is appointed to be on duty.

NURSES.

Two or more nurses are to be constantly on duty in each ward. They will perform any and all duties necessary in the care of the patients, under instructions from the surgeons received through the ward-masters.

DISPENSARY.

A dispensary will be established on each vessel, and one or more apothecaries will be placed in charge of it. They will be responsible for the medical stores and for their proper compounding, and issue upon requisitions of the surgeons through the ward-masters.

HOSPITAL PANTRY AND LINEN CLOSET.

These will be in charge of ladies, who will issue to ward-masters or nurses, or themselves administer and dispense, under proper control of the surgeons, special diet and drink and articles of bed and personal clothing for the patients.

WATCHES.

Ward-masters and nurses and all who have part in duty of a constant character, will be divided into two watches, which will be on duty alternately, as follows :

1. From 7 a. m. to 1 p. m. A
2. " 1 p. m. to 4 p. m. B, (dog watch.)
3. " 4 p. m. to 7 p. m. A. do. do.
   " 7 p. m. to 1 a. m. B
5. " 1 a. m. to 7 a. m. A
6. " 7 a. m. to 1 p. m. B, (2d day.)

TIME OF MEALS.

Breakfast.
One watch at 6.40 a. m., (being then off duty.)
The other at 7 a. m. do. do.

Dinner.
One watch at 12.30 p. m. do. do.
The other at 1.15 p. m. do. do.

Tea.
One watch at 6.40 p. m. do. do.
The other at 7 p. m. do. do.

HOUSE DIET.

BREAKFAST.
To be ready at 7 A M.
Bread (or Toast) with Butter,
Coffee or Tea.

DINNER.
To be ready at 1.15 P. M.
Beef Soup and Boiled Beef or Beef Stew
Boiled Rice or Hominy,
Bread or Crackers.

TEA.
To be ready at 7 P M.
Bread or Toast or Crackers, with Butter.
Coffee or Tea.

When practicable, the house diet will be served at tables to such patients as are able to come to them. When not practicable to arrange tables, such patients as may be designated by the surgeons, will be divided into squads of forty, and a squad-master appointed to each, who will receive and distribute to the rest, the prepared diet, as may be found most convenient. Patients not able to leave their beds will not be included in these squads, but house diet will be served to them by the nurses of their wards, if ordered by the surgeon.

SPECIAL DIET.

The surgeons will ascertain from the administrative agent, or from the ladies, what articles of diet are available on the vessel, and in their morning rounds direct what choice shall be made from these for the diet of each patient, for whom the house diet would not be suitable, during the succeeding twenty-four hours. The ward-master on duty at the hour for surgeon's morning rounds will, in regular order, be on duty at each meal time during the following twenty-four hours, and will consequently be able to direct the entire diet of each patient from verbal instructions. He should, as soon as possible, notify the proper person (no rule in this respect being practicable for all vessels) of the quantity of each article of special diet which will be required at each meal in his ward, and at the proper time should (if

necessary) send the nurses for it, and see it properly distributed.

SURGEONS' ROUNDS.

Surgeons' rounds should commence at 9 a. m., and at 8 p. m. The ward-master on duty will closely attend the surgeon, and receive his instructions as he passes through his ward. The ward-master off duty may also attend the surgeon at this time, for the benefit of receiving instructions directly. The surgeon may make this a duty, otherwise it will be optional.

ALL HANDS.

In receiving and discharging patients, or in any emergency which makes it necessary, ward-masters and nurses may be required to do duty in their watches off. In cleaning, fitting, or repairing the vessel for hospital purposes, they will act under orders of the administrative agent.

RECEIVING AND DISTRIBUTING PATIENTS.

Before patients are taken on board, the vessel should be properly moored or placed ; gangways, or other means of entrance arranged, and, if possible, all duties completed, for the time being, in the performance of which the crew of the vessel are required. The surgeon, who should have previously informed himself of the character of the accommodations for patients in all parts of each ward, should detail a sufficient number of guides and bearers to convey the patients, and of all necessary attendants at the gangway, and within the wards. These should remove their boots, and each squad of bearers should be instructed that all orders will be given them by their guide alone, and that no one else is to speak aloud while carrying a patient, or passing through the wards. All persons not having a specified duty to perform in receiving patients, should be put where they will not be in the way or disturb the patients, but where they can be readily called on it the force engaged is found insufficient.

As each patient is brought on board, he will be examined by the surgeon in charge, who will direct where he shall be taken : at the same time notes will be taken, as follows :

Name, Age, Company, Regiment, Residence, Disease.

The administrative agent will, at the same time, cause a corresponding number to be placed on the effects of the patient, which he will take care of, to be returned to the patient on his leaving the vessel. If practicable, the patients **may,** before being taken to their berths or cots, be **washed** and supplied with clean clothing.

It will not usually be in the power of the surgeon in charge to select patients for his vessel. It may, however, be proper for him to protest against taking patients whose illness is not of a sufficiently serious character to warrant their withdrawal from the seat of war, or those for whose cases there is less suitable provision on the vessel than in the hospitals they are leaving, or those already in a dying condition, whose end will have been accelerated or whose suffering aggravated by their removal ; also, when going to sea, against taking cases of compound fracture of the lower extremities.

FRED. LAW OLMSTED, General Secretary.

A broadside detailing the work of the United States Sanitary Commission's Hospital Transport Service. (*Courtesy The New-York Historical Society*)

112,000 men, proposing to advance up the Peninsula between the York and James Rivers and capture Richmond.

The Army encamped for a brief period at the village of Hampton, not far from the Fortress, and then once again was on the move along the Yorktown Road, which ran through a low, swampy, pestilential region. Yorktown, a Rebel stronghold and McClellan's next port of call, was only twenty-three miles from Hampton, but it took all the determination and energy of veterans to march half the distance in a day. Marching through the mud and mire was difficult even for the mules.

Food rations were soon exhausted, but more provisions did not arrive. It seemed impossible to get a supply train over the muddy road. Miles of corduroy bridges had to be constructed before a team could make the trip, and the horses were as badly off for forage as the men. Foragers made frequent excursions from camp to buy food from the nearby Southern homes while the Army bivouacked on the wet ground in front of Yorktown and prepared for a long siege.

Meanwhile, McClellan's secret service, headed by Allan Pinkerton, brought back exaggerated reports of the size of the Confederate Army, and "Little Mac" frantically wired Washington for more troops. Scouts and spies were sent to Yorktown to determine the strength of the Rebel fortifications, and Professor Thaddeus Lowe made balloon reconnaissances, transmitting the results of his observations to McClellan by telegraph.

There was a great deal of activity but no battles of any significance would take place on the Peninsula before the end of May.

But there was fighting going on around Winchester, Virginia. General Banks drove Stonewall Jackson out of the Lower Shenandoah Valley in March, and won the first Battle of Kernstown near Winchester.

JANE AND CHARLEY HAVE GONE TO THE PHILHARMONIC

Abby Howland Woolsey

On April 26th, 1862, Abby Woolsey writes to her mother who had gone to Washington to see what was keeping Georgy happy there.

We are all bright and well this fine morning. Jane and Charley have gone to the Philharmonic rehearsal and Carry is practicing some of her old music on the piano, in a way to make you, who love to hear it, happy. Mr. Prentiss came in last night to see us, looking well, but queer, as he always does in a black stock. He had been hard at work, moving his books, and did not intend to go to prayer meeting, and evidently didn't suppose we had gone, or he wouldn't have come to spend the evening with us. He told us much that was pleasant and funny about his visit in Washington, which, short as it was, paid him well, he thought, for going. . . . He hopes Eliza and Georgy will get their wishes and go to Fort Monroe, as they are in a state of mind to be fretted and troubled if they don't. . . .

Very few of the wounded brought by the *Cossack* from Newbern were landed here. . . . All were crazy to get home, all full of spirits and fun. The five or six who were carried to the N. E. Relief only fretted at having to spend a night longer on the road. The man with both legs gone smoked his pipe and read his newspaper. His chief anxiety was to go into New Jersey by a certain train. . . . Five or six ladies were at the rooms, Jane among them, yesterday, a lady apiece and several men to each volunteer. . . . No wonder it dazed an Irishman just released from four months' imprisonment in Richmond. "Begor," he said, "I can't pay for all this!" . . . Jane says there is nothing much for the present set of ladies to do, except to rearrange the piles of shirts, etc., on the closet shelves—changing them about from the way she had fixed them! They immediately proceeded to that work, and each new set of ladies will have *that*, at least, to occupy them. As for the Park Barracks, a portion of them have been scrubbed and whitewashed, the bunks taken down, neat iron beds all made and put up. Mrs. Mack is to live there as Matron, and, for the purpose of a mere halting place and infirmary, it is as good an one as they could have, though too many ladies were on hand, switching things over with their hoops, giving unlimited oranges to men who had the dysentery, and making the surgeons mad. There were, beside, half the medical students in the city, all staring and eager for jobs;—no difficulty in the men's having all, and more than all, the attention they want. One good thing Mrs. Woodruff did, at Mrs. Buck's suggestion—sent over to the Astor House for a steward, and through him ordered a good dinner brought in of tender beef, fresh eggs, etc., for the twenty or thirty New York and New Jersey men who were resting there. It will be charged to New York State, which supports the Barracks. . . . We have Lloyd's map of Virginia under the front parlor picture of the Virgin, along the back of the sofa, and we sit there and read the papers and study it.

THEY HAD JUST RECEIVED THEIR MARCHING ORDERS

Georgeanna M. Woolsey

Washington, March 10, 1862.

All strange rumors come on Sunday. Josepha Crosby, Hatty,* and I went down to spend the afternoon at the Patent Office Hospital.

During the week the camps had been emptied of convales-

* Harriet Roosevelt Woolsey, her sister.

cents, sent North to recover, and their places in the hospitals were occupied by others. The Patent Office is full again, four rows of beds and very sick men in them. . . . Coming away I hurried up to Mrs. Captain Rodgers' house and heard the story of the Merrimac fight. The first intimation they had of it was in church on Sunday morning, when, during service, a messenger came in and was seen to whisper something to General Meigs, who immediately left the church. A little later General Totten was summoned, and then a Commodore somebody, by which time the congregation was in a state of suppressed excitement miserable to bear. Dr. Pine preached an unusually long sermon, and finally, the people rushed out and heard the bad news.

While I was talking at the door with Mrs. Rodgers a four-horse ambulance was standing at McClellan's door, and we sat down on the steps intending to see who got into it, and which way it went, a determination shared by plenty of other people on their way from church. At last a servant brought blankets, and McClellan and Franklin got in and started on their way over the Potomac; and then I came home, and presently Colonel McClure came in and told us that Heintzelmann, with whom he had been sitting an hour, expects to move in the morning and that Manassas was reported evacuated. Contrabands brought word of it to Kearney's quarters; he made an armed reconnaissance and discovered the truth; word was sent to Mc-Clellan, and his ride on Sunday P.M. was in consequence. Mrs. Rodgers came in as we were in our petticoats, getting ready for bed, and confirmed it all.

From the Journal *of Eliza Woolsey Howland:*

We went to bed in a state of great excitement and were awakened early Monday morning by a knock from George and a note from Joe saying it was all true. He wrote at 2 A.M., having been up all night. They had just received their marching orders —the brigade to leave at 5 A.M., the rest of the corps at 9. I sent George over at once with a note to J., and he found him on horseback just starting, the regiments formed and ready, and the General and staff in their saddles, all off for Fairfax Court House, which they reached, J. writes me, at 5 P.M., all in good spirits, having borne the march well. The Rebs have abandoned both Centreville and Manassas, falling back, the *Star* says, as far as the Rapidan and Gordonsville—whether by panic or by a preconcerted plan is unknown.

J. writes the climate at Fairfax C. H. is lovely and the air dry, pure, and very sweet, but the country is utterly desolate, houses burnt or pulled to pieces, fences gone, and the inhabitants, except a few miserable Negroes, fled.

From the Journal *of Georgeanna M. Woolsey:*

March 11.

So the great move was made, the thing we had been looking forward to for so many months. The entire army was in motion, troops on the other side the river advancing, troops on this side taking their place. All day Monday and far into the night regiments marched over the bridges into Virginia—fifty thousand over the Long bridge, they say, and to-day we drove up to the Chain bridge, and they told us fifteen thousand crossed there yesterday. We walked down towards the Long bridge to-day; crowds of people were collected on 14th street to see the move. As we crossed the canal, mother, Charley, and I, swinging along with the rest, three large army wagons brought up the rear, marked T.E., carrying the telegraphic apparatus for the Engineers, and the wires must have been laid last night, for this morning General Williams had the announcement from McClellan (who slept at Fairfax Court House), that our troops are in possession at Manassas.

STONEWALL JACKSON IN DISGUISE

Charlotte E. McKay

In March, 1862, after the deaths of her husband and only child, Charlotte E. McKay "turned the key in the door of her house" and left her home in Massachusetts to serve in a hospital in Frederick City, Maryland.

I arrived on March 24, 1862, the day after the Battle, and started my nursing duties in two old stone buildings dating back to the time of Washington which had been converted into a temporary hospital. I had no time to brood about my personal sorrow for the sick and wounded were brought in from the battlefield in increasing numbers. Our first care for them was sometimes before they were taken from the ambulances—to administer food and slightly stimulating drinks; wash them, dress their wounds, comb their hair and replace their bloody and torn garments by others clean and whole.

One Sunday while superintending the distribution of dinner in my ward, I heard footsteps coming down the long walk and looking up saw the Chief Medical Officer preceded a little by a gentleman in citizen's dress, whose appearance at once riveted my attention. There was nothing very striking in his brown suit, white cravat, sallow complexion, heavy grey beard, and anxious expression; and yet on the whole he was remarkable, and I stood looking at him as he passed down, his keen eyes seeming to take in everything, especially the dinner that was being served out to our men, until with a slight bow he turned and passed out the side door. . . .

"Do you know what strange gentleman inspected our hospital today?" I asked of a . . . friend . . . as I walked across the hospital grounds.

"Oh, yes. That was Dr. George. He was a surgeon in the Crimean War . . . a good Union man."

A few weeks afterwards when our hospital and town were occupied by the Rebel army, I compared notes with one of the soldiers and learned that this man was Stonewall Jackson.

"He often goes into your lines in disguise . . . and so acquaints himself with what is going on in your army. . . ."

After the war was over, the report of my Rebel friend was confirmed by one of Stonewall Jackson's staff officers. . . . He said that he was acquainted with the fact of General Jackson's visit to Frederick about three weeks before Lee's invasion of Maryland, and that he visited the hospitals, introducing himself as Dr. George.

SHE DISCHARGED A PISTOL AT ME

Sarah Emma Edmonds

Emma was often sent out alone on foraging expeditions for the Army of the Potomac and met with many interesting adventures, one of which is recorded here.

One morning I started, all alone, for a five-mile ride to an isolated farmhouse . . . which report said was well supplied with all the articles of which I was in search. I cantered along briskly until I came to a gate which opened into a lane leading directly to the house. It was a large old-fashioned two-story house, with immense chimneys built outside, Virginia style. The farm appeared to be in good condition, fences all up, a rare thing on the Peninsula, and cornfields flourishing as if there were no such thing as war in the land.

I rode up to the house and dismounted, hitched my horse to a post at the door, and proceeded to ring the bell. A tall, stately lady made her appearance, and invited me in with much apparent courtesy. She was dressed in deep mourning, which was very becoming to her pale, sad face. She seemed to be about thirty years of age, very prepossessing in appearance, and evidently belonged to one of the F.F.V.'s. As soon as I was seated she inquired: "To what fortunate circumstance am I to attribute the pleasure of this unexpected call?" I told her in a few words the nature of my business. The intelligence seemed to cast a deep shadow over her pale features, which all her efforts could not control. She seemed nervous and excited, and something in her appearance aroused my suspicion, notwithstanding her blandness of manner and ladylike deportment.

She invited me into another room, while she prepared the articles which she proposed to let me have, but I declined, giving as an excuse that I preferred to sit where I could see whether my horse remained quiet. I watched all her movements narrowly, not daring to turn my eyes aside for a single moment. She walked round in her stately way for some time, without accomplishing much in the way of facilitating my departure, and she was evidently trying to detain me for some purpose or other. Could it be that she was meditating the best mode of attack, or was she expecting someone to come, and trying to detain me until their arrival? Thoughts like these passed through my mind in quick succession.

At last I rose up abruptly, and asked her if the things were ready. She answered me with an assumed smile of surprise, and said: "Oh, I did not know that you were in a hurry: I was waiting for the boys to come and catch some chickens for you." "And pray, madam, where are the boys?" I asked; "Oh, not far from here," was her reply. "Well, I have decided not to wait; you will please not detain me longer," said I, as I moved toward the door. She began to pack some butter and eggs both together in a small basket which I had brought with me, while another stood beside her without anything in it. I looked at her; she was trembling violently, and was as pale as death. In a moment more she handed me the basket, and I held out a greenback for her acceptance; "Oh, it was no consequence about the pay"; she did not wish anything for it. So I thanked her and went out.

In a few moments she came to the door, but did not offer to assist me, or to hold the basket, or anything, but stood looking at me most maliciously, I thought. I placed the basket on the top of the post to which my horse had been hitched, took my seat in the saddle, and then rode up and took my basket. Turning to her I bade her good morning, and thanking her again for her kindness, I turned to ride away.

I had scarcely gone a rod when she discharged a pistol at me; by some intuitive movement I threw myself forward on my horse's neck and the ball passed over my head. I turned my horse in a twinkling, and grasped my revolver. She was in the act of firing the second time, but was so excited that the bullet went wide of its mark. I held my seven-shooter in my hand, considering where to aim. I did not wish to kill the wretch, but did intend to wound her. When she saw that two could play at this game, she dropped her pistol and threw up her hands imploringly. I took deliberate aim at one of her hands, and sent the ball through the palm of her left hand. She fell to the ground in an instant with a loud shriek. I dismounted, and took the pistol which lay beside her, and placing it in my belt, proceeded to take care of her ladyship after the following manner: I unfastened the end of my halter strap and tied it painfully tight around her right wrist, and remounting my horse, I started, and brought the lady to consciousness by dragging her by the wrist two or three rods along the ground. I stopped, and she rose to her feet, and with wild entreaties she begged me to release her, but, instead of doing so, I presented a pistol, and told her that if she uttered another word or scream she was a dead woman. In that way I succeeded in keeping her from alarming anyone who might be within calling distance, and so made my way toward McClellan's headquarters.

After we had gone in that way about a mile and a half, I told her that she might ride if she wished to do so, for I saw she was becoming weak from loss of blood. She was glad to accept the offer, and I bound up her hand with my handkerchief, gave her my scarf to throw over her head, and assisted her to the saddle. I marched along beside her, holding tight to the bridle rein all the while. When we were about a mile from McClellan's headquarters she fainted, and I caught her as she was falling from the horse. I laid her by the roadside while I went for some water, which I brought in my hat, and after bathing her face for some time she recovered.

For the first time since we started I entered into conversation with her, and found that within the last three weeks she had lost her father, husband, and two brothers in the Rebel army. They had all belonged to a company of sharpshooters, and were the first to fall. She had been almost insane since the intelligence reached her. She said I was the first Yankee that she had seen since the death of her relatives, the evil one seemed to urge her on to the step she had taken, and if I would not deliver her up to the military powers, she would go with me and take care of the wounded. She even proposed to take the oath of allegiance, and seemed deeply penitent.

Soon after this conversation we started for camp, she weak and humbled, and I strong and rejoicing. None ever knew from that day to this the secret of that secesh woman becoming a nurse. Instead of being taken to General McClellan's headquarters, she went direct to the hospital, where Dr. P. dressed her hand, which was causing her extreme pain.

The next day she returned to her house in an ambulance, accompanied by a hospital steward, and brought away everything which could be made use of in the hospitals, and so took up her abode with us. Her name was Alice M., but we called her Nellie J. She soon proved the genuineness of her conversion to the Federal faith by her zeal for the cause which she had so recently espoused. As soon as she was well enough to act in the capacity of nurse she commenced in good earnest, and became one of the most faithful and efficient nurses in the Army of the Potomac.

A SECRET EXPEDITION FOR MC CLELLAN

Sarah Emma Edmonds

Through the Army chaplain, who was a friend of hers, Emma learned that one of General McClellan's spies had been executed at Richmond, and that it would be necessary to fill his place at once. The perilous undertakings of a Union spy seemed far more enticing to her adventurous spirit than nursing, which had grown monotonous, and she went to Washington to apply for the position. After a careful examination by a group of generals, Emma, who was of course known to the military only as Franklin Thompson, was accepted as a member of the secret service and given her first assignment. Disguised as a Negro boy, she was sent behind enemy lines at Yorktown to learn about the Rebel fortifications there.

My arrangements were soon made, and I was ready to start on my first secret expedition toward the Confederate capital. With a few hard crackers in my pocket and my revolver loaded and capped, I started on foot, without even a blanket or anything which might create suspicion. At half past nine o'clock I passed through the outer picket line of the Union army, at twelve o'clock I was within the Rebel lines, and had not so much as been halted once by a sentinel. I had passed within less than ten rods of a Rebel picket, and he had not seen me. I took this as a favorable omen, and thanked heaven for it.

As soon as I had gone a safe distance from the picket lines I lay down and rested until morning. The night was chilly and the ground cold and damp, and I passed the weary hours in fear and trembling. The first object which met my view in the morning was a party of Negroes carrying out hot coffee and provisions to the rebel pickets. This was another fortunate circumstance, for I immediately made their acquaintance, and was rewarded for my promptness by receiving a cup of coffee and a piece of corn bread, which helped very much to chase away the lingering chills of the preceding night. I remained there until the darkies returned, and then marched into Yorktown with them without eliciting the least suspicion.

The Negroes went to work immediately on the fortifications after reporting to their overseers, and I was left standing alone, not having quite made up my mind what part to act next. I was saved all further trouble in that direction, for my idleness had attracted the notice of an officer, who stepped forward and began to interrogate me after the following manner: "Who do you belong to, and why are you not at work?" I answered in my best Negro dialect: "I dusn't belong to nobody, Massa, I'se free and allers was; I'se gwyne to Richmond to work." But that availed me nothing, for turning to a man who was dressed in citizen's clothes and who seemed to be in charge of the colored department, he said: "Take that black rascal and set him to work, and if he don't work well tie him up and give him twenty lashes, just to impress upon his mind that there's no free niggers here while there's a D——d Yankee left in Virginia."

So saying he rode away, and I was conducted to a breastwork which was in course of erection, where about a hundred Negroes were at work. I was soon furnished with a pickaxe, shovel, and a monstrous wheelbarrow, and I commenced forthwith to imitate my companions in bondage. That portion of the parapet upon which I was sent to work was about eight feet high. The gravel was wheeled up in wheelbarrows on single planks, one end of which rested on the brow of the breastwork and the other on the ground. I need not say that this work was exceedingly hard for the strongest man; but few were able to take up their wheelbarrows alone, and I was often helped by some good-natured darkie when I was just on the verge of tumbling off the plank. All day long I worked in this manner, until my hands were blistered from my wrists to the finger ends.

The colored men's rations were different from those of the soldiers. They had neither meat nor coffee, while the white men had both. Whiskey was freely distributed to both black and white, but not in sufficient quantity to unfit them for duty. The soldiers seemed to be as much in earnest as the officers, and could curse the Yankees with quite as much vehemence. Notwithstanding the hardships of the day I had had my eyes and ears open, and had gained more than would counterbalance the day's work.

Night came, and I was released from toil. I was free to go where I pleased within the fortifications, and I made good use of my liberty. I made out a brief report of the mounted guns which I saw that night in my ramble round the fort, viz.: fifteen three-inch rifled cannon, eighteen four-and-a-half-inch rifled cannon, twenty-nine thirty-two-pounders, twenty-one forty-two-pounders, twenty-three eight-inch Columbiads, eleven nine-inch Dahlgrens, thirteen ten-inch Columbiads, fourteen ten-inch mortars, and seven eight-inch siege howitzers. This, together with a rough sketch of the outer works, I put under the inner sole of my contraband shoe and returned to the Negro quarters.

Finding my hands would not be in a condition to shovel much earth on the morrow, I began to look round among the Negroes to find someone who would exchange places with me whose duty was of a less arduous character. I succeeded in finding a lad of about my own size who was engaged in carrying water to the troops. He said he would take my place the next day, and he thought he could find a friend to do the same the day following, for which brotherly kindness I gave him five dollars in greenback; but he declared he could not take so much money—"he neber had so much money in all his life before." So by that operation I escaped the scrutiny of the overseer, which would probably have resulted in the detection of my assumed African complexion.

The second day in the Confederate service was much pleasanter than the first. I had only to supply one brigade with water, which did not require much exertion, for the day was cool and the well was not far distant; consequently I had an opportunity of lounging a little among the soldiers, and of hearing important subjects discussed. In that way I learned the number of reinforcements which had arrived from different places, and also had the pleasure of seeing General Lee, who arrived while I was there. It was whispered among the men that he had been telegraphed to for the purpose of inspecting the Yankee fortifications, as he was the best engineer in the Confederacy, and that he had pronounced it impossible to hold Yorktown after McClellan opened his siege guns upon it. Then, too, General J. E. Johnson* was hourly expected with a portion of his command. Including all, the Rebels estimated their force at one hundred and fifty thousand at Yorktown and in that vicinity.

When Johnson arrived there was a council of war held, and things began to look gloomy. Then the report began to circulate

* General Joseph E. Johnston.

that the town was to be evacuated. One thing I noticed in the Rebel army, that they do not keep their soldiers in the dark as our officers do with regard to the movements and destination of the troops. When an order comes to the Federal army requiring them to make some important movement, no person knows whether they are advancing or retreating until they get to Washington, or in sight of the enemy's guns, excepting two or three of the leading generals.

Having a little spare time I visited my sable friends and carried some water for them. After taking a draught of the cool beverage, one young darkie looked up at me in a puzzled sort of manner, and turning round to one of his companions, said: "Jim, I'll be darned if that feller ain't turnin' white; if he ain't then I'm no nigger." I felt greatly alarmed at the remark, but said, very carelessly, "Well, gem'in, I'se allers 'spected to come white some time; my mudder's a white woman." This had the desired effect, for they all laughed at my simplicity, and made no further remarks upon the subject. As soon as I could conveniently get out of sight I took a look at my complexion by means of a small pocket looking-glass which I carried for that very purpose—and sure enough, as the negro had said, I was really turning white. I was only a dark mulatto color now, whereas two days previous I was as black as Cloe. However, I had a small vial of nitrate of silver in weak solution, which I applied to prevent the remaining color from coming off.

Upon returning to my post with a fresh supply of water, I saw a group of soldiers gathered around some individual who was haranguing them in real Southern style. I went up quietly, put down my cans of water, and of course had to fill the men's canteens, which required considerable time, especially as I was not in any particular hurry just then. I thought the voice sounded familiar, and upon taking a sly look at the speaker I recognized him at once as a peddler who used to come to the

Federal camp regularly once every week with newspapers and stationery, and especially at headquarters. He would hang round there, under some pretext or other, for half a day at a time.

There he was, giving the Rebels a full description of our camp and forces, and also brought out a map of the entire works of McClellan's position.

On the evening of the third day from the time I entered the camp of the enemy I was sent, in company with the colored men, to carry supper to the outer picket posts on the right wing. This was just what I wished for, and had been making preparations during the day, in view of the possibility of such an event, providing among other things a canteen full of whiskey. Some of the men on picket duty were black and some were white. I had a great partiality for those of my own color, so calling out several darkies I spread before them some corn cake, and gave them a little whiskey for dessert. While we were thus engaged the Yankee Minié balls were whistling round our heads, for the picket lines of the contending parties were not half a mile distant from each other. The Rebel pickets do not remain together in groups of three or four as our men do, but are strung along, one in each place, from three to four rods apart. I proposed to remain a while with the pickets, and the darkies returned to camp without me.

Not long after night an officer came riding along the lines, and seeing me he inquired what I was doing there. One of the darkies replied that I had helped to carry out their supper, and was waiting until the Yankees stopped firing before I started to go back. Turning to me he said, "You come along with me." I did as I was ordered, and he turned and went back the same way he came until we had gone about fifty yards, then halting in front of a petty officer he said, "Put this fellow on the post where that man was shot until I return." I was conducted a few rods farther, and then a rifle was put into my hands, which

I was told to use freely in case I should see anything or any-body approaching from the enemy. Then followed the flattering remark, after taking me by the coat collar and giving me a pretty hard shake, "Now, you black rascal, if you sleep on your post I'll shoot you like a dog."

The night was very dark, and it was beginning to rain. I was all alone now, but how long before the officer might return with some one to fill my place I did not know, and I thought the best thing I could do was to make good use of the present moment. After ascertaining as well as possible the position of the picket on each side of me, each of whom I found to be enjoying the shelter of the nearest tree, I deliberately and noiselessly stepped into the darkness, and was soon gliding swiftly through the forest toward the "land of the free," with my splendid rifle grasped tightly lest I should lose the prize. I did not dare to approach very near the Federal lines, for I was in more danger of being shot by them than by the enemy; so I spent the re-mainder of the night within hailing distance of our lines, and with the first dawn of morning I hoisted the well-known signal and was welcomed once more to a sight of the dear old stars and stripes.

I went immediately to my tent. . . . After removing as much of the color as it was possible for soap and water to do, my com-plexion was a nice maroon color, which my new costume showed off to good advantage. Had my own mother seen me then, it would have been difficult to convince her of our relationship. I made out my report immediately and carried it to General McClellan's headquarters, together with my trophy from the land of traitors. . . . The rifle was sent to Washington, and is now in the Capital as a memento of the war. . . .

6 The Fleet of Mercy

EARLY IN 1862, WHEN THE BATTLEFRONTS HAD OPENED ALL ALONG the waterways in the West, the Medical Department had had no means of getting to the scene of action to treat the sick and wounded nor of transferring them to the general hospitals. Many military men still believed that when there was active fighting, the fighting power would be weakened and the Army personnel unnecessarily burdened if transportation were used to carry the sick and wounded and medical stores.

To meet this new emergency, the United States Sanitary Commission, chiefly through the efforts of its General Secretary, Frederick Law Olmsted, took over certain large steamers not being used by the Government and fitted them up as floating hospitals with medical supplies, sanitary stores, and their own hospital corps, at no expense to the Government. It was Mr. Olmsted's plan to have the boats kept in readiness so that when a battle occurred they would be prepared to receive the sick and wounded, and if necessary to treat them on the spot.

While the states of the Union had been celebrating the fall of Forts Henry and Donelson, hundreds of the soldiers who had been wounded in winning these battles were taken from the bloodstained snow with their garments frozen on them. They had been left lying where they fell that bitter morning until they froze to the ground. The Army had no time to look after them—there were no available places to be used as hospitals and many of the men lay suffering with their clothes on and their wounds undressed until they perished on the battlefield. This

146

harrowing situation did not end until the arrival of the hospital steamer *City of Memphis,* loaded with Sanitary Commission stores taken on at Cairo. Telegrams for medical aid were sent to Chicago and physicians arrived on the first trains. Two days later a number of Sanitary Commission steamers brought efficient relief.

The United States Sanitary Commission transport system got started in the East after many tedious delays. The sudden transfer of the scene of active war from the high banks of the Potomac to a low and swampy region intersected by a network of rivers and creeks demanded facilities for the proper care of the sick and wounded that had not been anticipated by the Government arrangements. After postponements and disappointments of various kinds—one fine large boat having been assigned, partially furnished by the Commission, and then withdrawn—an order was at length received authorizing the United States Sanitary Commission to take possession of any of the Government transports not in actual use that were lying at Alexandria.

The only vessel then lying at Alexandria hardy enough for ocean passage from Virginia to New York or Boston proved to be the *Daniel Webster,* an old Pacific coast steamer of limited capacity. She had recently been stripped of everything movable but dirt, so that the task of turning her into a hospital boat was no mean one. But within a very few days the *Daniel Webster* was ready for service, scrubbed and whitewashed to the steerage, the bulkhead of the wings of the engineroom section knocked away so as to get a through draft from stem to stern, with new bunks and an apothecary shop.

At the end of April the *Daniel Webster* made its first trip to York River, and was soon followed by the steamer *Knickerbocker,* and a whole succession of other boats assigned to the Commission. Among the first women to serve in the East were

Georgeanna Woolsey, her sister, Eliza Howland, and Katharine P. Wormeley, on the *Wilson Small,* and Eliza Harris on the *Vanderbilt.* The hospital transports plowed back and forth up and down the rivers carrying their human cargo from the battlefield to the bases nearest the hospitals in Washington. Yorktown, White House, and Harrison's Landing became the successive bases on the Potomac.

The workers in the hospital transport service were taxed to the utmost. No duty was said to be more exhausting in its character nor more important in its results. The number of lives saved through this on-the-scene care as envisioned by Mr. Olmsted is incalculable. The efficiency with which the hospital service carried on its program is a great tribute to the men and women who served with the Sanitary Commission in this field. When freight or hospital cars from the battlefields or ambulances and stretchers from the nearby hospitals arrived at the wharves, the fleet of mercy was ready for them. Stretchers were carried up the companionway or elevated and then lowered to the cabins by pulleys and the men then hoisted to the berths or placed on cots. Often these terrible processions came so thick and fast that every berth was filled and the men packed in so closely that there was hardly room enough to go around them. After a bloody battle the cabin of one hospital boat where operations were performed "ran in streams of blood, and legs and arms as they were rapidly dismembered formed a stack of human limbs." Often the boats were directly in the line of shell and gunfire, and the Commission surgeons and nurses aboard risked their own lives as they stood by prepared to minister to the critically injured. Hospital boats were usually anchored alongside each other with their gangways connected, the nurses running through four or five boats at a time.

A second squad of the Hospital Corps was detailed to accompany the patients from the battlefield bases to hospitals in New York, Philadelphia, Boston, and other Northern cities.

The transport system was in complete working order when McClellan marched up the Peninsula with his Army of the Potomac, after leaving his elaborate defenses at Yorktown to go in pursuit of the retreating Confederates, and finally pushed his pickets to within four miles of Richmond.

Then, on May 30, just when things were beginning to look up for McClellan, there was a torrential storm. The Chickahominy overflowed, threatening to sweep away McClellan's bridges. McClellan's advance forces that had crossed the river earlier were now separated from the bulk of the Army by the swollen Chickahominy. The Rebels took advantage of the desperate plight of the bluecoats and at one o'clock in the afternoon made a violent attack upon Casey's division, followed by an equally formidable one on General Couch in the vicinity of Fair Oaks Station. Total annihilation of the Federals seemed to be the enemy's goal and it looked very much as if they would be successful in driving the Yankees into the Chickahominy unless reinforcements arrived. General Heintzelman quickly ordered two brigades of Kearny's division to move a quarter of a mile in front of Savage's Station in support of Casey, and the enemy was held until they were reinforced by Generals Sedgwick and Richardson. The Battle of Fair Oaks (or Seven Pines) was the greatest fought in the Eastern theater of the War up to this time.

The Rebels were driven back and McClellan retained his position. They attempted to renew the fight on Sunday morning but were beaten back at every point. Losses on both sides were heavy, and the efficiency of the transport service was put to a crucial test.

From the Battle of Fair Oaks at the end of May to the great Seven Days' Battle that began on June 25, more and more women became involved in hospital duty on the Peninsula. At Mechanicsville, Gaines's Mill, Garnett's Farm, Peach Orchard, Savage's Station, White Oak, Glendale, New Market, and Malvern Hill the women of the North were under gunfire on the shore and on the waterways.

McClellan failed to take Richmond. At the end of the bloody week of fighting, White House Landing on the York River, where the Sanitary Commission had a large hospital center and supply base, had to be abandoned, and a quick getaway managed almost under Rebel shot and shell. Here the efficiency of the transport system was put to a still further test as the women saw to it that all the sick and wounded were taken from tents and hospitals before the boats sailed down the river in the wake of McClellan's retreating army. A new base was established at Harrison's Landing on the James River.

Tens of thousands of soldiers were ill with malaria from the Chickahominy swamps, and these men with the wounded who accumulated more rapidly than the transports could carry them away kept part of the Woolsey family, Eliza Harris, and others well occupied throughout July and August. At Harrison's Landing the condition of the sick and wounded was pitiful. The Medical Department seems to have become demoralized at this point. All the things required for the patients were lacking. The pasty adhesive mud was everywhere, and the hospital tents, old, mildewed, and leaky, were pitched in it, with no floors provided. Where tents were supplied they were either of the "wedge" pattern or the bivouacking kind of black cloth which was no protection against the hot Virginia sun. Many of the patients had to be put into cabins and miserable shanties in the vicinity, sometime seven in the attics of such places. Here they were left without food or drink unless some of the Sanitary Commission agents or women connected with other organizations, like Eliza Harris, agent for the Philadelphia Aid Society, looked after their needs. Hard tack, salt junk, fat salt pork, and cold greasy bean soup was the diet provided for the men suffering from typhoid fever and from wounds that rendered liquid food indispensaable. Soft bread had been promised to the men, but it did not arrive until it was time to break up camp.

On July 22, Dr. Henry W. Bellows reported that "The Hospital Transport System had worked better and better up to this date. It has fully realized our expectations in the amount of comfort, diminution of suffering, and of saving human life. . . . No money could ever reckon the service it has accorded. It has disappointed us only in one respect, but that is a cardinal point. . . . It has not provoked the imitation of the United States Government in its own transport for the sick and wounded men. They do not appear to be any better for our example. . . . They do not seem to be improving nor even to attempt to adopt our standards nor to follow our style of organization. . . . Mr. Olmsted doubts whether it is possible for the medical authorities to pay much attention to the example or advice of unofficial co-workers like ourselves. . . . We have succeeded both in the East and West in bringing a large share of more than half of all our sick and wounded men throughout the army to healthy and comfortable hospitals of the North. . . . There has been inevitable jealousy in our transport service. We have had to push our salubrious boats upon the medical directors who are more ready to use their own simply because they own their own. I do not yet see a thorough statement of this jealousy even under Dr. Hammond. Perhaps it is too much to expect of official human nature. . . .

"But from this time on the transport service will be less important. The Government is very wisely changing its policy . . . or the lack of it. It has been compelled to bring North its sick and wounded as fast as possible. . . ."

When the United States Sanitary Commission hospital transport service came to an end, the whole staff of the *Wilson Small* fell back on Washington. Katharine Wormeley came home on the old hospital ship the *Daniel Webster*, in charge of the last load of wounded from the Peninsula, and Georgeanna and Eliza went to New York for a visit before returning to hospital duty in Washington.

RUN FOR THE RIVER—THE REBELS ARE COMING!

Belle Reynolds

Although this account is from the Western front it reveals the effective use to which the United States Sanitary Commission transports were put before they appeared on the Eastern front.

Belle Reynolds had remained with her husband's regiment, following it in all its campaigning. In the early part of February, 1862, General Grant began the campaign that terminated in the capture of Corinth and Memphis and the opening of the upper part of the Mississippi Valley. Mrs. Reynolds was present at the Battle of Pittsburgh Landing, having embarked on March 21 on the Steamer D. A. January for this battleground. Ten miles above the landing the passengers disembarked and camped about three miles from the river "on a most romantic spot." Deserted cabins were everywhere. Shiloh Meeting House and the cool spring were all that made the place look as if ever trod by the foot of man.

She wrote:

April 4. The long roll has called the regiment out, and we know not what an hour may bring forth. Pickets have been driven in, and skirmishing is going on at the front. Distant musketry and the rumbling of artillery past my tent give the situation a look of reality which I had not dreamed of an hour ago. Although so near the enemy's lines, we feel no fear. Mrs. N. and myself are the only ladies in camp, and our tents are adjoining.

April 17. On Sunday morning at sunrise we heard the roll of distant musketry; but supposing it to be the pickets discharging their pieces, we paid no attention to it. In about an hour after, while preparing breakfast over the campfire, which Mrs. N. and I used in common, we were startled by cannon balls howling over our heads. Immediately the long roll was beaten, and orders came from the commanding officer of the brigade to fall in. Knowing my husband must go, I kept my place before the fire, that he might have his breakfast before leaving; but there was no time for eating, and though shells were flying faster, and musketry coming nearer, compelling me involuntarily to dodge as the missiles shrieked through the air, I still fried my cakes, and rolling them in a napkin, placed them in his haversack, and gave it to him just as he was mounting his horse to assist in forming the regiment. His last words to me, as he rode away, were, "What will you do, Belle?" I little knew then what I should do; but there was no time to hesitate, for shells were bursting in every direction about us. Tents were torn in shreds, and the enemy, in solid column, was seen coming over the hill in the distance. Mrs. N. and I, thinking we might have time to pack our trunks, were doing so, when the wagon-master told us we must run for our lives; so, snatching our travelling baskets, bonnets in hand, we left the now deserted camp. We passed the large parade ground, close by our camp, where the cavalry was forming. Balls were flying and shells bursting among the terrified horses and fearless riders. On reaching General Ross's headquarters, supposing ourselves at a perfectly safe distance from the Rebels, we took possession of a deserted tent, and sat resting ourselves, when Lieutenant Williams, acting quarter-master, passing by, saw us sitting there, apparently regardless of the flying missiles. "For God's sake," exclaimed he, "run for the river; the Rebels are coming!" We were by this time convinced of their close proximity; for we had scarcely left when a shell exploded close by, the pieces tearing through the tent, and a solid shot passed through headquarters. The troops were now moving up from the river, pouring along by thousands, fresh and hopeful, and sanguine as to the result of the conflict in which they were hastening to engage. Others were going towards the river, many sick, and scarcely able to drag themselves along through the almost impassable roads; and we, while hurrying along, were constantly asked, "What's the matter back here, ladies?" But soon enough they ascertained, for the enemy were pressing closer and closer, and the musketry coming nearer and nearer each moment. When within about half a mile from the river, we came upon a number of ambulances, from which the wounded were being taken and laid upon the ground for the surgeons' attention. We stopped, took off our bonnets, and prepared to assist in dressing their wounds; but in less than ten minutes an orderly came dashing up, with orders to move the wounded immediately to the river, as the Rebels were pressing so closely, they were not safe where they were. The surgeon said we had better go to some of the boats, as we should find plenty to do. So we made our way to the steamer *Emerald*, Captain Norton's headquarters; and, just as we were going aboard, General Grant and staff came up from Savannah. Anxious faces they all wore, though they little knew what lay before them. We were rejoiced to find that Mrs. C., one of our nurses, had arrived from Illinois, with quite a large supply of hospital stores, for they came not an hour too soon. A few moments after our arrival (about ten o'clock A.M.), Sergeant Autcliff, Company A, was brought on board, supported by two comrades. Both arms were broken. His greeting to Captain Norton was, "Well, captain, they have winged me." To see that strong man, now utterly helpless, and almost fainting from loss of blood, and exhausted from a walk of nearly two miles, was a piteous sight indeed.

Soon the wounded came pouring in upon us, and for thirty-six hours we found no rest. At night we had three hundred and fifty wounded on board our boat. I dared not ask the boys if my husband was unharmed, and feared each moment to see him among the almost lifeless forms that were being brought on board the boat.

Through the day the thunder of artillery had almost deafened us; the air seemed filled with leaden hail, and the spent balls would patter upon the deck like a summer shower. Solid shot, directed at the ammunition boat, which was close by us, would pass over our heads and drop into the water. As the sun went down our army was gradually nearing the river: resistance to the infuriated masses opposed to them had been impossible. The Rebels now occupied all the camps of the Federal army, and the alternative to perish beneath the waves of the Tennessee, or surrender to the exultant foe was before them. Never had the fate of an army been more desperate, or its ruin more inevitable. Panic seized the half-crazed men, and rushing down the steep declivity, they came pouring along by hundreds, each intent on securing his own safety, regardless of others. Many attempted to crowd upon the hospital boats; others swam to the opposite shore. Captain N. guarded the gangplank with a revolver in each hand, and giving me another, I stationed myself upon the hurricane deck, prepared to execute any orders he might give me. But deliverance came to the disheartened army; the gunboats *Lexington* and *Tyler* arrived from below, and steaming up to the mouth of a little stream, called Licking Creek, they opened a deadly fire upon the Rebel army. Broadside after broadside of sixty-four-pounders was discharged into the midst of the now terrified foe. Fresh courage seemed infused into our dispirited ranks, for now across the river we could see the long-expected troops hurrying forward at double quick to our rescue. How we cheered them! All the transports were put in requisition to ferry them across, that they might add to the waning strength of the almost defeated army. Every effort was made to inspire the panic-stricken hundreds with fresh courage, but without effect. At the Landing it was a scene of terror. Rations, forage, and ammunition were trampled into the mud by an excited and infuriated crowd. Officers were rushing around, vainly endeavoring to collect the stragglers from their commands, and lead them once more to the scene of conflict. Trains were huddled together on the brow of the hill and in sheltered places. Ambulances were conveying their bleeding loads to the different boats, and joined to form a Babel of confusion indescribable. None were calm, and free from distracting anxiety and pain, save the long ranks of dead, ranged for recognition or burial, at the hospital on the hillside. Night closed the scene. The two armies rested for the morrow's conflict; ours sad and disheartened, theirs hopeful and almost victorious. The gunboats were doing a great work; one after the other would send a broadside; and we, watching from the deck, would listen until the explosion, and then shout for joy. They were tokens of remembrance sent to our beleaguered friends. Soon the rain came pouring down. What a blessing to the wounded on the battlefield! Hour after hour passed, and the storm increased; but above all was the solemn thunder of the gunboat cannon. Towards morning we dropped down to Savannah, and unloaded the wounded; and morning found us again at work, dressing the wounds of others, who had but just been brought from the field.

In all this time I heard nothing of my husband. I dared not ask those who had come from the field. I would wait until I should hear that all was well with him, or see him face to face.

The mud and rain made it impossible to extend our labors beyond the boat; and reports were continually coming to us that the rebels were retreating, and that our army, strengthened and encouraged by the arrival of Buell's command, would probably push them to Corinth. They had passed beyond our camps, and the way was strewn with dead and dying. Lieutenant Colonel Smith came from the regiment about dark, with a message to me from my husband. He had passed through that terrible battle unharmed, though his horse had been shot under him. How thankful I was none can know but those who have endured like suspense and anxiety. There had been no preparation made for a two days' battle when the army left their comfortable quarters on Sunday morning, and no rations had been provided. I knew there was a large supply of bread on hand, and making arrangements with the cook for a dozen loaves, I supplied the colonel with some impromptu saddlebags, and filling them to the brim, and tying each end, he threw them across his horse, and started off. Fortunately for him, darkness enveloped him, or he might not have arrived with his precious freight. That night we rested, though the storm was still raging. Wednesday morning the sun came forth upon a scene of blood and carnage such as our fair land had never known. The roads were almost impassable; yet we felt it our duty to go out, and do all we could for those were were in the hospital.

MY PAPER IS THE COVER OF THE SUGAR BOX

Georgeanna M. Woolsey

The women on the transports were often able to observe the entire proceedings of a battle, and any other goings-on on land or water.

Georgeanna takes time out from her duties to write her mother from aboard the steamer Knickerbocker.

If my letter smells of "Yellow B." sugar, it has a right to, as my paper is the cover of the sugar box. Since I wrote I have been jumping round from boat to boat, and Saturday came on board the *Knickerbocker* at Mr. Olmsted's request, with Mrs. Strong and some others, to put things in order, and, privately, to be on hand to "hold" the boat, which had been made over to the Commission, over the heads of the New Jersey delegation. Dr. Asch was on board, and we had the New Jersey dinner table abolished and fifty-six Sanitary Commission beds made on the dining-room floor that night. The two hundred wounded and sick brought down to Fortress Monroe under our care were transferred to the shore hospital, where we stole some roses for our patients on the *Small*. Saw regiments embarking for Norfolk, which surrendered the next day. Saw Mr. Lincoln driving past to take possession of Norfolk; and by Tuesday had the boat all in order again, with the single exception of a special-diet cooking stove. So we went ashore at Gloster Point [sic] ransacked all the abandoned Rebel huts to find one, coming down finally upon the sutler of the "Enfants Perdus," who was cooking something nice for the officers' mess over a stove with *four* places for pots. This was too much to stand; so under a written authority given to "Dr. Olmsted" by the quartermaster of this department, we proceeded to rake out the sutler's fire and lift off his pots, and he offered us his cart and mule to drag the stove to the boat and would take no pay! So through the wretched town filled with the debris of huts and camp furniture, old blankets, dirty cast-off clothing, smashed gun carriages, exploded guns, vermin and filth everywhere, and along the sandy shore covered with cannon balls, we followed the mule—a triumphant procession, waving our broken bits of stovepipe and iron pot-covers. I left a polite message for the Colonel "Perdu," which had to stand him in place of his lost dinner. I shall never understand what was the matter with that sutler, whose self-sacrifice was to secure some three hundred men their meals promptly.

We set up our stove in the *Knickerbocker*, unpacked tins and clothing, filled a linen closet in each ward, made up beds for three hundred, set the kitchen in order, and arranged a black hole with a lock to it, where oranges, brandy, and wine are stored box upon box; and got back to Yorktown to find everybody at work fitting up the *Spaulding*. I have a daily struggle with the darkeys in the kitchen, who protest against everything. About twenty men are fed from one pail of soup, and five from a loaf of bread, unless they are almost well, and then no amount of food is enough.

One gets toughened on one's fourth hospital ship and now I could stop at nothing; but it is amusing to see the different ways taken to discover the same thing. Dr. McC.: "Well-my-dear-fellow-is-anything-the-matter-with-your-bowels-do-your-ears-ring-what's-your-name?" Dr. A.: "Turn over my friend, have you got the dia*ree*?" Dr. A. was in a state of indignation with Miss Dix in the shore hospital at Yorktown. She has peculiar views on diet, not approving of meat, and treating all to arrowroot and farina, and by no means allowing crackers with gruel. "*Them* does not go with this," as Dr. A. gracefully puts the words into Miss Dix's mouth.

I WISH TO JOIN THE HOSPITAL TRANSPORT SERVICE

Katharine P. Wormeley

British-born Katharine Prescott Wormeley had many rare qualities that endeared her to people of all levels of society, and

*made her one of the most discussed women of her day. Mary A.
Livermore and Frances E. Willard called her the "woman of
the century." A sketch of her life appeared in* Who's Who in
America *in 1908-9 and numerous magazine articles were devoted
to her life.*

*Katharine Wormeley was born on January 14, 1830, in Ips-
wich, England, the second of the three daughters of Ralph
Randolph, a Rear Admiral in the British navy, and Caroline
Wormeley. When she was about eighteen years old her family
moved to the United States, where she was to live for the rest
of her life. Had she wished, Katharine might have led a sheltered life devoted to esoteric literary writing, the translation of
the works of noted French authors, particularly Balzac, to whom
she devoted herself from the early eighties until her death, or
correspondence with Thackeray and other writers and leaders of
European society with whom she hobnobbed while still living
in England. She was in Paris at the time of Napoleon's second
funeral, which she described vividly later in* Napoleon's Return
from Helena, *published in 1908 by Putnam.*

*But Katharine Wormeley loved her fellow man too much to
exclude herself from even the most sordid of situations. This
philanthropic side of her nature manifested itself in her Civil
War work and in the responsible part she played in the activities of numerous charitable organizations, especially those
which dealt with the work of women and girls and their instruction in domestic science. She founded the Girls' Industrial
School at Newport, Rhode Island, and bore its expense for
three years, after which it was taken over by the public school
system.*

*When the Civil War began, Katharine associated herself with
the work of the United States Sanitary Commission, which she
liked to describe as "an organization of 'private gentlemen'
whose voluntary and unpaid services were accepted by the gov-*

*ernment at the beginning of the War of the Rebellion to supply
the deficiencies of the Medical Department of the army."*

*During General George McClellan's Peninsula Campaign in
1862, she served on hospital transports, joining the service on
the second voyage of the* Daniel Webster.

Newport, R. I., April 27, 1862.

The Sanitary Commission has today sent off from Washington a large steamship to be fitted up as a hospital transport. Mrs. Griffin has gone down in her with Mr. Olmsted, and by his request. I have great cofidence in her. She is a lady whose presence is guarantee enough that I, or any other woman, may go there with propriety. She is very efficient, and I should be satisfied in working under her. . . . I have written to her to send for me if they want me; the letter went yesterday. . . . My work here is closing. Colonel Vinton [Quartermaster General in New York] sends me today the flannel for the last ten thousand shirts, which closes my present contract; I have just drained the community dry as to hospital supplics, and the churches have lately sent in $1,800 (making $5,500 which I have received since we began in April, 1861).

May 7.

I received a telegram from Mrs. Griffin today, telling me that the *Daniel Webster* steamship had arrived at New York with the first load of sick and wounded, and that if I wish to join the Hospital Transport Service, I must be in New York tomorrow morning. So I leave tonight. Have telegraphed you to that effect.

U. S. Floating Hospital *Daniel Webster,*
Off Ship Point, May 10.

We left New York yesterday at 5 P.M., and . . . stayed on deck by moonlight till eleven o'clock, when I turned in, to sleep all night, and get up lazily to breakfast at nine this morning. Since then I have helped to make our hospital flag, and I have dreamed away the day, lying on deck in the sweet air, where I could see the bluest sky and the bluest water (when the vessel dipped), and nothing else. Four ladies are attached to the ship. . . . As far as I can judge, our duty is to be very much that of a housekeeper. We attend to the beds, the linen, the clothing of the patients; we have a pantry and storeroom, and are required to do all the cooking for the sick, and see that it is properly distributed according to the surgeon's orders; we are also to have a general superintendence over the condition of the wards and over the nurses, who are all men. What else, time and experience will show, I suppose.

I am inclined to like the surgeon-in-charge, Dr. Grymes, very much. He commands here; the captain, named Bletham—a truly honest, kindly, sailor-like man—being, under present circumstances, only second. Dr. Grymes is suffering from consumption, and today he is hanging about, languid and nerveless; they tell me that tomorrow he will be taut, tireless, hawk-eyed, and the spirit of an emergency. There are eight medical students on board ("dressers," they are called), and perhaps twenty other young men, wardmasters and nurses—all volunteers. The Government furnishes the vessel, and the rations of all on board. My stateroom, which I share with Mrs. Griffin, is on deck; it opens directly to the outer air, and has a large window and ventilator. . . .

I have done my first work—making the beds. How you would have laughed to see me, without a hoop, mounted on the ledge of the second tier of berths, making the beds on the third tier.

On May 12, 1862, Katharine Wormeley and the hospital staff of the Daniel Webstcr *were transferred to the* Wilson Small *where there were thirty-five badly wounded men—four or five amputations. Katharine took her first actual watch on the night of the 12th and felt adjusted to her work the following day. The patients were washed and given breakfast and then the surgeons and dressers made their rounds, opening the wounds, applying the remedies, and replacing the bandages. This was an awful hour. Katharine pressed her hands to her ears to shut out the cries of the men. When the surgeons had finished, the nurses put the wards in order once more.*

The *Elm City*, filled with wounded men, sailed this morning. The *S. R. Spaulding*, a large ocean steamship, is to be fitted up for hospital service; and that appears to be our next work. Meantime, Georgy* has returned with another vessel, the *Knickerbocker*, in perfect order. It seems that the Quartermaster's department ran away with the boat for some purpose of its own, carrying the ladies in her—for Georgy is a lady. . . . They made the most of their time, and have brought back the runaway boat in perfect hospital order. I've just been over her. They have had her cleansed . . . from the hold to the hurricane deck. The *Knickerbocker* is a large river steamboat, and is intended for surgical cases. Then they prepared the cots, mattresses, and bunks, and made the beds; arranged every ward with all necessary appliances; filled the linen closets with the proper quantity of bed linen, hospital clothing, socks, bandages, lint, rags, etc., got ready the hospital kitchen, stole a stove for it, as far as I can make out, and had all the necessary stores unpacked and moved into places where they would be at hand when needed. These girls must be splendidly efficient. It is not the doing it, but the knowing how it should be done and handling the whole affair with as much ease as if they were arranging a doll's house that delights me.

We are all now sitting idly on carpetbags or on the floor, in a

---

* Georgeanna Woolsey, her friend.

little covered saloon or passage onto which our staterooms open. Our dinner table, the stove, is being removed, and Dr. Ware is improvising a better, with a plank across the railing of the stairs. The moment the pressure is taken off, we all turn to to be as funny as we can.

I am astonished at the cheerful devotion—whole-souled and whole-bodied devotion—of the surgeon and medical students attached to this boat. These young men toil day and night at the severest work, quick, intelligent, and tender. Their business is to ship the men, move them carefully from one boat to another, and register their names and all their belongings; to attend to the dispensaries, keeping them amply supplied with stores; to give medical and surgical attendance, dress the wounds, and often to sit up all night, after working hard all day. Then they turn in wherever a mattress comes to hand, take a long sleep, and come out of it refreshed and full of fun—in which we join until the next work comes, and then we are all fresh to work in cheerful concert together. This seems the best way to do the work; nothing morbid comes of it, which is the danger.

We are now making ready to run up the Pamunkey River as far as the advance of the army at Cumberland. This boat, the *Wilson Small*, is disabled. She was twice run into today, the second time by the huge *Vanderbilt*, which nearly demolished her. We are to be towed by the *Knickerbocker* (for we can't even get up steam) as far as West Point, where there is a shipyard. You must get a good map and follow us and the army—or rather the army and us. General Franklin's corps, with those of Porter and Sedgwick, are at Cumberland and New Kent Court-House. This is the *right* wing. The *left* is moving towards the Chickahominy at Bottom Bridge, where the enemy are supposed to be rallying for a stand. Meantime McDowell is coming down from Fredericksburg *at last*, Banks from the direction of Gordonsville, and perhaps Burnside may get up along the line of the Petersburg Railway. The general opinion is that a fearful struggle will take place before Richmond. Alas! But it is not a battle which destroys so many lives as it is the terrible decimating diseases brought on by exposure and hardships and the climate of marshes and watercourses. The majority of the cases of illness which I have seen were men who dropped exhausted from the army on its march, and had painfully made their way to the banks of creeks and rivers, where they were picked up by passing boats and brought down to us. A number of men who came to-day (one lad who died almost immediately) were in the battle of West Point, and took the fever from exposure and fatigue afterwards.

A telegram is just brought on board, saying that a hundred sick men are waiting at Bigelow's Landing for transportation; the telegram says, "They are dying in the rain." This message is to the United States Medical officer at Yorktown; but he seems to think the obvious thing to do is to hand it over at once to the Sanitary Commission. Mr. Olmsted is not on board; when he is found I suppose we shall start. The *Knickerbocker* is all ready for three hundred men, and I think it likely we shall run up in her and be at work all night; but nothing is too much with such efficiency as we have on board—order, calmness, promptitude. I only wish we might be kept working together. . . .

Wilson Small, Sunday, June 1, 1862.

I write amid the distant booming of cannon and the hourly arrival of telegrams from the scene of action. The battle* began yesterday afternoon. Up to 11 P.M. the accounts received were not wholly favorable. The attack was made on our weakest point, General Casey's division, which is the advanced body on the Chickahominy. It was attacked on front and flank, and retreated; but being reinforced by General Heintzelmann, the

* Fair Oaks, otherwise called Seven Pines.

ground and a lost battery were recovered. The second telegram to Colonel Ingalls was written off by the operator on the envelope of your letter of the 26th; I shall keep it as a souvenir. It says: "General Kearny has driven the enemy a mile at the point of the bayonet. General Heintzelmann is driving back the enemy. Prisoners, General Pettigru and several field and staff officers." A little later, and we heard: "We are driving them before us at every point"; and now the *last* word is, "Our victory is complete."

The wounded are pouring in. *All our ships*, except the *Spaulding*, are here. Even the *Elm City*, which started with five hundred sick for Yorktown at four o'clock this morning, has just returned, beds made and all—a triumph for her hospital company! The *Commodore*, a Pennsylvania boat, the *Vanderbilt* and *Whilldin*, Government boats, are full. The *Knickerbocker* filled up, before we left her, with three hundred men from Casey's division—a sad sight. We left her this afternoon, after the men were comfortably settled, in the hands of those who are to take her to Newport News, and came home here, *Wilson Small*, with all our belongings. Mrs. M. and Georgy went off soon after to fit up the *Daniel Webster No. 2*.

I am writing on our little afterdeck by the light of the moon. The shore resounds with cheering; even the wounded are elated. All around me lie hundreds, well-nigh thousands, of the poor fellows. Noble boys!

Wilson Small, June 2.

Dear A.,

The *Daniel Webster* is filling, to sail tonight. . . . What a day and night we have had! What a whirlwind of work, sad work, we have been in! . . . Yesterday, Mrs. Griffin and I were whisked away in a little boat, at the peril of our lives, and hustled, tumbled, hoisted, first into the *State of Maine*, where we lost our way amid frightful scenes, until we finally reached the *Elm City*, where we were going as night watch to relieve the ladies belonging to her, who had been up all the night before. She had four hundred and seventy wounded men on board. We passed the night up to our elbows in beef tea, milk punch, lemonade, panada, etc. The men were comfortable. The surgeons let them, for the most part, have a night's rest before their wounds were opened. Not so, however, on the *State of Maine*, where operations were going on all night; the hideous sounds filling our ears even in the midst of our own press of work. . . .

THE *Daniel Webster* CAME TO DOCK

Abby Howland Woolsey

New York, May 7, 1862.

The *Daniel Webster* came to the dock at dusk yesterday. Charley went down at once, thinking there was a possible chance of your being on board, or at all events, some of the 16th sick. Mrs. Griffin, who came up to care for the men, had gone, and several of the officers had landed, but the men were to remain till morning. . . . I am thankful you were not on board, for your own sakes. *Five men* died and more are dying today, and will die in the act of being landed. . . . McClellan's dispatches today are not very hopeful. He will do the best he can—the rebels outnumber him greatly, are fighting fiercely; will contest every inch of the way; strongly intrenched, etc., etc. Yesterday he called it a "brilliant success." . . . Your letter, Georgy, to Charley, of Saturday and Sunday, is received this morning. It furnishes us the missing links in the story, and will instruct Charley whom to apply to about his duties and his passage, etc. He felt that your telegram, with merely your signature, did not authorize him to go aboard and assume duty. . . . Mrs. Griffin sent us your penciled note as soon as she landed, with one from herself, saying she had left you well—"lovely and active," I think were her expressions. She asked if I knew anything about Mrs. Trotter's decision as to going to the front. The latter was here yesterday. She said she should love dearly to go, but she believed she couldn't, her mother couldn't spare her just now.

Later . . . Charley went down yesterday and saw Mr. Strong, and was inducted as *Purser* of the ship *Daniel Webster*. Mr. Strong gave him a sum of money, and he has been on board today paying the medical cadets and the contrabands. Came home just now for a lunch and has gone down again to finish. He thinks he may have to sleep on board. The vessel is not cleaned up or ready yet. . . . They *may* get off to-morrow afternoon. Mrs. Trotter is to send up to-night to see what we have heard. She is going to join the *Daniel Webster* on its return trip.

THE DEAD LAY BY THE LIVING

Sophronia E. Bucklin

We succeeded in getting on board just as the boat pushed out into the river, where it again lay until morning, crowded to its fullest capacity. Upper and lower decks were packed with soldiers going to the front to fill the ranks which had been decimated by the late battles. The cabin was filled with officers, several of whom vacated sofas—one of which each of us occupied during the night after rolling them closely together.

Two other women—one a State agent and the other in the employ of the Sanitary Commission, the latter from Williamsburg, New York—made them each a bed close together on the floor, while the officers lay around like sheep in a packed fold. Many persons were ill, and the suffocating atmosphere increased the distress until the suffering was general.

On the afternoon of the third day we reached the White House, on the Pamunkey River. It had been the home of Gen. Fitz Hugh Lee, son of the Rebel commander, and under its roof Gen. Washington was married—therefore much interest was associated with it in my mind. All that remained of it now were two stacks of blackened chimneys, and a row of Negro huts made of hewn logs, standing on the brink of the river. The narrow river, with its ragged banks, was somewhat like a city harbor, being filled with boats of every description. It was necessary in making a landing to lay planks from one boat to another— and over these we walked, to the extent of half the width of the river, to the thronged shore.

On the ground men and mules lay together asleep—the mules still in the harness, lying forward on their knees—the soldiers with their trusty guns beside them. They had been walked over, till the dust half-covered them; some so deeply that their heads only were visible, and they crawled up upon the legs of the animals to keep from being earthed alive.

The huge army wagons, still attached to the creatures, were loaded with all manner of supplies, and underneath and about them many lay sleeping amid the noise and confusion. . . .

Between five and six hundred contrabands—old, young, male, and female—cannon, cattle, prisoners of war, and squads of soldiers added to the strangeness of the scene. Some were running with tents, others with the pole; some with a box of crackers, others with a piece of pork; some gathering sticks for a fire, others boiling their coffee—and each intent on his own peculiar errand.

Mr. Shafer, the gentleman who had come on from Washing-

ton in our company, tried vainly for two hours to procure a
conveyance to take us nurses up to the hospital ground, which
lay a mile and a half away. Each one was for himself, and cared
little for those less fortunate. Everything was strongly guarded,
in fear of lurking Rebels, as White House was in the rear of
Cold Harbor, where a battle had been fought only a day or two
previous. . . .

We reported to the surgeon for duty, and he said, if possible,
a tent should be put up for us—so we sat down on the grass till
the chill of evening was upon us. A night in the open air, without even a blanket to cover us, seemed inevitable. When I had
settled it thus in my mind and nerved myself to endure it with
all the fortitude of my soul, I saw the welcome face of one of our
stewards, whom I had known at Camp Stoneman. Never was a
faithful friend greeted with greater joy. After learning of our
forlorn condition, he said, "I am going down to the landing,
and, if I can get them by any means, I will bring each of you a
blanket."

Before the sun's last rays streaked up into the darkening sky
we had a tent erected, and, shivering with cold, although in the
month of June, we were glad to crawl under its white wings,
and try to sleep. Presently we heard a scratch on the canvas
(which answers to a rap on a civilized house-door), and, following it, came a blanket for each of us, from generous hands.

We were without supper—the supplies not having arrived yet
—and tired, cold, and hungry, we rolled ourselves up in our new,
clean blankets, and, with our satchels under our heads, lay down
to rest on the bare ground. I had lain on the uncovered slats of
a Government bedstead, on straw, on husks, on shavings, and
on the bare floor, but never before on the ground, which was
chilly with the heavy fall of dew.

Rebels were on every hand; we knew not at what moment

they might dash down through our pickets, on whom we distinctly heard them firing at intervals. . . .

We knew we must have relief soon, or we should be rendered unfit for the duty which had brought us hither, and it was uncertain how long we must wait for government supplies. Presently, in the stillness of the bright morning, I heard the sound of a hammer, and looking out across a little creek, which ran babbling through the tall, dewy grass, I saw another tent going up, and the familiar face of Mrs. Brainard, Michigan State agent, appeared very close by it. I had known her at Gettysburg, and knew that we would not apply to her for relief in vain.

I called upon her and stated our failure to obtain food from the Sanitary Commission. She said, "Our table is spread, and the delegates are now breakfasting—come in, and partake of what we have." And it seemed a feast as she named over good soft bread and butter, raw ham, and plenty of tea and coffee. "You are welcome to eat here until your supplies come," she added, as I departed with the glad tidings to my tentmates.

We were waiting for our work during those bright and warm June days. . . .

A Government kitchen was going up; a dispensary was being erected and the medicines arranged in their proper places; the commissary was getting the hospital supplies ready for use; boxes of bandages were opened, and the hurry of preparation was on every hand. Tents were being spread, and the ambulances came upon the field with their ghastly, bloody freight—unloading them, dying and groaning under the sun—the small number of tents being entirely insufficient to shelter the constantly arriving throngs.

Equipped for labor, with a box of bandages, a box of lint, adhesive plaster, sponge, shears, and chloroform, we went out to begin our labor of mercy, and found them lying in every imaginable position on the bare ground. Men were in attendance to bring us the water, with which to wash the gore from the lacerated bodies. We worked under the scorching sun from early morn till late at night, the ambulances still bringing them in steadily.

I never beheld any worse sights than here met my gaze in every hand. I had seen as distressing wounds, but the awful circumstances which heightened the distress of the wretched, dying men had never been more glaringly presented to my sight before.

Men lay all around me, who had been left for days on the battleground, wet with the dews of night, disfigured with powder and dirt, with blood oozing from their torn flesh, and worms literally covering the festering wounds—dying with thirst, starving for food, unable to attend to nature's wants, groaning in delirious fever, praying to die, to be rid of the intense pain which wracked the poor body.

Such dreadful suffering I hope never to witness again. The field was one vast plain of intense mortal agony, tortured by the sun, and chilled by the night dews. Everywhere were groans and cries for help; everywhere were the pleading and glassy eyes of dying men who were speechless in the delirium of death. It was a scene to appall the stoutest hearts, but the excitement nerved us to shut our senses to everything but the task of relieving them as fast as possible. The dead lay by the living; the dying groaned by the dead, and still one hundred ambulances poured the awful tide in upon us.

We soon had our quarters arranged quite comfortably. A stove, bedsteads, straw ticks, with one blanket, and a table made by driving sticks into the ground and laying boards upon them, completed the inventory of our tent furniture. We also had a boy detailed to cook for us. . . .

We dreaded the nights, for we lay, through the dark hours, insufficiently protected from the cold, yet knowing there were

hundreds of wounded in the open air who had far less covering
than we.

The Sanitary and Christian Commissions were on the ground
at work. . . .

The cry for food was the standing one in the hastily constructed field hospitals. . . .

I FOUND GENERAL KEARNY IN THE THICKEST OF THE FIGHT

Sarah Emma Edmonds

*Assuming another one of her many roles, Emma Edmonds
(Franklin Thompson) describes the dramatic fashion in which
she went to see about reinforcements for Kearny's division during the Battle of Fair Oaks.*

At this time I was in military uniform, mounted upon my
Rebel horse, and was acting orderly for General K.* Several
aides and orderlies had been sent with messages and dispatches,
but no reinforcements had yet arrived, and, taking a Federal
view of it, the picture presented a gloomy appearance. General
K. reined in his horse abruptly, and taking from his pocket an
envelope, he hastily wrote on the back of it with a pencil: "In
the name of God bring your command to our relief, if you have
to swim in order to get here—or we are lost." Handing it to me,
he said, "Go just as fast as that horse can carry you to General
G.,† present this with my compliments, return immediately,
and report to me."

I put poor little Reb over the road at the very top of his speed
until he was nearly white with foam, then plunged him into

* General Philip Kearny.
† Emma must be referring to General McClellan by his first name, George.

the Chickahominy and swam him across the river. I met General G. about a hundred rods from the river making the best of his way toward the bridge. Engineers were at once set to work strengthening the crazy structure, which was swaying to and fro with the rushing tide. The eager, excited troops dashed into the water waist deep, and getting upon the floating planks went pouring over in massive columns. I preferred to swim my horse back again rather than risk myself upon such a bridge, for I looked every moment to see it give way and engulf the whole division in the turbid waters of the swollen creek. However, all reached the other side in safety, and started along the flooded road on the double quick. This was cheering news to carry back to General K., so I started again for the field in order to claim the reward of "him who bringeth good tidings."

I found General K. in the thickest of the fight, encouraging his men and shouting his orders distinctly above the roar and din of battle. Riding up to him and touching my hat, I reported: "Just returned, sir. General G., with his command, will be here immediately." It was too good to keep to himself, so he turned to his men and shouted at the top of his voice, "Reinforcements! reinforcements!" then swinging his hat in the air he perfectly electrified the whole line as far as his voice could reach, and the glorious word "reinforcements" was passed along until that almost exhausted line was reanimated and inspired with new hope.

While I was thus watching with delight the effects of this joyful news upon the soldiers, my attention was directed to another object. General H.,* who had made himself conspicuous by his gallant conduct, was struck by a ball which shattered his arm badly. He was only a few rods from me and there was none near to help him. I asked General K. if I might go to him, leaped from my horse, and hitched him near by. I then removed the clothing from his arm, gave him some water, poured some

* General Oliver O. Howard.

on the wound, and went to my saddlebags to get some bandages, when my Rebel pony laid hold of my arm with his teeth and almost tore the flesh from the bone. Not content with that, he turned his heels in an instant and kicked with both feet, sending me about a rod. My arm was now almost as bad as General H.'s, and I could do but little to help him, for in ten minutes it was swollen terribly, and I could not raise to it my head; finally I was ordered back to an old sawmill about a mile and a half from the field, where were considerable quantities of quartermaster's and commissary stores, with orders to have them removed further to the rear; and all who were able to come to the front, together with the surgeon and a portion of the hospital corps who had been left there in charge of the sick, were to lose no time in reporting themselves for duty on the field.

Upon arriving at the old sawmill I found it crowded with wounded men who had crawled there from the battlefield, to have their wounds dressed if possible, and if not to lie down and suffer where the shot and shell could not reach them. I delivered my orders. In a few moments more there was not a soul left to minister to those poor fellows who were huddled together in that mill by the score; all had gone to the front, and I was left there in a sad plight.

I put my vicious little Reb in a building near the mill, where there was plenty of hay and corn, but did not dare to unsaddle him. I then examined the extent of the injury done to my arm, and found it was worse than I had supposed. It was badly mangled by the horse's teeth, and in one place a large piece of flesh was torn from the arm and hung by small shreds. But the arm was not the worst; he had kicked me in the side, which had lamed and bruised me sadly. Yet this was no time to groan over a slight kick from a horse, when so many lay around me with shattered limbs and ghastly saber wounds, some of them even now in the very agonies of death. I bound up my arm in a sling, and set about removing the blood-clotted clothing from the wounds of those who needed it most; but having neither knife or scissors, I was obliged in many instances to use my teeth in order to tear the thick woolen garments stiffened and saturated with blood, the very remembrance of which now makes me feel rather uncomfortable in the gastric region; but then there was no unpleasant sensation.

The next thing to be thought of was, how I could procure some bandages. . . . There were two houses within a mile, and I decided to try my fortune in that direction. First of all I went among the sick, who were left there by the surgeon, and inquired if there were any who were able to assist me in dressing wounds. Yes, I found two; one a little mail-carrier, and the other a commissary sergeant, both of whom were scarcely able to stand alone. These two set to work pouring cold water upon the wounded limbs occasionally, and giving the men water to drink until I returned.

At the first house I went to they would not let me in at all, but raised the window and wished to know what was wanted. I told them, anything that would admit of tearing up for bandages. No, they had nothing of the kind, and closed the window again. I limped along to the next house. A man came to the door, holding it, to prevent my attempting to get in. The same question was asked, and a similar answer returned. By this time my patience and strength were both exhausted, and my mind was made up with regard to the course I should pursue. Therefore, drawing both my pistols from my belt, I demanded some cotton, new or old—sheets, pillow-cases, or any other article which would answer the purpose for bandages. The man trembled from head to foot, and called his wife to know if she could let me have anything of the sort; yes, she could, if I would pay her for it; and of course I was willing to pay her; so she brought me an old sheet, a pair of pillow-cases, and three yards of new factory cotton cloth, for which she demanded five dollars. Happening to have only three dollars in change, I told her I thought that would be sufficient; and so saying, I left immediately.

I did not know, until I had proceeded some distance, that the blood was running from my arm in a perfect stream. In my excitement and determination, I had grasped one of my pistols with the lame hand and started those terrible gashes bleeding afresh. I grew faint and dizzy, and sat down by the roadside to gather a little strength, before proceeding further. . . .

I made my way slowly toward the mill. . . . The wounded were coming in faster than ever, and I was busy tearing up the cotton in strips, and trying to bind up some of the poor mangled limbs, the little sick sergeant being my right-hand man. . . .

All that weary night my heart burned with indignation, and I seemed endowed with supernatural powers of endurance, for when morning came and found me still at my post, without having tasted food for twenty-four hours, I felt stronger and fresher than I had done the day before. My two young sick friends had been persuaded to lie down, and were now fast asleep, side by side with the wounded.

Night brought a cessation of hostilities to the weary troops, but to neither side a decided victory or defeat. Both armies bivouacked on the bloody field, within a few rods of each other. There they lay waiting for the morning light to decide the contest. The excitement and din of battle had ceased; those brief hours of darkness proved a sweet respite from the fierce struggle of the day, and in the holy calm of that midnight hour, when silence brooded over the blood-washed plain, many brave soldiers lay down on that gory field. Sunday, the first of June, dawned beautifully, a day of hallowed rest and promise to the millions who rose to their devotions, ere the bell called them to the house of prayer, but not of rest to the weary, broken armies

the drum-beat called from their wet and muddy beds to renew the contest. At a quarter past seven o'clock the battle again
commenced, and raged fiercely until about noon. Both armies
fought with determination and heroic bravery until the Rebels
were compelled to yield, and victory once more perched upon
the banners of the National troops.

I came on the field about ten o'clock, and remained until the
close of the battle, but could do little more than look upon the
terrible scene. General McClellan was on the field when I arrived. I saw him ride along the entire battle front, and if I had
not seen him, I could not have long remained in ignorance of
his presence—for the cheers from all parts of the Federal lines
told as plainly as words could express that their beloved commander was with them, amid that desperate struggle for victory.
It was a terrible slaughter—more than fifteen thousand lay upon
the field. It was enough to make angels weep, to look down upon
that field of carnage. The dead and wounded of the enemy fell
into the hands of the Unionists, which added fearfully to the
labors of that exhausted, battle-worn army.

On the evening of the third of June, General McClellan issued the following address to his troops, which was read on
dress parade, and was received with tremendous cheering:

"Soldiers of the Army of the Potomac! I have fulfilled at least
a part of my promise to you. You are now face to face with the
Rebels, who are held at bay in front of their capital. The final
and decisive battle is at hand. Unless you belie your past history,
the result cannot be for a moment doubtful. If the troops who
labored so faithfully at Yorktown, and fought so bravely, and
won the hard fights at Williamsburg, West Point, Hanover
Court-House, and Fair Oaks, now prove themselves worthy of
their antecedents, the victory is surely ours. The events of every
day prove your superiority; wherever you have met the enemy,

you have beaten him; wherever you have used the bayonet, he has given way in panic and disorder.

"I ask of you, now, one last crowning effort. The enemy has staked his all on the issue of the coming battle. Let us meet him, crush him here, in the very center of the rebellion. Soldiers! I will be with you in this battle, and share its dangers with you. Our confidence in each other is now founded upon the past. Let us strike the blow which is to restore peace and union to this distracted land. Upon your valor, discipline, and mutual confidence, the result depends."

Every battle fought on the Peninsula fearfully reduced the strength of the Army of the Potomac, and proved a demonstration that the enemy far outnumbered the Union forces. Still there were no reinforcements, notwithstanding McClellan's daily urgent dispatches to the President and Secretary of War, and the great impending battle in front of the Rebel Capital so near at hand.

The next day McClellan sent another dispatch, as follows:

"Please inform me at once what reinforcements, if any, I can count upon having at Fortress Monroe or White House, within the next three days, and when each regiment may be expected to arrive. It is of the utmost importance that I should know this immediately. The losses in the battle of the thirty-first and first will amount to seven thousand. Regard this as confidential for the present. After the losses in our last battle, I trust that I shall no longer be regarded as an alarmist. I believe we have at least one more desperate battle to fight."

The day after the battle of Fair Oaks, a splendid sword was presented to me. It had been struck from the hand of a Rebel colonel, while in the act of raising it to strike one of our officers after he had fallen from his horse. Oh, how proud I felt of that beautiful silver-mounted trophy, from the bloody field of Fair

Oaks, which had so recently been wielded by a powerful arm, but powerless now, for he lay in the agonies of death, while his splendid sword had passed into my feeble hands. I presume if he had known this, it would have added another pang to his already agonized spirit. The sword was presented by General K.,* to whom I gave my Rebel pony, with the comforting assurance that he was only intended for ornament, and not for use; for generals were too scarce on the Peninsula to risk their precious lives by coming in contact with him. The General was delighted with him, and without paying the slightest attention to my suggestion deliberately walked up to the pony and commenced patting him and handling his limbs as if he were the most quiet creature in the world, while Reb stood eyeing his new master with apparent satisfaction, and seemed to rejoice that he had passed from my insignificant hands, and was henceforth to be the honored bearer of shoulder straps. After thoroughly examining him he said: "He is certainly a splendid horse, and worth three hundred dollars of any man's money; all he requires is kind treatment, and he will be as gentle as any one could desire."

But Reb very soon gave him to understand decidedly that he was overrating his good qualities; for no sooner had the General turned his back toward him that he struck him between the shoulders with both hind feet, sending him his full length upon the ground; and as soon as he attempted to rise he repeated the same performance until he had knocked him down four or five times in succession. By that time the General was pretty thoroughly convinced that Reb's social qualities were somewhat deficient, his bump of combativeness largely developed, and his gymnastics quite impressive.

* Philip Kearny.

ESCAPING FROM STONEWALL JACKSON

Eliza Woolsey Howland

Eliza writes her husband the latest news of the Hospital Transport Service while ashore at White House.

June 20.

I am much entertained by the regiment's vote of thanks to ME for the hats with which I had nothing whatever to do.

Joe Howland had ordered straw hats for the 16th to help guard against the intense heat of the Chickahominy swamp and gave them in his wife's name.

Quartermaster Davies has gone off with an order for the delivery of the musical instruments, and you will probably receive them tomorrow. . . .

We ran down at daybreak yesterday to Yorktown to see the floating hospital, the *St. Mark,* just arrived from New York with Drs. Agnew, Draper, Carmalt, and others on board. . . .

Later: The *Small* came back during the evening and brought Dr. Agnew and Dr. Carmalt and a number of the *St. Mark* force to go out to the front today. We all spent most of the evening in the tent (on shore) with the front curtains down and the back ones open to let in the blaze of the camp fire, over which on the pothooks hung the kettles of tea and coffee and soup which we were preparing for 200 or 300 sick who are expected down on the trains. . . .

Another party, the third of Congressional picknickers, came down today but were refused transportation to the front by General McClellan's orders. I rejoice in it. . . .

Eliza writes in her Journal about her experiences.

Aboard *Wilson Small*, June 23.

A very anxious day. An orderly from Brigade Headquarters brought word from Captain Hopkins that Joe was ill and unable to write. I at once put up a basket of stores for him . . . to go by the orderly, and Charley telegraphed Generals Slocum and Franklin to know the truth, while Mr. Olmsted arranged with Captain Sawtelle for a pass to take me to the front tomorrow morning. My mind was relieved, however, by the telegraphic answers and better accounts, and I have given up the idea of going out.

June 25. General Van Vliet says that if I want to go to the front at any time and will send him word he will have his wagon meet me and take me over to J.'s camp. This morning Dr. Bigelow came back to our boat from the front.

June 26. Running away down the Pamunkey again as fast as we can go, escaping from Stonewall Jackson!

All night the wood choppers were at work cutting down the woods at White House (Landing) to give the gunboats a chance to command the land beyond, and just now as we passed the banks were shorn and the pretty little place laid bare. The pickets had been driven in, and Jackson was supposed to be close at hand. Eighty wounded were brought down last night and put on board the *Knickerbocker*. Twelve more and a few sick came down this morning. . . .

The rumor today is that all communication with the front is stopped to conceal an advance of our army.

June 28. We went as far as West Point, followed by a train of schooners and barges running away like ourselves. There we lay through the evening and night, watching for the flames of burning stores at White House which did not burn, and for booming of guns which did not boom. Without news or orders until after dinner, when we turned and ran up the river again in search of both. Near Cumberland we met the *Arrowsmith* with Surgeon Vollum on board, who hailed us and told us of all we yet know of yesterday's action at the front. Colonel Vollum then pushed on up to Washington for medical supplies and we kept on up here to White House again.

News that Joe Howland had been wounded reached Eliza and Georgy at White House; the accident had occurred during the Battle of Gaines's Mill on June 27, the first of the terrible Seven Days' Battle before Richmond. The Staff Surgeon at Army Headquarters had wired that "Colonel Howland has a slight flesh wound. He is in my tent and will be taken good care of until he can be sent down." At almost the same moment communications with the front were cut. The Rebels were advancing. General Stoneman sent in word that they were in sight. The Wilson Small stood by as long as it could and then went off into the dock. The next day Georgy wrote her mother:

The telegraph wires had just been cut as we received the news of Joe's wound, and a mounted messenger announced the enemy at Tunstall's. Stoneman's cavalry were worrying them until we were all safely off, when he would fall back, and the Rebels would walk into our deserted places. So we steamed away watching the moving of the last transports, and the *Canonicus* (Headquarters boat for the army officers at White House) with Colonel Ingalls, Captain Sawtelle, and General Casey and staff. The most interesting thing was the spontaneous movement of the slaves who, when it was known that the Yankees were running away, came flocking from all the country about, bringing their little movables, frying pans, old hats, and bundles to the riverside. There was no appearance of anxiety or excitement among them. Fortunately there was plenty of deck room for them on the forage boats, one of which as we passed seemed filled with women only, in their gayest dresses and brightest turbans, like a whole load of tulips for a horticultural show. The black smoke began to rise from the burning stores on shore (fired to keep them from the enemy), and now and then the roar of the battle came to us, but the slave women were quietly nursing their children and singing hymns. . . . All night we sat on the deck of the *Small*, watching the constantly increasing cloud of smoke and the fireflashes over the trees toward the White House as we moved slowly down the river.

FOR GOD'S SAKE, GIVE US BREAD

Eliza Harris

There seem to be no limits to the panegyrics employed by nine-teenth-century biographers when extolling womanhood and the weakness of the weaker sex. Eliza Harris of Philadelphia was said to be pale and delicate, yet proved able to work like a horse when her services were needed. A woman of refinement and education, she was the wife of Dr. John Harris, a "somewhat eminent physician" in Philadelphia, and lived in comfort. "She seemed to be one of those least fitted to endure hardships," one of her contemporary biographers notes, but goes on to say that "beneath that quiet and frail exterior there dwelt a firm and dauntless spirit."

It took a dauntless spirit to travel aboard the Government transport Vanderbilt, *which brought the wounded from the bloody field of Fair Oaks. Mrs. Harris went as the agent for the Philadelphia Aid Society, which had been organized on April 26, 1861. Although she was secretary of the Society, she preferred to work in the field and distribute the supplies they sent to her. Mrs. Harris's stay on the* Vanderbilt *was unexpectedly prolonged, as the officers were not able to get the necessary supplies on board. Mrs. Harris witnessed the removal of the wounded from the battlefield of Fair Oaks to the* Vanderbilt.

There were eight hundred on board. Passageways, staterooms, floors from the dark and fetid hold to the hurricane deck were all more than filled; some on mattresses, some on blankets, others on straw; some in the death struggle, others nearing it, some already beyond human sympathy and help; some in their blood as they had been brought from the battlefield of the Sabbath previous, and all hungry and thirsty, not having had anything to eat or drink, except hard crackers, for twenty-four hours.

The gentlemen who came on with us hurried on to the White House, and would have had us go with them, but something held us back; thank God it was so. Meeting Dr. Cuyler, Medical Director, he exclaimed: "Here is work for you!" He, poor man, was completely overwhelmed with the general care of all the hospitals at Old Point, and added to these, these mammoth floating hospitals, which are coming in from day to day with their precious cargoes. Without any previous notice, they anchor, and send to him for supplies, which it would be extremely difficult to improvise, even in our large cities, and quite impossible at Old Point. "No bakeries, no stores, except small sutlers." The bread had all to be baked; the boat rationed for two days; *eight hundred* on board.

When we went aboard, the first cry we met was for tea and bread. "For God's sake, give us *bread*," came from many of our wounded soldiers. Others shot in the face or neck begged for liquid food. With feelings of a *mixed* character, shame, indignation, and sorrow blending, we turned away to see what resources we could muster to meet the demand. A box of tea, a barrel of cornmeal, sundry parcels of dried fruit, a few crackers,

ginger cakes, dried rusk, sundry jars of jelly and of pickles, were
seized upon, soldiers and contrabands impressed into service,
all the cooking arrangements of three families appropriated, by
permission, and soon three pounds of tea were boiling, and many
gallons of gruel blubbering. In the meantime, all the bread we
could buy, twenty-five loaves, were cut into slices and *jellied*,
pickles were got in readiness, and in an incredibly short time, we
were back to our poor sufferers.

When we carried in bread, hands from every quarter were
outstretched, and the cry, "Give us a piece, O please! I have had
nothing since Monday"; another, "Nothing but hard crackers
since the fight," etc. When we had dealt out nearly all the
bread, a surgeon came in, and cried, "Do please keep some for
the poor fellows in the hold; they are so badly off for everything." So with the remnant we threaded our way through the
suffering crowd, amid such exclamations as "Oh! please don't
touch my foot," or, "For mercy's sake, don't touch my arm";
another, "Please don't move the blanket; I am so terribly cut
up," down to the hold, in which were not less than one hundred
and fifty, nearly all sick, some very sick. It was like plunging into
a vapor bath, so hot, close, and full of moisture, and then in
this dismal place, we distributed our bread, oranges, and pickles,
which were seized upon with avidity. And here let me say, at
least twenty of them told us next day that the pickles had done
them more good than all the medicine they had taken. The tea
was carried all around in buckets, sweetened, but no milk in it.
How much we wished for some concentrated milk. The gruel,
into which we had put a goodly quantity of wine, was relished,
you cannot know how much. . . . After hours spent in this way,
we returned to the Hygeia Hospital, stopping on our way to stew
a quantity of dried fruit, which served for supper, reaching the
Hygeia wet through and through, *every garment* saturated. Dis-
robed, and bathing with bay rum, was glad to lie down, every

bone aching, and head and heart throbbing, unwilling to cease work where so much was to be done, and yet wholly unable to do more. There I lay, with the sick, wounded, and dying all around, and slept from sheer exhaustion, the last sounds falling upon my ear being groans from the operating room.

Two days afterward I was on the *Knickerbocker*, one of the Sanitary Commission transports, and headed for White House Landing, where, with Miss Charlotte Bradford, I spent the whole night on the transport *Louisiana* looking after the wounded. When I left the boat at eleven o'clock the next night, I *was obliged to wash all my skirts as they were saturated with the mingled blood of the Union and Confederate soldiers which covered the floor as I kneeled to wash their faces.* I had torn up all my spare clothing for bandages and compresses.

I SEE SOMETHING WHITE AMONG THE TREES

Katharine P. Wormeley

The Battle of Malvern Hill to which Katharine Wormeley refers in this letter to her mother was the violent concluding engagement of the Seven Days' Battle.

Off Berkley, Harrison's Bar, James River,
Tuesday, July 1, 1862.

We arrived here yesterday to hear the thunder of the battle and to find the army just approaching this landing. Last night it was a verdant shore; today it is a dusty plain. The feelings with which we came up the James River I can't describe, our anxiety, excitement, and breathless desire to know something were so great. Not a vessel was in sight after we left Newport News, except the *Canonicous*, Quartermaster's Department boat, which was just ahead of us. No one could guess what knowledge any moment might bring to us.

We were just admiring a fine old colonial house, when someone standing in the bows cried out: "I see something white among the trees to the right!" and in a few minutes more we made them out to be army wagons. We had met our army! What next were we to learn? Never shall I forget the look of the first officers who came on board—one a major, the other a chaplain. They were gaunt and haggard, their hair stood out from their heads stiffened with dust and dirt, their faces were nearly black, and to their waists they were literally moulded in Virginia clay. "Oh, what is this?" we cried. "It is a defeat?" "Defeat! No, we have retreated, but we never turned our backs on them. We have faced and fought and beaten them for five days!"

Just as we arrived, General McClellan came down on the *Galena* to see Colonel Ingalls. Think what a relief it must have been to his anxious mind to learn the perfect success of our removal from White House, and to know that supplies were already here, and following us up the river, for his exhausted army! I saw the gunboat he was on, but I did not see him; and he was gone almost immediately. . . .

Wilson Small, Harrison's Landing, July 3.

As I write I glance from time to time at the Army of the Potomac, massed on the plain before me—an army driven from its position because it could not get reinforcements to render that position tenable; forced every day of its retreat to turn and give battle; an army just one third less than it was; and yet it comes in from seven days' fighting, marching, fasting, in gallant spirits, and making the proud boast for itself and its commander that it has not only marched with its face backward to the enemy, but has inflicted three times the loss it has borne, and that the little spot of its refuge rings with its cheers.

And yet the sad truth cannot be concealed: our position is very hazardous. What I hear said is such as this: "Unless we have reinforcements, what can we do? Must McClellan fight another bloody battle in a struggle for life, or surrender? Give us reinforcements, and all is well. We have got the right base now. We could not have it at first; we made another; that other the Government made it impossible for us to maintain. Day by day we saw it growing untenable. We now have the true base of operations against Richmond. The sacrifice? Yes! but *who compelled it?*"

THE PRESIDENT HAS COME TO HARRISON'S LANDING

Katharine P. Wormeley

After the Army of the Potomac was driven from its position because it could not get reinforcements in the Battle of Malvern Hill, Katharine wondered if McClellan would have to fight another battle "in a struggle for life or surrender." He had the right base now for operations against Richmond. "Give us reinforcements," Katharine wrote, "and all is well." She appears convinced that a "strong pull and pull together" would end the rebellion. On July 4, 1862, while aboard the Wilson Small, she learned of Lincoln's call for thirty thousand men and on the 8th the President came to Harrison's Landing to look over the situation himself.

For the last two hours I have been watching President Lincoln and General McClellan as they sat together in earnest conversation on the deck of a steamer close to us. I am thankful, I am *happy*, that the President has come—has sprung across that dreadful intervening Washington, and come to see and hear and judge for his own wise and noble self.

While we were at dinner someone said, chancing to look through a window: "Why, there's the President!" and he proved to be just arriving on the *Ariel*, at the end of the wharf close to which we are anchored. I stationed myself at once to watch for the coming of McClellan. The President stood on deck with a glass, with which, after a time, he inspected our boat, waving his handkerchief to us. My eyes and soul were in the direction of general headquarters, over where the great balloon was slowly descending. Presently a line of horsemen came over the brow of the hill through the trees, and first emerged a firm-set figure on a brown horse, and after him the staff and bodyguard. As soon as the General reached the head of the wharf he sprang from his horse, and in an instant every man was afoot and motionless. McClellan walked quickly along the thousand-foot pier, a major general beside him, and six officers following. He was the shortest man, of course, by which I distinguished him as the little group stepped onto the pier. When he reached the *Ariel* he ran quickly up to the afterdeck, where the President met him and grasped his hand. I could not distinguish the play of his features, though my eyes still ache with the effort to do so. He is stouter than I expected, but quicker, and more *leste*. He wore the ordinary blue coat and shoulder straps; the coat, fastened only at the throat, and blowing back as he walked, gave to sight a gray flannel shirt and a—suspender!

They sat down together, apparently with a map between them, to which McClellan pointed from time to time with the end of his cigar. We watched the earnest conversation which went on, and which lasted till 6 P.M.; then they rose and walked side by side ashore—the President in a shiny black coat and stovepipe hat, a whole head and shoulders taller, as it seemed to me, than the General. Mr. Lincoln mounted a led horse of the General's, and together they rode off, the staff following, the dragoons presenting arms and then wheeling round to follow, their sabres gleaming in the sunlight. And so they have passed over the brow of the hill, and I have come to tell you about it. The cannon are firing salutes—a sound of strange peacefulness to us, after the angry, irregular boomings and the sharp scream of the shells to which we are accustomed. . . .

MOTHER CANNOT STAND THE ANXIETY MUCH LONGER

Abby Howland Woolsey

8 Brevoort Place, Saturday, July 5, '62.
Georgy's and Charley's letters from Harrison's [Landing] have just arrived, the last date being a postscript Thursday, July 3, which brings us into close correspondence again, you see. These letters have relieved the painful anxiety that began to possess us, about Joe's condition and whereabouts. We thought perhaps that if his wound were really slight, he had been tempted to rejoin the regiment, and had shared in that horrible battle of White Oak Swamp. . . . Mother says that if it is Charley's *desire* to stay a little while longer, she consents; he is evidently so useful that she should not have the heart to insist on his coming back. As for Georgy, if you leave her behind, we shall never forgive you. She *must* come. Mother cannot stand the anxiety much longer, nor can Georgy bear the constant strain. By-and-by, perhaps, if necessary, she could go back; *now* she must come home with you. We should be better pleased to have Charley and all once more together, at the end of this battle year, and before we all begin on other years of separation and distress. Have C. come too. Poor, poor Colonel Marsh! Mortally wounded at Gaines's Mill. What a mercy it would have been

had he been killed on the spot. . . . We shall never know all that this week of desperate fighting has cost us; our dead and wounded being left behind, or crawling painfully along in the trail of the retreating army. Here and there an officer picked up in a passing ambulance, as Joe rescued the four you speak of. Our great, beautiful "Army of the Potomac," dwindled down to an exhausted handful. . . . Fifty thousand in all destroyed by fever and wounds, in McClellan's brief campaign! No wonder if the President has hesitated to send more troops to be used up in swamps, when so little was being done to show for it. . . . Any fool might have known that Beauregard and the bulk of his army had come to Richmond; but then our generals are not even fools, but something less if possible. . . . It may be God's will to destroy this nation by inches. It is certainly the devil's will to put dissension into the hearts of our leaders, and blundering darkness into their minds. God overrules all evil, even this, I suppose, to his own glory. I have no question that this and all other defeats are intended to drive us, as a nation, to a higher moral ground in the conduct and purpose of this war. As things stand, the South is fighting to maintain slavery, and the North is trying to fight so as to put it down. When this policy ceases, perhaps we shall begin to have victory, if we haven't already sinned away our day of grace.

I don't know who kept Fourth of July yesterday; there was not much for public rejoicing though many families had private mercies and deliverances, like ours, to be thankful for. Hatty and Carry went with the Bucks to Bedloe's Island, with a tug load of ice cream and cake, and flowers and flags, and a chest of tea, forty quarts of milk, and butter, and handkerchiefs, papers and books, to set out a long table and give a treat to two hundred in hospital there. To their distress they found that H—— B—— (malisons on him) had ordered away the day before, back to their regiments (via Fort Monroe I suppose), all who were strong enough to move about. They cannot possibly carry their knapsacks or guns, and must go into hospital again for relapse.

The forty convalescents left on the Island had a glorious feast, the doctor giving his full consent that even the twelve sick ones, in bed, should have as much *ice cream* as they wanted. Mr. Lasar, the singer, and one or two others, went about twice in the course of the day, from tent to tent, singing patriotic songs and hymns, winding up with "Lord, dismiss us," by particular request of the men; and then the men escorted the whole party, after tea, back to the tug, with three cheers and overwhelming thanks. Each man had at least a quart of ice cream, Carry thinks, and each a glass of Catawba wine, and a good slice of cake, and no doubt there will be many made sick, and the ladies will be blamed as the cause.

If you have a hold on Hammond, do get him to look into the hospital rations in the hospitals here: Bedloe's and David's Islands. There seems to be no "special diet" provided—nothing but coffee (no tea), dry bread and stew, rank with onions and white with grease. I have written to the ladies at New Rochelle, begging them to take David's Island in hand, and open a "ladies' kitchen," a "gruel kitchen" as Sarah says theirs in New Haven is called. But they say the surgeon looks with disfavor on the visits of ladies, and they feel "satisfied that the men are *well* taken care of." . . . They will find out by-and-by that surgeons and hospital stewards are not all angels in uniform. . . .

People kept coming yesterday, having seen Joe's name in the newspaper lists, and to-day we have notes of inquiry from all directions. . . .

Edward Walker's account of the fight at Gaines's Mill agrees with the Tribune reporter's—black masses of men coming upon our guns with *orderly joy* determined to take them, and falling under our fire in solid blocks, others pressing forward to fill the gaps.

HOW DID YOU TAKE TO CIVILIZATION?

Katharine P. Wormeley

Katharine Wormeley had hardly regained her land legs when she was offered the directorship of Portsmouth Grove Hospital in Rhode Island. Surgeon General Hammond himself went to see her to urge her to take the position. Miss Wormeley then wrote to Georgy Woolsey, asking her cabin mate from the Wilson Small, to join her in Rhode Island.

Newport, R.I., July 25, 1862.

We left Harrison's Landing on Thursday in the *Daniel Webster*, with two hundred and thirty sick on board. At Fortress Monroe Mrs. Griffin came off the *Euterpe** to ask me to take her cousin, a captain in the regular army, to his friends in Newport. We had some difficulty in getting him on board, for the sea was running very high at midnight, when Mr. Olmsted put the *Webster* as close to the *Euterpe* as he dared. The captain had typhoid fever, with a good deal of low delirium; but he did very well during the voyage, having a comfortable berth on deck under cover. When we reached New York I took him over to the Newport boat in an ambulance, hunted up Captain Brown, and made him establish my patient on his stretcher in the airiest part of the boat. It was rich to see the state of fuss into which that worthy man was thrown, and to hear him exhort *me* to "keep calm!" As soon as I could, I went below, and made the stewardess give me oceans of warm water, out of which I emerged a new creature. When I went back to my captain I found a lady sitting by him—his mother, who happened to be going to Newport on that boat! So I gave up my

---

* Sister ship to the *St. Mark.* She was used as a receiving hospital in Hampton Roads. Mrs. Griffin took charge of the women's department on her for several weeks.

last patient into better hands—though at night, when I found him moved out of the fresh air, so essential to him, into the close cabin, I wished I had held command over him till we landed, and sighed over the follies of private nursing.

The Hospital Transport Service is ended. We left the *Elizabeth* well supplied, and moored to the long wharf at Harrison's Landing, where the surgeons and chaplains and quartermasters can get at her with ease. Dr. Jenkins and Dr. Douglas remain to superintend the issue of stores and inspect the condition of camps and regiments; but the transports are given back to the Quartermaster's Department: our reign is over. I wonder who'll succeed to my cabin on the *Small*, and hang his clothes on my gimlets (used for pegs), and inherit my other little inventions of that nature?

There! my story is done. A short three months ago I wrote to tell you it was beginning; but what a lifetime lies between now and then.

Newport, R. I., July 21, '62.

Dear Georgy:

How did you take to civilization? I got along perfectly till I was caught going off the boat without paying my fare. Captain T.'s mother was on board, which was a capital thing, and induced him to behave himself. I found intimate friends on board who were dear to me because they escorted me to supper. Georgy! if you ever take passage on the *Metropolis*, go down to supper for my sake and imagine how it affected me. My friends rather apologized for their desire to go down; for my part all I could do was to conceal my disappointment at not being able to eat everything. It seemed to me there was everything good that I had ever heard of, ending with peaches and ice cream.

I put the wounded captain into an express wagon (the nearest thing to an ambulance) and got home myself at 4 o'clock, to be finely cackled over by Mother. The next day the town called on me, beginning, like a Fourth of July procession, with the mayor and clergy. The next day I stayed in bed till after visiting hours. By-the-by, isn't a bed delicious? I can't believe it is the same mattress, the same blanket and sheets that I had before I went away. Of course you know that Dr. Wheaton with seventeen hundred men is here (six miles from here). Excursion boats run from here and from Providence to the camp. It is the fashionable drive, and the dear creatures are all female sutlers with baskets of *pies* and cakes and pickles and sweetmeats. Colonel Vollum is here. I have sent him word that if I can do anything sensible with authority I will, meanwhile I do not intend going near the camp. . . . I am truly sorry that Colonel Howland's furlough is shortened. Fanny Russell told me about it, and we spent all the time we were together in adoring "Mrs. H." I have said one hundred times "I will tell that to Georgy," but behold I have forgotten everything. Yesterday was a happy day to me, the dear little chapel was so peaceful and full of love and praise. I thought of Mr. —— as I sat there. . . . No large mind doubts God or the excellence of life with Him merely through looking at the mean lives of others.

Good-bye, love to Mrs. Howland and C.W.W.

THE SOLDIERS HAVE COME

Jane Stuart Woolsey

After joining Katharine Wormeley at Portsmouth Hospital, Georgeanna suggested that both Jane Woolsey, her sister, and

* Husband of Eliza Woolsey Howland.

Sarah Woolsey, her cousin, transfer to this hospital. Jane, Sarah,
and Georgeanna then established themselves at the hospital six
miles from Newport in a "jolly little thin board house built for
the nursing staff." Jane wrote to her sister Abby.

This morning in the grey (I don't know how she managed to
be up and seeing) Sarah looked in at the ventilator and announced, "Girls, there's a big black steamer off the hospital
dock. The soldiers have come!"

She proved to be the *Daniel Webster* with two hundred
ninety men from FREDERICKSBURG, many of them! There
she lies at this writing, two o'clock, no tug having been got up
from Newport, and the tide being so excessively low that she
can't move in. They have boarded her in boats, however, and
report the men very comfortable—short, delightful trip from
Fortress Monroe, plenty to eat and no very bad cases on board.
Everything is ready for four hundred fifty. Clean wards, clean
beds, clean clothes, and the best of welcomes. Georgy and I,
who have the medical division, will not profit much. We shall
get the sulky old "chronics" and "convalescents," and Sarah and
H. Whetten will have all the surgical cases; but we shall go to
see them all the same, and they shall have all our stores, soft
towels, jelly, and oranges.

Shingling the barracks goes on bravely. I think things will be
all so much finished to the satisfaction of Mr. *Jefferson Davis*,
by spring, that he will perhaps retain us in office!

7 P.M. The men are all safely landed, housed, and suppered,
and all the surgeons are busy dressing wounds. They must work
all night. The men are bright as buttons and jolly. Tell Harriet
Gilman that her shirts are blessing *Fredericksburg men to-night.*

Dr. Edwards, surgeon in charge, in the handsomest way offers to turn *out* anybody we wish and put *in* anybody we wish,

so if you know of any first-rate candidates amenable to female influence, forward us their names.

Their services at Portsmouth Grove lasted only about five months. Sarah was the first to be called home, the family greatly alarmed over an outbreak of smallpox of the worst variety, with a number of deaths among the men. Sarah had to obey the call, leaving Georgeanna in charge of her wards and this scrap of a note:

Number 41 ought to have soda-water and egg beaten in wine every day—Eastman, near the door; be good to him and to D. and C. and M., and read the Pickwick Papers to the poor fellow who blew himself up with gunpowder.

Sarah came back for a little while, later, but their staff was broken up; Jane and Georgeanna yielded to the home demand, went back to New York, and did not return.

Sarah Chauncey Woolsey expressed the sentiments of them all: "Civilization is even more revolting than I supposed, and I pine all the time for our beloved Bohemia."

Georgeanna wrote to her mother from Fishkill: "If you have any difficulty in deciding what we shall have for dinner, the Surgeon General's diet table for each day will be found among my papers; what is good enough for our soldiers will be even too good for us."

Portsmouth Grove was before long turned into a convalescent camp.

7 Hearts Were Heavy with Despair

IN SEPTEMBER OF 1862, A SERIES OF BATTLES TOOK PLACE THAT are referred to as Second Bull Run or the Second Battle of Manassas. Once again at Bull Run Creek the Confederates, led by General Stonewall Jackson, defeated the Army of the Potomac under the command of General John Pope. Rebel President Jefferson Davis saw that "God has again extended his shield over our patriotic army and has blessed the cause of the Confederacy with a second signal victory. . . ."

In the trail of the Union Army were thousands of wounded, and three thousand convalescent soldiers had to be moved from Washington to Philadelphia in order that space would be available for the more serious cases from Bull Run. Signs went up on street walls calling for volunteer nurses, "each to bring a bucket or a tin cup, a bottle of brandy and, if possible, transportation from the battlefield."

For some women, hospital work had begun with the fall of Fort Sumter; for others it began much later when the great casualties of a particular battle created a desperate need for more nurses.

POPE'S ARMY RETREATED FROM BULL RUN

Julia Susan Wheelock

Julia Wheelock left her home in Ionia, Michigan, in September, 1862, because she had received word that her brother, Orville,

199

had been seriously wounded in the Second Battle of Bull Run.
The news was brought to Julia while she was listening to a
recitation in the little red schoolhouse where she had been
teaching ever since she completed two years of study at Kalama-
zoo College in Michigan. She decided that her brother "must
not suffer alone" and set out for Washington with her sister-in-
law, Anna.

The following extract from Julia Wheelock's diary tells of her
trip to Washington in the fall of 1862.

At Detroit, we take the steamer *May Queen*, bound for Cleveland. . . . At eight o'clock, we leave the shores of Michigan and
soon are plowing our way through the blue waters of Lake
Erie. . . .

We land in Cleveland at five A.M., purchase tickets for Washington, via Philadelphia. After four weary hours of waiting, we
find ourselves comfortably seated in the cars and are hurried
on toward our destination. We arrive at Pittsburgh at two P.M.,
where we change cars and hasten away, leaving the dingy, smoke-
wreathed city in the distance. As we approach the Alleghenies,
scenery becomes picturesque and grand, often approaching the
sublime. We pass Harrisburg in the night so we have not even
a glimpse of the capitol of the old Keystone State. All is hushed
and still. We have just composed ourselves for a little sleep
when suddenly there is a crashing and jarring which throws
many from their seats; but in a few minutes, all is explained—
the cars are off the track. The first thought is that some villain-
ous "Reb" has placed obstructions on the track but the truth
is soon known; an innocent horse is the cause of the accident
and "Johnny Reb" is for once wrongly accused.

No one is seriously hurt; only a few minutes' delay; the passengers are crowded into the few remaining cars and we are soon

on our way again, leaving the poor horse on both sides of the track.

We arrive in Philadelphia at four A.M., where we wait for the eleven o'clock train to Baltimore. We saw but little of the city, being very tired; and having our minds constantly occupied with thoughts and fearful forebodings, we felt no desire for sightseeing.

After a short delay, once more the shrill whistle was heard and again we are moving on toward the Nation's capital where we arrived in good time. The first object that attracts our attention is that magnificent building—the Capitol. . . .

It being too late to go to Alexandria—the boats having already stopped running—the fond hope of seeing the dear husband and brother that day had to be given up. . . . We passed thousands of our soldiers, some of them apparently having recently arrived—judging from their clean uniforms—while others had evidently seen hard service, looking worn and tired and well-nigh discouraged. We concluded they belonged to Pope's grand army which had so recently retreated from the disastrous battle-field of Bull Run. We wondered how such numbers could have been defeated. To us, having never before seen more than a single regiment at a time, it was a vast army. We began to realize that we had a mighty foe to contend with. . . .

Early next morning we hastened to the Provost Marshal's office to obtain passes for Alexandria. Arriving at the office, hope almost dies within us for we see this notice:

No Passes Granted on Sunday.

What is to be done now? Shall we retrace our steps and wait another twenty-four hours in such terrible suspense? No, we resolve not to leave until an effort has been made and the last argument exhausted, in setting forth the justice of our claims.

We enter the office, find it already filled with applicants, saw one after another as they applied and were refused. Tremblingly, we crowded our way to the Marshal's chair, and, with the greatest respect and more deference than is meet, or should be paid to mortals, request passage to Alexandria. He straightens himself up and, with the cold dignity of a prince, replies:

"Don't you know we don't give passes on Sundays? Why do you ask us to violate orders?"

Still acting as spokesman, I inquired: "Will no circumstances justify you in granting a pass today?"

"Well, what are the circumstances?" said he in the same strained manner.

Our story is briefly told after which, with some hesitation and watching us closely to see whether we were deceiving him, he directed the passes to be made out. Oh, what a load was that moment lifted from our hearts! Those little strips of paper, how precious! With tears of gratitude, we left the office and immediately started for the boat landing and were soon on the steamer *James* G. Y. and off for Alexandria, eight miles down the river. How delightful had we been on a pleasure excursion! . . .

Scenes and scenery so entirely new! The forts along the river, with those iron-throated monsters looking defiantly upon us, almost causing one to shrink back with terror, were a great curiosity. The beautiful residence of Gen. Robert E. Lee, now his no longer—having been forfeited by treason—on Arlington Heights, half hidden amid stately forest trees and luxuriant evergreens, was pointed out to us; also the Washington Navy Yard, the Arsenal, and the Insane Asylum. But what attracts our attention more than all else are the multitudes of soldiers with their snowy tents skirting the banks on either side of the river, and extending back as far as the eye can reach, covering every hillside and every valley, which, with the desolate appear-

ance of the country, remind us that we are in the presence of
WAR.

Soon the ancient city of Alexandria—ancient in American
history—heaves in sight. It presents a gloomy, dingy, dilapidated
appearance. As we set foot upon the "sacred soil," we experience
quickened heart-beatings, for we know that this terrible suspense will soon give place to, it may be, a dreadful reality. As
we pass up King Street we pause a moment to look at the building where the brave young Ellsworth* fell, drop a tear to his
memory, and hasten on. Turning from King into Washington
Street, we notice a soldier in full uniform with a shouldered
musket pacing to and fro in front of what appeared to be a
church. We are told by the guard that it is the Southern M. E.
Church, but now used for a hospital. We enter the building,
make known the object of our visit but find he is not there. My
poor sister could go no farther. . . .

I hastened to the next hospital but met with the same reply
as before. I cross the street to the Baptist church, which is also
used for a hospital, my fears every moment increasing. Happening to look back before entering this hospital to the one I had
just left, I saw someone beckoning me to return. Hope began to
revive; I hurried back and was told he was there, and doing well,
though still very weak. My informant asked if I would see him.
"No," I replied, "Not until I have informed his wife." . . . I hurried back with a light heart and a quick step to the hospital
where my sister was waiting in such agony of suspense. She
heard my voice before reaching the hospital, exclaiming at almost every step: "I've found him! I've found him! Oh, Anna,
come quickly!" I did not realize that I was in the streets of a
city, attracting the notice of passers-by, nor did I much care,

* Colonel Elmer Ellsworth, leader of the Firemen Zouaves, was shot in
May, 1861, in Alexandria after removing a Confederate flag from a hotel.

for a deep anxiety and long days of suspense had given place to joyful hopes and sweet anticipations.

She rose to accompany me, hesitated a moment, and then sank back upon her seat, and with a look almost of despair, says: "Julia, are you *sure*, have you seen him?" I assured her that though I had not seen him, there could be no mistake, for they certainly would not have said he was there, had he not been. Thus reassured she rose the second time, took my arm, and we started. We had gone but a few steps when our ears were saluted with the sad and mournful tones of the fife and muffled drum, and on looking back we saw a soldier's funeral procession approaching—a scene I had never before witnessed, but one with which I was destined to become familiar. How unlike a funeral at home! No train of weeping friends follow his bier; yet one of our country's heroes, one of the "boys in white," lies in that plain coffin. He is escorted to his final resting-place by perhaps a dozen comrades, who go with unfixed bayonets, and arms reversed, keeping time with their slow tread to the solemn notes of the "Dead March," plaintively executed by some of their number. . . .

In a few minutes we are at the Lyceum Hospital where heart-rending tidings await us. He who, but a few moments before was the bearer of such good news again makes his appearance. . . . "I was mistaken, he is not here." But something either in his tone or manner indicated that he had been there, and at the same moment we inquired: "Oh, where is he?" "He is dead!" was the reply. . . .

Julia went to Washington with Anna to find out if the widow could receive a pension. While in the capital, she engaged a room for the night "at Treadway's, a family from Detroit, now residing at number 541 H Street, which has since become noted as the place where that dark assassination plot was concocted which robbed the nation of its chosen leader. . . ."

Julia decided not to return home with Anna. Thirty years old and unmarried, there was no reason why she should not remain in Washington "to do for others as I would have done for my brother." She became an agent for the Michigan Relief Association.

MANY ARE SLEEPING AT BULL RUN

Charlotte E. McKay

Early in September after the Federal defeat at Manassas (Second Bull Run), the Union forces were driven back to Washington City and word came that the Rebel Army was advancing on Frederick City. There was panic in the town. Many civilians fled. Charlotte McKay, however, was one of those who remained behind in the hospitals.

As the town could not be defended, the citizens prepared to give Lee as silent a reception as possible. The Home Guard was sent off and everyone based in the hospital who could walk hurried to the outskirts of town where teams were seized to carry them to a safe distance. Immense quantities of government clothing, blankets, and other stores were heaped in piles and burned on the ground. . . .

All through the town window blinds were closed on the houses and even the streets became silent and deserted. In our hospital remained a few patients who could not be removed and the medical officers with a few attendants and nurses. All through the long night of September 5th we watched and waited anxiously for their coming, wondering what would be our fate as

prisoners. . . . At length at about ten o'clock on the morning
of the sixth, the glitter of long rows of polished bayonets was
flashing on the top of the hill to the east. . . . Stuart's cavalry,
followed by Jackson's infantry, entered the town. As they poured
rather lazily through the main street a miserable band with a
few cracked and battered instruments attempted to play "Maryland, My Maryland" . . . but the music soon died away. A squad
of horsemen from the vanguard dashed up into the hospital
yard and, presenting drawn sabres to the few medical officers
who stood leaning on the balcony of one of the old stone buildings, demanded, in the name of the Confederate states, the surrender of the post.

The surrender was made, protection promised, and guards
stationed at every door of the yard. During a brief delay in
finding the chief medical officer, there was time for a short
colloquy.

"Our men must have been asleep to let you come into Maryland," said a hospital steward.

"Yes," replied a young Rebel officer, "Many of them are sleeping at Bull Run, more on the Peninsula."

Soon a brigade of Virginia troops marched up and encamped
on the hospital grounds. As they filed in we could see that nearly
every soldier had a watermelon on his shoulder, captured from
a neighboring field.

They quickly set themselves in squads on the ground and began to eat, throwing the refuse around about our nicely policed
grounds. Before the week was out the place which had been a
model of neatness was turned into a pen of filth. . . . Yet these
men were by no means ruffians. Seeing me at the window they
would sometimes stop and ask politely for food . . . and whenever I gave whatever I had at hand they received it with gratitude. Many of them I found to be intelligent, thoughtful, even

Christian men, having implicit faith in their cause, in God as their special leader and next to him, in Stonewall Jackson.

On parting with our soldiers they shook hands cordially and hoped it might never be their fortune to meet on the battlefield. Some of the officers manifested a more haughty temper.

"Are you tired, soldier, after your long march?" I asked of one.

"No, I shall not be tired until I get to Philadelphia."

"But do you know that many of you poor fellows will find a grave before you get to Philadelphia?"

"We expected nothing else, Madam, when we came out and our homes and our little children are as dear to us as any others."

"But you are all caught in a nice trap and we shall soon see you rushing out of this town much faster than you came in."

"Perhaps you haven't heard, Madam, how we fight the Yankees down in Virginia."

"No, how is that?"

"We fight with our muskets until the powder is all gone; then we break our gunstocks over their head; then we take the fence rails and break them all up; then fling rocks at them."

"Very well," I said, "our soldiers can fight with fence rails and rocks as well as you and by the time you get to Philadelphia you'll have plenty of that sort of work. . . ."

8 Sufferings of War

THE BLOODY BATTLE OF ANTIETAM WAS FOUGHT IN WESTERN Maryland a few miles north of Harper's Ferry, on September 16 and 17, 1862, with General McClellan leading the Federals and Lee commanding the Rebel Army. Although it brought victory to the North, it also brought such "horrors and sufferings of War" as they had never previously experienced. Nearly ten thousand Federal wounded besides many of the Confederates were left shelterless in the woods and fields of Sharpsburg without any adequate supply of surgeons, and with not "a tenth part of needed medical stores," which were locked up in the block of the railroad between Baltimore, the base of supply, and the battlefield. Those on the battlefield had been captured at Manassas. The Quartermaster's Department was taxed to the utmost to forward supplies of food and ammunition, and consequently the medical supplies were left behind. The officers of the Sanitary Commission at Washington had been notified of the coming battle and fortunately were able to send supplies by other routes, as the Commission had wagons and horses of its own.

On Sunday, the 14th of September, Clara Barton loaded an Army wagon with supplies and started to follow the march of General McClellan. Her only companions were Mr. Cornelius M. Welles, the teacher of the first contraband school in the District of Columbia, and one teamster. She traveled three days along the dusty roads of Maryland, buying bread as she went and sleeping in the wagon by night. She reached Burnside's corps after dark on the night of the 16th when the air was dark and thick with fog "and with the smoke of campfires and premonitory death." Firing on the right was resumed in the morning. Reinforcements soon began to move along the rear to Hooker's support. Clara, who believed the place of danger was the place for her, ordered her mules to be harnessed and joined the train of artillery that was passing. When they reached the scene of action they turned into a field of tall corn and drove through it to a large barn now close upon the line of battle. Rebel shot and shell flew thickly around and over them. Men, torn and bleeding, lay amid the corn. Army medical supplies had not yet arrived, the small stock of dressings was exhausted and the surgeons were trying to make bandages of corn husks. Clara unpacked her stock of dressings and with her compainions began distributing bread dipped in wine to the wounded. Before the day was over she had commandeered twenty-five men who had come to the rear with the wounded and set them to work administering restoratives, bring and applying water, lifting the men to more comfortable positions and stopping hemorrhages.

Meanwhile, help for the wounded had been coming in from other sources. A wagon train loaded with medical stores had been sent forward daily to meet the anticipated difficulty, and before the battle was over they were on the field. For four days the medical director received no Government supplies and the wounded were mainly dependent on the stores of the Sanitary Commission. Through the system of Sanitary Commission depots, hospital transports, hospital cars, diet kitchens, and relief stations and by the quick effective movements of agents in the field, such as lifting the soldiers from the battlefields onto stretchers and ambulances, plying them with restoratives, placing them in clean cots, clothing them with new uniforms, the Sanitary Commission often preserved the wounded until adequate medical and nursing care could take over. In this way the Sanitary Commission assumed the major role it was to hold throughout the war—that of getting medical and sanitary supplies to the men at the front to the seats of immediate battle far in advance of the Medical Department.

Within one week of the Battle of Antietam, the Sanitary Commission had distributed through its agents on the field enormous supplies of dry goods, medicine, first aid material, and food, as well as bottles of wine and cordials. It had succeeded in transporting from the medical purveyor's office in New York to the depot at Frederick, four thousand sets of hospital clothing and one hundred twenty bales of blankets. The women of the country were stirred anew by the gravity of the situation and the great need for their services in the field.

In November, 1862, a Council of representatives from the principal aid societies, numbering four hundred sixty-two at this period, was held in Washington. Its main purpose was to discuss ways and means of arousing the public to meet the great needs of the Sanitary Commission for medical supplies, food, and clothing, and to plan to have such supplies delivered with a greater system and regularity. Immediately after a battle, but too late for the exigency, there would be an influx followed by a lull. The Woman's Central Relief Association urged its auxiliaries to send a monthly box. It also urged the *Federal* principle, which meant that all supplies brought in would be bestowed upon United States troops and not on individuals or regiments. At the close of the session, the women were granted an interview with President Lincoln.

SCENES OF HORROR

Anna Holstein

Anna Holstein and her husband were living in their beautiful home in Upper Merion, Montgomery County, Pennsylvania, when the Civil War broke out. They were people of wealth and social position and were greatly honored and loved by their neighbors.

During the early days of the War, Anna Holstein remained at home working for the Soldiers' Aid Society in her own valley because, as she wrote, "there was an irresistible impulse to act. Anything but idleness when our armies were preparing for the combat."

Six of Anna Holstein's neighbors offered their services for a few weeks to nurse the wounded, but she shrank from the idea of joining them in this kind of work until her husband returned from the battlefield and told her of the desperate sufferings of the wounded. Hesitating no longer, they gave up their "sweet country home and from that date were 'dwellers in tents' " with the exception of periodic trips home when her husband needed to rest. They lost no time in returning to the battlefield where their services were so greatly needed.

In the following extract from her journal, Anna Holstein describes her arrival at Antietam with food, clothing, and medicine for the soldiers.

At that early day in the history of the war, we found our noble United States Sanitary Commission here, doing a vast amount of good. From their storeroom were sent, in every direction, supplies to relieve the greatest suffering. And to it, strangers as we were to them, we daily came for articles which we found, in our visits to the hospitals, were most urgently needed, and which our own more limited stores could not furnish. They were as freely given to us for distribution as they had been in like manner intrusted to them by friends at home.

My imperfect notes of this date are filled with names of terribly wounded men, who are scattered over the entire extent of the field, recalling most vividly scenes that can never be forgotten. Those were fortunate who were in barns, where they were sure of a little hay or straw upon which to rest their shattered limbs. . . .

In a miserable little log house near the Potomac, thirty men lay upon the floor, ill with fever; some had a little straw, but no pillows were to be found; at that time it was unavoidable, but their food was hardly fit for well men; medicines very scarce; this house the counterpart of many others, both as to occupants, food, etc.

On the same road were several places filled with wounded Rebels; in their hurried flight, they had been left by thousands, and now had to be provided for. The Episcopal church in the town had also been taken for their use. The rest of the churches, and half the houses in the place, were crowded with our wounded troops.

The 26th of October, the army, which had been resting for more than a month in the vicinity of the battlefield of Antietam, took up its line of march southward; by the evening of the same day their camping-grounds were nearly all vacated. The 30th of the month, the last of the troops were moving, and the town looked deserted; but in the hospitals the duties continue the same, and cases of the deepest interest are daily found. Of the numbers we had known upon our first arrival, many had gone to their "dreamless sleep" by the side of comrades who had early fallen.

Another trip to Antietam and Harper's Ferry, and Mr. H. returned, ill with the fever; fortunately, it was not a serious attack. We remained there only long enough to nurse him through it, when our trips to the hospitals at Antietam and Frederick City were resumed. While in the latter place, our home was the house of a well-known loyal family. They felt, what we at the North knew nothing of, that loyalty meant life was at stake, homes deserted, property destroyed, and the friends of early, happier years, all given up—for what? devotion to the country and the flag!

As Stonewall's men marched through the town, they manifested their contempt for the "Starry Flag" by trailing it in the dust, at their horses' feet, as they rode along. Our friends, pained to know of their ill deeds, and unwilling to look upon the disgraceful act they were powerless to prevent, closed their doors and windows, that they might be out of sight. Their old neighbors pointed them out to the Rebels, as they passed exultingly through their streets, as hated Unionists. But their joy was of short duration; soon driven out by our forces, and many prisoners taken, a long line of the captured were marched by their door. Now was their hour of triumph; the flag which had been so cautiously concealed, and sacredly guarded, was brought from its hiding-place, and secured to the staff. Mrs. J——, an elderly lady, a Virginian by birth, determined they should again pass under the flag they had dishonored.

> In her attic window the staff she set,
> To show that one heart was loyal yet.
> She leaned far out on the window sill,
> And shook it forth with a royal will.

The Rebels could only threaten, as they moved on, that if again in possession of the city, they and their home were doomed. Some months after this had occurred, I stood by that attic window as she related the story, and pointed out how defiantly she had waved it over them. Its weight was as much as I could raise, and yet, in the excitement, my friend was all unconscious of it. It was long after, before I saw or heard of Whittier's "Barbara Frietchie"—that charming story, so told that it will live for ages to come; and have often wondered whether his original and my friend were the same.

LITTERS AND AMBULANCES GOING IN ALL DIRECTIONS

Eliza Harris

The following extracts from a letter written just after the Battle of Antietam in 1862 gives a picture of the sufferings Eliza witnessed that autumn.

Night was closing in upon us—the rain falling fast; the sharpshooters were threatening all who ventured near our wounded and dying on the battleground; a line of battle in view, artillery in motion, litters and ambulances going in all directions; wounded picking their way, now lying down to rest, some before they were out of the range of the enemy's guns, not a few of whom received their severest wounds in these places of imagined safety; added to this, marching and countermarching of troops, bearers of dispatches hurrying to and fro; eager, anxious inquirers after the killed and wounded; and the groans of the poor sufferers under the surgeons' hands—and you may form some faint idea of our position on that eventful evening. Reaching a hospital but a few removes from the cornfield in which the deadliest of the strife was waged, I found the ground literally covered with the dead and wounded—barns, hayricks, outhouses of every description, all full. Here and there a knot of men, with a dim light near, told of amputations; whilst the shrieks and groans of the poor fellows, lying all around, made our hearts almost to stand still. The rain fell upon their upturned faces, but it was not noticed; bodily pain and mental anguish—for many were brought to meet the king of terrors face to face, and would have given worlds to evade his cold touch—rendered them indifferent to their surroundings. Most of the sufferers were from General Meagher's Irish brigade, and were louder in their demonstrations of feeling than are the Germans, or our own

native born. We could do little that night but distribute wine
and tea, and speak comforting words. . . . Then we sang. . . .
The sound stopped the shrieks and groans of the brave men.
They listened. They all seemed comforted. . . . We remained
at this hospital until the evening of the 19th; we had slept a few
hours on the straw upon which our soldiers had lain, and upon
which their lifeblood had been poured out. We prepared tea,
bread and butter, milk punch, and eggnog; furnished rags, lint,
and bandages, as needed, and then came on to French's Division
Hospital, where were one thousand of our wounded, and a
number of Confederates. The first night we slept in our ambulance; no room in the small house, the only dwelling near,
could be procured. The next day was the Sabbath. . . . Almost
every hour I witnessed the going out of some young life. No
words can describe the wonderful endurance: not a murmur,
not a word of complaint or regret. Many such expressions as
the following have been heard: "Yes, I have struck my last
blow for my country; whether I have served my country well
others may judge. I know I love her more than life."

Passing over the battleground . . . such sights as might cause
the general pulse of life to stand still met our eyes.

Stretched out in every direction, as far as the eye could reach,
were the dead and dying. Much the larger proportion must
have died instantly—their positions, some with ramrod in hand
to load, others with gun in hand as if about to aim, others still
having just discharged their murderous load. Some were struck
in the act of eating. One poor fellow still held a potato in his
grasp. Another clutched a piece of tobacco; others held their
canteens as if to drink; one grasped a letter. Two were strangely
poised upon a fence, having been killed in the act of leaping it.
How my heart sickens at the recollection of the appearance of
these men. . . . Begrimed with dust, heads and bodies bloated
and blackened, a spectacle of sickening horror, objects of loath-
ing, the worm already preying upon them!

9 A Sad Day for the Army of the Potomac

GENERAL MC CLELLAN WAS RELIEVED OF HIS COMMAND. MAJOR General Ambrose Burnside took his place, whereupon Sarah Emma Edmonds wrote: "That was a sad day for the Army of the Potomac." Her sorrow, needless to say, was not universal.

The new commander immediately marched the Army to Falmouth opposite Fredericksburg where Lee with his 72,000 men was waiting for Ambrose Burnside and his 113,000 men.

Then came December with cold and rain followed by an unexpected snowstorm. The Army in the East was much better supplied than the one in the West, but the medical officers were not prepared for the sudden change in weather. They welcomed the otherwise unattainable supplies of woolens—blankets, shirts, drawers, and stockings—provided by the Sanitary Commission.

On a foggy Saturday morning, Burnside's men charged the Rebels on Marye's Heights. As the General observed there was "enough bloodshed to satisfy any reasonable man." Charge after charge was made until sheets of flame covered the enemy stronghold as the boys in blue marched to their death. The butchery finally ended at nightfall, and 12,500 Union boys were killed or maimed. Some burned to death in long dry grass that had been set afire by cannons. Others died of exposure in the bitter cold. The President's heart was heavy at the news.

As quickly as was possible the wounded were removed by rail to Aquia Creek. At the landing the Sanitary Commission agents quickly established a feeding and relief station where six hundred men were fed and looked after on the first night.

216

Great numbers of wounded men were brought to Washington from the battlefield.

To their great relief, General Burnside allowed the beaten troops to rest for a month before he started "dragging them up the river" to force his way through one of the fords for another assault on the Rebels. Men waded ankle deep in a rain storm while the pack trains "foundered in bottomless mire"—sickness dogged the weary men.

Dorothea Dix sent several nurses on board the Government transport steamer *Rockland* in the command of Captain Oris Ingraham to Aquia Creek, to look after the wounded en route to Washington hospitals after Fredericksburg. Those who were not wounded from battle soon became ill after being dragged up the Rappahannock by Ambrose Burnside who is known to posterity not for his deeds but for the sideburns he inspired.

The nurses often had to leave the transports, going in the ambulances to pick up the wounded, carrying food and drink to those who must wait longer. Now and then a nurse was forced to spend a night in the ambulance on the battlefield, very near the enemy. No one dared to make a fire or light a match. One intrepid girl wrote later that she "drank water from holes made by the horses' feet in the mud; it tasted good and sweet." After lying all night in the mud and water, the infantry were detailed to cut logs and carry them on their back to build a corduroy road so that the heavy guns and baggage wagons might be lifted out of the mud which was so thick that on one occasion fourteen horses tried vainly to pull one gun from its hold, but the wheels sank to the hub. Famished boys came to the Army nurses offering five dollars, or all the money they had, for something to eat.

In a letter dated December 22, 1862, Louisa Lee Schuyler, the tireless directress of the Woman's Central Relief Association in New York, mentioned a widespread lack of interest in giving.

The situation did not improve. By January, 1863, as a result of the great requirements of the armed forces in the battles of Antietam and Fredericksburg, all Sanitary Commission supplies had been exhausted. Once again there was a great need, but the lull on the home front continued. People were not giving as readily as they had in the initial stages of the war. Some were not giving at all. The Aid Societies everywhere and agents at the Sanitary Depots near the front began to feel the pinch.

This failure to replenish the supplies was too serious to be treated casually. The correspondence between Louisa Schuyler and Henry Bellows and between Miss Schuyler and the branch representatives during this period reveals the concern of the leaders. To meet the crisis there was a great deal of reorganization within the ranks of the Sanitary Commission. New branches were established in the different states, embracing greater sections. Attempts were made to reach people in every walk of life.

This sudden lack of incoming hospital supplies was attributed to a great many factors besides waning interest and ignorance of the situation. The potential benefactors had to consider "the very high price of material of all kinds . . ." and, in Miss Schuyler's words, ". . . the difficulty which the people of the little villages—more zealous than those of large towns—find in paying the transportation expenses."

Many railroad companies in the East and West had already been helpful, giving prompt and free transportation for Sanitary Commission stores and granting free passes for agents or representatives of the Commission. But too many did not, and the time had come when all railroads—the Hudson River, New Haven, Erie, New York Central, and the Shore Line of the Long Island Railway—had to be asked to "put their shoulder to the wheel once again, and allow all packages plainly marked

'United States Sanitary Commission' to pass over their lines free of charge."

Before long gratuitous and unlimited use of the telegraph lines was permitted for the "relief of the anxious friends of the soldiers and the furtherance of the various modes of the Commission's work." Aid from such sources as these as well as the press enabled the Commission to use the money it received for relief work alone.

Women everywhere were asked to rally their forces and spur the people to donate. The main thing, according to Louisa Schuyler, was to have the people realize "the necessity of constant contributions, not to work upon impulse, but from a sense of duty which must last as long as the war."

There were many who mistrusted the aims and purposes of the Commission, and others, jealous of its activities or in sympathy with the South, were only too willing to nurture this distrust. Reports were sometimes circulated by returning soldiers that they had been sick in hospitals and had not received any of the comforts sent to the Commission; that if dried foods, jellies, etc., were in the hospitals, they were enjoyed by the officers and their friends. These prejudicial rumors had to be explained away as people were too willing to use them as an excuse not to give.

Agents of the Commission (every state had its own) were sent out on lecture tours around the country to tell the people of the true needs of the soldiers at the front, of the great service performed by the Sanitary Commission and its workers and, what was equally important, to what use the supplies were being put.

The winter of 1862-63 was a period of general discouragement throughout the North. People had only begun to realize, as President Lincoln had observed back in November, that they had "to buckle down to the determination to fight this war,"

and that the war was going to last longer than they had anticipated.

In January of 1863, General Hooker was put in command of
the Army of the Potomac and Burnside with the Ninth Army
Corps was ordered to the Western Department. Emma Edmonds had been attached to this Corps for some time, and asked
permission to be transferred with it.

TIMES WERE GLOOMY THEN AT WASHINGTON

Jane C. Hoge and Mary A. Livermore

*In November the Sanitary Commission called a convention at
Washington of its various members and branches. It was desired that each Branch Commission in the North should be
represented by two women who were acquainted with the work-
ings of the society, and who had been connected with it from
the beginning. Mary Livermore and Jane Hoge were duly appointed by the Chicago Branch. When they reached the Capital, they met President Lincoln.*

Eight o'clock P.M. was designated as the hour for the interview. We were accompanied by Mr. Olmsted, Mr. Bloor, Corresponding Secretary of the United States Sanitary Commission,
and an officer of the U.S. Army. We waited some minutes in
the private drawing room before the President appeared.

Times were gloomy then at Washington. The army was en-
trenching or entrenched—burning to advance but held back
alternately by its leader and the autumnal rains and little substantial advantage had been gained. The men were suffering
greatly from low fevers and chronic dysentery. . . . As we sat in
silence, partaking of the general gloom, Abraham Lincoln, the

Emancipator, the honest patriot, the Christlike man, entered. His brow was deeply furrowed, his face oppressively sad, his form slightly bowed, and his step feeble. He seemed to be literally staggering under a nation's burden and, we surmised, had just left a perplexed and depressed meeting of the Cabinet.

As we rose to greet him, he shook each one's hand with his awful but touching cordiality as Mr. Olmsted introduced us, one by one. When he took his seat, Mr. Olmsted remarked we were a company of women representing the patriotic benevolence of various sections of the country and had come to pay our respects to our honored Chief Magistrate and receive words of encouragement from him that would stimulate home effort. His face did not relax and a pause ensued. He then said: "Ladies, no one has the interest of the army more at heart than I have. I always rejoice to know they are remembered and cherished; still, great care must be taken not to tangle the lines of the big team. You know, when a coach and six runs off down hill, 'tis a desperate struggle to stop it; still one hand must hold the reins."

We said we were well aware of that and were happy to say we represented an organization that deprecated any interference with government. We afterwards learned that, so great had been the fears of intermeddling entertained by the Medical Bureau, even our good President had imbibed the doubt which was, afterwards, fully dispelled. After this wise caution, he proceeded to talk most kindly of the humanity, energy, and perseverance of good women all the world over. I said: "Mr. President, have you not an encouraging word as to our country's prospects that we may take back to the Northwest? A token from you would inspire the people."

With the sadness deepening on his worn face, he replied, "What if I have none to give?"

A silence that might be felt followed these ominous words.

yet made up their minds that we are at war with the South. They haven't buckled down to the determination to fight this war through; for they have got the idea into their heads that we are going to get out of this fix, somehow, by strategy! That's the word—*strategy!* General McClellan thinks he is going to whip the Rebels by strategy; and the army has got the same notion. They have no idea that the war is to be carried on and put through by hard, tough fighting, that will hurt somebody; and no headway is going to be made while this delusion lasts."

Someone ventured to remonstrate against this, and reminded the President how hundreds of thousands had rushed to arms at the call of the country; how bravely the army and navy had fought at Forts Henry and Donelson, Pea Ridge, Shiloh, and New Orleans; and how gloriously they had triumphed.

He admitted this, but returned to his first statement. "The people *haven't* made up their minds that we are at war, I tell you!" he repeated, with great positiveness. "They think there is a royal road to peace, and that General McClellan is to find it. The army has not settled down into the conviction that we are in a terrible war that has got to be fought out—no; and the officers haven't either. When you came to Washington, ladies, some two weeks ago, but very few soldiers came on the trains with you—that you will all remember. But when you go back you will find the trains and every conveyance crowded with them. You won't find a city on the route, a town, or a village, where soldiers and officers on furlough are not plenty as black-berries. There are whole regiments that have two thirds of their men absent—a great many by desertion, and a great many on leave granted by company officers, which is almost as bad. General McClellan is all the time calling for more troops, more troops; and they are sent to him; but the deserters and fur-loughed men outnumber the recruits. To fill up the army is like undertaking to shovel fleas. You take up a shovelful," suiting the word with an indescribably comical gesture; "but before you can dump them anywhere they are gone. It is like trying to ride a balky horse. You coax, and cheer, and spur, and lay on the whip; but you don't get ahead an inch—there you stick. . . . The desertion of the army is just now the most serious evil we have to encounter. At the Battle of Antietam, General McClellan had the names of about one hundred and eighty thousand men on the army rolls. Of these, seventy thousand were absent on leave granted by company officers, which, as I said before, is almost as bad as desertion. For the men ought not to ask for furloughs with the enemy drawn up before them, nor ought the officers to grant them. About twenty thousand more were in hospital, or were detailed to other duties, leaving only some ninety thousand to give battle to the enemy. General McClellan went into the fight with this number. But in two hours after the battle commenced thirty thousand had straggled or deserted, and so the battle was fought with sixty thousand—and as the enemy had about the same number, it proved a drawn game. The Rebel army had coiled itself up in such a position that if McClellan had only had the seventy thousand absentees, and the thirty thousand deserters, he could have surrounded Lee, captured the whole Rebel army, and ended the war at a stroke without a battle.

"We have a Stragglers' Camp out here in Alexandria, in connection with the Convalescent Camp, and from that camp, in three months, General Butler has returned to their regiments seventy-five thousand deserters and stragglers who have been arrested and sent there. Don't you see that the country and the army fail to realize that we are engaged in one of the greatest wars the world has ever seen, and which can only be ended by hard fighting? General McClellan is responsible for the delusion

that is untoning the whole army—that the South is to be conquered by strategy."

(That very week, General McClellan had been removed from
the command of the army, and General Burnside—of whom the
President spoke most eulogistically—had been appointed in his
place, but none of us knew it that night.)

The next day my friend, Mrs. Hoge, and myself had another
interview with the President, on business entrusted to us. If we
were shocked the night before at his haggard face, how much
more were we pained when the broad light of day revealed the
ravages which care, anxiety, and overwork had wrought. In our
desperate condition it was difficult to control our feelings so as
not to weep before him. Our unspoken thought ran thus: "Our
national affairs must be in the very extremity of hopelessness if
they thus prey on the mind and life of the President. The country has been slain by treason—he knows it, and that it cannot
recover itself."

Our business ended, before we withdrew we made one more
attempt to draw encouraging words from the reluctant head of
the nation. "Mr. President," we said timidly, "we find ourselves
greatly depressed by the talk of last evening; you do not consider our national affairs hopeless, do you? Our country is not
lost?"

"Oh, no!" he said, with great earnestness, "our affairs are by
no means hopeless, for we have the right on our side. We did
not want this war, and we tried to avoid it. We were forced into
it; our cause is a just one, and now it has become the cause of
freedom." (The Emancipation Proclamation had just been promulgated.) "And let us also hope it is the cause of God, and
then we may be sure it must ultimately triumph. But between
that time and now there is an amount of agony and suffering
and trial for the people that they do not look for, and are not
prepared for."

THE FIELD RAN RED WITH BLOOD

Sarah Emma Edmonds

The following is an extract from Sarah Emma Edmonds' journal, written on the battlefield the second day after the Yankees had crossed the Rappahannock River.

Battlefield, Fredericksburg, Va.
December 13, 1862.

In consequence of one of General H.'s staff officers being ill I have volunteered to take his place, and am now aide-de-camp to General H.* I wish my friends could see me in my present uniform! This division will probably charge on the enemy's works this afternoon. God grant them success! While I write the roar of cannon and musketry is almost deafening, and the shot and shell are falling fast on all sides. This may be my last entry in this journal. God's will be done. I commit myself to Him, soul and body. I must close. General H. has mounted his horse, and says "Come!"

Of course it is not for me to say whose fault it was in sacrificing those thousands of noble lives which fell upon that disastrous field, or in charging again and again upon those terrible stone walls and fortifications, after being repulsed every time with more than half their number lying on the ground. The brave men, nothing daunted by their thinned ranks, advanced more fiercely on the foe.

But when it was proved by a demonstration that it was morally impossible to take and retain those heights, in consequence of the natural advantage of position which the Rebels occupied, and still would occupy if they should fall back—whose

* Emma had volunteered to act as orderly for General Orlando Metcalfe Poe, not General H.

fault was it that the attempt was made time after time, until the field was literally piled with dead and ran red with blood?

Among the many who fell in that dreadful battle perhaps there is none more worthy of notice than the brave and heroic Major Edward E. Sturtevant, of Keene, New Hampshire, who fell while leading the gallant Fifth in a charge upon the enemy. He was the first man in New Hampshire who enlisted *for the war*. He was immediately authorized by the Governor to make enlistments for the First New Hampshire Volunteers, and was eminently successful. He held the commission of captain in the First Regiment, and afterwards was promoted major of the Fifth.

During the progress of that battle I saw many strange sights —although I had been in many a fierce battle before. I never saw, till then, a man deliberately shoot himself, with his own pistol, in order to save the Rebels the satisfaction of doing so, as it would seem.

As one brigade was ordered into line of battle, I saw an officer take out his pistol and shoot himself through the side—not mortally, I am sorry to say, but just sufficiently to unfit him for duty; so he was carried to the rear—he protesting that it was done by accident.

Another officer I saw there, a young and handsome lieutenant, disgraced his shoulder straps by showing the white feather at the very moment when he was most needed.

I rode three miles with General H. to General Franklin's headquarters, the second night we were at Fredericksburg, and of all the nights that I can recall to mind that was the darkest. On our way we had numerous ditches to leap, various ravines to cross, and mountains to climb, which can be better imagined than described. It was not only once or twice that horse and rider went tumbling into chasms head first, but frequently.

As we passed along, we stopped at the headquarters of General Bayard (General of Cavalry) a few minutes—found him enjoying a cup of coffee under a large tree, which constituted his headquarters. We called again when we returned, but he was cold in death, having been struck by a stray shot, and died in a short time. He was killed just where we had left him, under the tree. He was a splendid officer, and his removal was a great loss to the Federal cause. His death cast a gloom over his whole command which was deeply felt. . . .

Of the wounded of this battle I can say but little, for my time was fully occupied in the responsible duties which I had volunteered to perform; and so constantly was I employed that I was not out of the saddle but once in twelve hours, and that was to assist an officer of the Seventy-ninth, who lay writhing in agony on the field, having been seized with cramps and spasms, and was suffering the most extreme pain. He was one of the brave and fearless ones, however, and in less than an hour, after having taken a powerful medicine which I procured for him, he was again on his horse, at the general's side. . . .

A council or war was held by our generals, and the conclusion arrived at that the enterprise should be abandoned, and that the army should recross the Rappahannock under cover of darkness. Everything was conducted in the most quite manner; so quiet, indeed, that the enemy never suspected the movement, and the retreat was accomplished, and the bridges partially removed, before the fact was discovered.

THE SICK LAY ON THE SIDEWALKS

Mary Phinney von Olnhausen

The disastrous Battle of Fredericksburg, with its great number of killed and wounded, took place on December 13, 1862. Worn

out with excitement and fatigue, and justly indignant at the in-
adequacy of the preparations for caring for the suffering men,
Mrs. von Olnhausen wrote:

Monday night, December 15, 1862.

Today has been such an awful day, bringing in the wounded
from Frederick. The whole street was full of ambulances, and
the sick lay outside on the sidewalks from nine in the morning
till five in the evening. Of course, places were found for some;
but already the house was full; so the most had to be packed
back again and taken off to Fairfax Seminary, two miles out.
I have been so indignant all day—not a thing done for them,
not a wound dressed. To be sure, they got dinner; but no supper. They reached town last evening, lay in the cars all night
without blankets or food, were chucked into ambulances, lay
about here all day, and tonight were put back into ambulances
and carted off again. I think every man who comes a-soldiering
is a fool!

Sunday night, December 21, 1862.

This has been as blue a week as ever I passed. Tuesday night
(I mean Tuesday week) two women arrived, one to see her sick
son and the other her husband; one came from western Wisconsin and the other from northern New York. Dr. S. had just
made a new law forbidding visitors to stay in the house; but
they were so very poor, and had come so far and felt so bad, I
could not bear to see them. So I, bold as a sheep, really decided
to face the doctor and to beg him to let them stay. At first he
said decidedly, "No"; but you know how I hang on and grow
braver; so finally—to get rid of me, I guess—he said, "Yes, if you
will take them into your own room." Oh, dear! now I had just
got so nicely settled and so snug; but of course I could not refuse and would not under the circumstances. . . .

We have been sending off this week every one who could be moved; and you may believe it's been a pretty blue time with me; I have had so many of them so long under my care. All have been sent to New York on the *Daniel Webster;* thanks to that last splendid box, I have been able to make many of them comfortable. Not one left without some warm garments. I expect they will suffer much as it is, but I'm glad they are getting near home. Poor fellows! some of them are so lean and miserable. . . .

ONE THOUSAND DOLLARS OR YOUR RIGHT LEG?

Mary A. Bickerdyke

One of the most eloquent, direct speeches delivered to the folks at home by a woman who had been living and working at the battlefront from the very beginning of the war was a talk delivered by Mother Bickerdyke. For the first and only time during the War, this faithful woman had broken down and was forced to take a leave of absence from her hospital duties. The hardships she had passed through, her work, her fastings, her anxieties "had been sufficient to kill a dozen women," and she came North to recuperate. People tried to honor her then as they had before when she had come North for special supplies, but she declined all such invitations. In Milwaukee the people were holding a fair for the relief of the sick and wounded soldiers, and, grateful for what Mary Bickerdyke had done for the Wisconsin soldiers in the Western Army, insisted on her visiting their city. Mary Livermore accompanied her as Mary Bickerdyke refused to go anywhere to be lionized unless someone was with her to "bear the brunt of the nonsense" as she is said to have phrased it. The woman was "overwhelmed with attentions." The Milwaukee Chamber of Commerce made an appropriation

of twelve hundred dollars a month for hospital relief to be con-
tinued throughout the war until the end of the war. And she
was, according to her Boswell, invited to their handsome hall to
receive from them a formal expression of gratitude for her care
of the boys of the home state. Ladies were invited to occupy
the gallery, which they packed to the utmost. The President of
the Board of Trade, on behalf of the state of Wisconsin, spoke
first, and Mother Bickerdyke was thanked for her "patriotic
labors" and informed then of the recent pledge of the Board.
Then Mary, who disliked speaking publicly, particularly about
herself, rose to make her reply.

I am much obliged to you gentlemen for the kind things you
have said. I haven't done much, no more than I ought; neither
have you. I am glad you are going to give twelve hundred dollars
a month for the poor fellows in the hospitals; for it's no more
than you ought to do, and it isn't half as much as the soldiers in
the hospitals have given for you. Suppose, gentlemen, you had
got to give to-night one thousand dollars or your right leg,
would it take long to decide which to surrender? Two thousand
dollars or your right arm; five thousand dollars or both your eyes;
all that you are worth or your life?

But I have got eighteen hundred boys in my hospital . . . who
have given one arm, and one leg, and some have given both, and
yet they don't seem to think they have done a great deal for
their country. And the graveyard behind the hospital, and the
battlefield a little farther off, contain the bodies of thousands
who have freely given their lives to save you and your homes and
your country from ruin. Oh, gentlemen of Milwaukee, don't let
us be telling of what *we* have given, and what *we* have done! *We*
have done nothing, and given nothing, in comparison with
them! And it's our duty to keep on giving and doing just as
long as there's a soldier down South fighting or suffering for us.

THE SORROWS OF A NATION WERE BEARING HIM DOWN

Julia Susan Wheelock

On the evening of January 31, 1863, Julia Wheelock attended a meeting of the various relief associations in the capitol in Washington at which Admiral Foote and Andrew Johnson were the speakers.

The address of each was characteristic of the man who delivered it. Admiral Foote, as might have been expected, recognized the hand of God in the war, and recommended the people to exercise more faith in His overruling providence, firmly believing that all would eventually work out, not only for God's glory, but for the best interest of our country. Mr. Johnson spoke at length of the state of affairs in Tennessee, and of the nation generally. He believed in meting out to traitors their just deserts—that stern justice, without any sprinkling of mercy, should be the portion of their cup. A slight change in his policy since then!!!! During the evening, President Lincoln and several members of his cabinet came in. As they entered, the audience rose to their feet; ladies waved their handkerchiefs, gentlemen threw up their hats, while cheer after cheer went up for our chieftain, which echoed and reverberated through the halls and great dome of the Capitol. Every heart seemed to beat in unison with the great heart of Abraham Lincoln, whose careworn face too plainly told that it was not the weight of years, but the sorrows of a nation, which were bearing him down. None could look upon his sad countenance without feelings of pity and a willingness to share the responsibility which rested with such crushing weight upon his shoulders; and many were the expressions heard, like the following: "Poor Father Abraham!" "God bless him!" "Long live our President."

10 No End to All the Horror

IN THE EAST IN THE SPRING OF 1863, GENERAL LEE, SUPPORTED BY Jackson, renewed his offensive and sought to break through to the North, "to levy tribute," and get food and clothing. A cavalry raid was anticipated in Alexandria and the streets of the town were stockaded. The gates were open for carriages to pass through only at certain hours. Foot passengers "clambered over the steps," wrote Sophronia Bucklin, and a "feverish anxiety because of the closeness of the Rebel lines kept the Northerners on the alert at all times." When the magazine at Fort Lyon was blown up, the explosion was great and it was believed the Rebels had come. This terrible accident sent twenty-two men to their death without warning.

Then on May 2 to 4 came the great Battle of Chancellorsville. The Union Army was defeated, but the Confederates lost a beloved General, Stonewall Jackson.

Thousands of the wounded who had been brought from the field were dead or dying, while still other thousands lay in hospitals suffering unimaginable agonies. They are said to have suffered more than on any other occasion during the war, as not only the regular medical service but the supplementary service of the Sanitary Commission as well "was baffled by the fortunes of war." More than seventeen thousand men died.

During the period between the battles of Chancellorsville and Gettysburg, the Army of the Potomac was depressed and discouraged. The great battle which had been so long in anticipation had been lost and, with it, thousands of precious lives.

Of those who had been brought wounded from the field, thousands were dead or dying, while still other thousands were lying in hospitals, suffering unimaginable agonies. It was indeed a time to try the bravest souls. Deep mud and impassable roads precluded travel, and for a few weeks nothing happened. Then, on June 13, orders were received at the Eastern front to break up the Second Corps hospital at Falmouth. Quietly and rapidly, the order was obeyed. Ambulances were in readiness for all who could not walk, and in *two hours* the wounded and sick were on their way to the station. The Army of the Potomac was on the march.

WITH THE FIRST OF MAY CAME THE BATTLE OF CHANCELLORSVILLE

Charlotte E. McKay

In April when the Army of the Potomac crossed the Rappahannock, Charlotte McKay rode to the front in an ambulance and set up quarters in a brick house just a few miles from where the Battle of Chancellorsville was taking place.

With the first of May came the Battle of Chancellorsville. This was ten or twelve miles from our hospital along Potomac Creek on the south side of the Rappahannock. How faithfully are the . . . scenes of our life at Potomac Creek daguerrotyped on my memory! . . . At an early hour on Sunday morning, May 3, I left the hospital and went down towards the battlefield, my ambulance well loaded with sanitary supplies, a young soldier from the hospital for an assistant. Never can I forget that morning; the fearful roar of artillery which had scarcely been interrupted since daylight; the clear shining of the sun of the lovely spring morning; our way, partly through deserted camps—those

rude homes whence so many noble souls had just gone out . . .
long trains of Army wagons moving slowly towards the front;
couriers rushing back and forth. A mounted patrol dashed up
to us and demanded a halt but dismissed us politely when he
learned our purpose. Just across the river on our left the conflict
was raging in which the gallant Sedgwick with his 6th Corps
was contesting the heights of Fredericksburg. As we drew nearer
to United States Ford over which our Army crossed on their
pontoon bridges, we met squads of soldiers, slightly wounded,
making their way back to camp. They told us of this and of
that comrade or officer, killed or wounded. Among the latter,
the brave General Berry of our own Corps, whose lifeless body
was being borne back to Falmouth; and General Whipple,
mortally wounded; also that the 11th Corps had shown "the
white feather."

Just before we reached the river was a small house which had
been taken for an hospital. Horses were picketed around it in all
directions; quartermasters' wagons with their tents nearby; a
throng of soldiers coming and going.

Finding many wounded men lying in and around the house,
I immediately commenced the distribution of stimulants and
nourishment. . . .

After looking after some of the wounded that I found there,
Dr. Dexter, Corps Inspector, came late that night to me and
said he had been ordered to take charge of the wounded of our
Corps on the south side of the river and asked if I would go
over. It happened that the Chief Quartermaster of the post belonged to our division. He had sent word to me as soon as I
arrived that I should call on him for anything in his power to
do for me. I therefore sent to him immediately, requesting a
pass to Chancellorsville, which he readily gave, and in a few
moments, I was in my ambulance, leaving one scene of suffering

for another still more terrible. The way was difficult to find at night. Now we were entangled in a thicket and again blockaded by heavy army wagons. In going down a steep hill, my driver lost his balance and was thrown from his seat. Perhaps he had indulged a little too freely in the milk punch he had been helping to administer to the wounded. He recovered his seat but lost control of the horses and they were brought up by a train of wagons. It was nearly midnight when we got to the pontoon bridge across the Rappahannock, lying so smooth and white in the clear moonlight. At length, about three miles from the river, we found the large brick house to which the wounded of the 3rd Corps were brought from the battlefield. The wounded were lying all along the fences, all through the grounds . . . under the open heaven. . . . They were on the piazzas, under the piazzas, in the cellar, through the halls and in all the rooms above and below, while cries and groans broke out where the agony was too great to be suppressed. Some stimulants were given out and a closet not large enough for a man to stretch himself answered for my storeroom and dormitory. . . . We were within three miles of the front line of battle and could see artillery posted in various directions . . . word was brought that my brother had been shot through the heart . . .

Soon officers came in to report all things favorable to our side. "Tomorrow there will be a great battle. We shall have a victory and then go on to Richmond." But tomorrow comes and no sound of battle. What can it mean? The silence is now more portentous and perplexing than would be the roar of artillery. An order came to send off the wounded men which we supposed was preparatory to fresh arrivals for the coming battle. I was just giving directions for having the floors cleansed from stains and pools of blood when Dr. Harris of the Sanitary Commission came in and called me aside, told me I had better be in readiness to move at a moment's notice as the artillery was changing position and there was a probability that the house where we were might be shelled. I immediately began to pack up my remnants of supplies when I heard Dr. Dexter call for my ambulance driver and order him to load up and be off with me as quickly as possible or the house would be riddled with shells. . . .

Through all this, there was a vague terror of something still more fearful like a dark shadow on my thoughts. Our Army was going back, that grand Army of the Potomac which, only a few weeks before, we beheld passing in review before President Lincoln and his generals, was defeated. What if the enemy, flushed with success, had gathered up its forces, crossed the river and hurled them on our stunned and demoralized troops? Surely it could have been done. At length, the bridge was ready and we crossed the creek, the train of ambulances following, and among those who came out to bring nourishment to the wounded was sweet Helen Gilson, just returned from Fredericksburg. . . .

The carrying out of sudden orders for breaking up the hospitals and removing the sick and wounded to Washington. . . . Long lines of troops moving from all directions towards Aquia Creek, trains of cars quickly following one another, loaded within and without with our boys in blue. . . . Major Lee, riding back eleven miles in the early morning from the night's bivouac to embrace once more his young, tearful wife with that good right arm which a few days later was shot away from the shoulder-socket. . . .

When our Army left its base at Aquia Creek and moved on to meet the Rebel army in their second attempt on Pennsylvania, the field hospitals in Virginia were all broken up and the wounded sent to Washington. Thither I followed to remain in Washington until we should see where the next blow should fall.

DAYS OF DOUBT

Jane Stuart Woolsey

Spending a month in Washington in May, 1863, after the Battle of Chancellorsville, Jane Stuart Woolsey gives a very interesting description of activities there. From Washington she returned to Fairfax Seminary Hospital in Alexandria, of which she was the Superintendent.

Washington, May 25, 1863.

We have just been spending a month in Washington, my first visit since the war, and the city certainly looks like wartime, the white tents showing out of the green of all the hills, headquarters flags flying above all the remaining bits of wood, and everywhere on the highish places, the long, low, dun banks of earthworks you get to detect so soon, looking like a western river levee. Then it is strange not to be able to go in the ferry boat to Alexandria, or take an afternoon drive across the bridges into the country, without producing a document which sets forth over your names in full—men and women—that your purpose is pleasure visiting, and that you solemnly affirm that you will support, protect and defend the Government, etc., against all enemies, domestic or foreign, etc., any law of any State to the contrary notwithstanding, so help you God. It was odd, too, at the opera one night, to see an officer of the Provost Guard come into the theatre between the acts and accost the gentlemen in front of us: "Sorry to trouble you, Major; your pass if you please"; and so, to every pair of shoulder straps in the house. Then there are the great Barrack hospitals and the dwelling houses turned into hospitals, the incessant drum-beat in the streets and the going and coming of squads of foot and horse, the huge packs of army wagons in vacant lots, the armed sentinels at the public buildings, and all the rest of it. Washington certainly shows the grim presence. It is a calumniated city in some respects. It is as bright and fresh this springtime as any town could be. The sweet, early, half-southern spring is nowhere sweeter than in the suburbs of Washington; on the Georgetown Heights, as we drove with Dr. Bacon up the river-edges to the Maryland forts or the great new arch "Union" of the new aqueduct, or down the river-edges by the horrible road, or went on a little breezy rushing voyage in a quartermaster's tug to Mount Vernon to see Miss Tracy, the lady who lives all alone with the Great Ghost—all these little excursions are most charming. . . . But some days of our visit were dark ones—the three or four inevitable days of doubt and lying dispatches at the time of the Chancellorsville battles; then the days when the truth came partially out (Mr. Sumner told one of our party last week that it has never yet come out); then the days when the wrecks drifted in, hospitals filled up and our hotel, being a quiet one, became almost a hospital for wounded officers. In the evening we used to hear the tugs screaming at the wharf; soon after, carriages would drive up, a servant get out with one or two pairs of crutches, then a couple of young fellows, painfully hoisted upon them, would hobble in. Some were brought on stretchers. Then one day came our friends, Frank Stevens, 1st New York, shot through the knee, and Captain Van Tuyl, shot through both legs; then Lieutenants Asch and Kirby, one, arm gone, one, leg gone; then Palmer and Best of the 16th, etc. Stevens was left on the field at Chancellorsville, taken prisoner, sadly neglected. But it is astonishing to see the cheerful courage of these young men. I went to see Captain Bailey, 5th Maine, with superfluous condolences. "In six weeks I shall be in the service again; if they can't make me a marching leg I'll go into a mounted corps, you don't suppose I call *that* a 'disability'!" pointing to where his right leg used to be; lying, pale and plucky, encourag-

ing three other more or less mutilated men in the same room
with him; and much more in the same strain, like the music of
Carryl, "pleasant and mournful to the soul." We saw a long
train of Rebel prisoners come in, not by any means, I am bound
to say, ragged or gaunt or hungry-looking; dirty, of course, with
queer patchwork quilts in many cases for blankets; some without shoes, some without hats, but fighting men, not starvelings,
every one of them. Our friend Major Porter came up on the tug
with one detachment. They opened their haversacks and ate
their rations, which consisted in every case of crackers and sugar.
One young fellow brought his blanket and spread it by Major
Porter, to take a nap, saying, "Would you please wake me up,
sir, when we pass Mount Vernon? I'd like to take off my hat
when we come to the place where Gentleman George Washington lived." . . . None of us know much about the retreat and the
reason why. The President was anxious and restless in those
days, and went down to the tugs two or three times to see and
talk with wounded officers. Georgy met him by chance one
morning in the White House garden, and found him greatly
changed since last summer. He was walking slowly, eating an
apple, dragging Tad along by the hand, and gazing straight before him, afar off—older, grayer, yellower, more stooping and
harassed-looking. . . . "

IF MOSBY SHOULD MAKE A DASH IN HERE TONIGHT

Julia Susan Wheelock

*At the beginning of June, 1863, Julia received instructions to re-
turn to Fairfax Court House where she had been earlier in the
war, and to remain there until further orders. She was installed
in the hospital of the 6th Michigan Regiment. Here she dis-*

tributed supplies, did general cleaning, acted the role of a modern Red Cross Gray Lady, and in between times nursed the sick and wounded. On the evening of the 7th of the month, a messenger arrived from division headquarters with orders that the hospital hoist a red flag early the next morning, for it was reported that General Lee was advancing with troops in the direction of Fairfax.

Soon we were summoned to go to work making flags. Accordingly we assembled in the basement of the "Stoughton House," where a bright fire was blazing on the hearth, and went to work. We made two large flags, which at early dawn were spread to the breeze, in elevated positions, which we hoped would command the respect and consideration of the Rebel chief. After finishing the flags, I packed my trunk, that it might be in readiness to send to Washington in the morning, should the report be confirmed. As for myself, I resolved, with the other ladies, not to desert the sick, but stay and share their fate, whatever it might be. It was quite late when we retired that night, and I must confess my sleep was somewhat disturbed with unpleasant dreams: several times I awoke and listened to hear the tread of the advancing foe, but listened and looked in vain. . . .

Again, on the 26th instant, there was considerable excitement at our department. Mosby,* it was feared, would make a sudden dash into camp before morning, and carry off considerable plunder, if no prisoners. That evening Dr. Spalding was called to go to the camp of the Sixth—some nine miles distant—to see an officer who had been taken suddenly sick. Before leaving, he handed me the key to his trunk, saying: "If Mosby should make a dash in here tonight, try and secure my papers, and, if possible,

---

* Colonel John S. Mosby and his guerrillas were the terror of the Army of the Potomac. These raiders would appear without warning like the Commandos of World War II, on mountain ranges, in the woods, and even in open fields to attack the Federal forces on their Southbound march.

my money." But I did not have a chance to display my bravery, or to call into exercise my skill in secreting valuables; and yet our fears were not at all times groundless, for the country was infested with roving bands of guerrillas, ever ready for plunder. Occasionally a man shot on picket by these desperadoes was brought in, and not unfrequently a squad of cavalrymen was sent out to scour the country for these worse than Rebels. Skirmishes and battles were of frequent occurrence.

The 9th, a severe cavalry fight took place at Beverly Ford, on the Rappahannock, and, a week later, the Battle of Aldie. Everything indicated that an active, and we hoped, a decisive campaign was about to open.

The 14th, news was received that Hooker was on the move, and early the next morning this report was confirmed, for the wagon train of the Twelfth Corps was actually parked within sight. Soon the artillery began to come in, and then the infantry. All day and night troops continued to arrive, until the great Army of the Potomac was encamped around us. The thousands of campfires and the fine martial music discoursed by various bands made it a scene surpassingly grand. A day or two after, I witnessed the artillery review by General Hooker. I have no words to describe it.

But the ever-shifting scenes of war soon change the programme, and those weary, footsore troops are again on the move, as yet scarcely rested from their fatiguing march from Falmouth, through heat and dust almost intolerable. . . .

Later in the afternoon of the 24th, orders came to break up our hospitals, and before daylight the next morning the sick were all removed; at sunrise the cavalry were on the move. Mrs. Maryweather, matron of the Fifth, going with them on the march, Mrs. Manning had an opportunity to go to Washington, on horseback, while I was left alone to get away as best I could with the remainder of my stores. Oh, how lonely and desolate everything appeared! Tents struck, blankets, pillows, and dishes scattered about, nothing left in the line of edibles but "hard tack." Of all the loneliness I ever experienced, that day caps the climax. The first thing I did was what any silly woman would have done—gave myself up to a good cry; and then I went to work packing up, and trying to save the best of the bedding. About noon, a drizzling rain came on, which added gloom to loneliness. I had about made up my mind that I should not get away that day, and was trying to fix up some nice little speech to make to his excellency, Mr. Mosby, in case he should give me a call, which, in all probability, he would do before morning—when, as misery likes company, I was not a little comforted to find that Rev. Mr. Chapin, a "Christian Commission" delegate, had not left the place, but was also waiting an opportunity to remove his goods to the station, and who would likewise be honored with the company of this distinguished guest(!) But my little speech was never made, for about three o'clock transports came to remove the hospital stores. On the arrival of the first team, I hastily inquired of the driver if he would take a few things for me to the Station. "Yes," he replied, "and yourself in the bargain." What a sudden change came over the face of everything! Even the misty rain, a short time since so gloomy, is now just what we need to lay the dust. How pleasant and cheerful the plain, homely face of the driver looks: no fears now of "Mosby and Co." Being provided for myself, I next interceded, successfully, too, for Mr. Chapin. Our goods are soon piled into the wagon, and we quite comfortably seated on the top of the load with our heads reaching the canvas above; but a queen in her chariot was never happier than I. The farewell look is given Fairfax, and we are off for the station, but are too late for the train, so have to wait until six o'clock, when the last train leaves, and we have no more communication with the place for several months. The balance of army supplies not removed up to that time was burned. Arrived at Alexandria about eight o'clock, in the rain and mud.

In looking over the paper the next morning, about the first thing I noticed was "Mosby at Fairfax Court-House." Two Union ladies living a few miles from Fairfax, in the vicinity of Vienna, were made unwilling captives.

11 We Cannot Hallow This Ground

THE ARMY OF THE POTOMAC, AFTER THE WRETCHED RETREAT AT Chancellorsville, had lain along the Rappahannock, scouting here and there, burning Rebel sloops and bringing in contrabands, until Lee, who had not followed up his victory at once, put his forces in rapid march up the valley for the invasion of Pennsylvania, part of his Army reaching and occupying Gettysburg, June 26. The Army of the Potomac made quick marches to overtake the enemy, but by June 27 were only a little to the northwest of Baltimore. At this point Hooker was relieved of his command and Meade made the head of the Army of the Potomac, which he at once put in motion.

The Battle of Gettysburg followed—the great tragic duel between Meade and Lee—the slaughter of Pickett's men. The story is too well known to bear repetition here where we are concerned with the drama that went on behind the battle scenes, where sickness and death played the leading roles. And the shrieks and cries of the wounded—too many to be looked after on the fields—mingled with the shriek of shell and the roar of the cannon.

Because it was fought on their own soil this battle aroused the Pennsylvanians more than almost any battle had before. The "Germantown Field Hospital Association" was formed to aid in relieving the suffering among the soldiers, and is said to have become one of the most valuable aids to the United States Sanitary Commission to be found in Pennsylvania. Women who until that time had remained at home now were eager to help relieve the sufferings of the soldiers. Socially prominent ladies abandoned their summer plans and went to war. In Washington, Boston, and New York as well, women clamored for passes to the front. Mrs. Jane Newton Woolsey hastened with her daughter, Georgeanna, to offer their services at the Sanitary Commission Lodge. Young ladies left their homes to join the procession of Lincoln's Daughters of Mercy. Others already in Government hospitals pleaded with Dorothea Dix for permission to go to the front lines.

Never before had the country been so aroused. Never before had medical and nursing care in the Army been so extensive and so well organized.

The enormous losses of the war necessitated a draft to fill the depleted regiments. Thousands of the men re-enlisted after serving the official two years, but idlers and "the evil-minded" resisted. There were serious outbreaks in Boston and other cities, but New York's disorders were outrageous and frightening.

The Sanitary Commission agents accompanied the Federal Army on its forced marches to Gettysburg. Its wagons of supplies, replenished continually from Washington, were put at the disposal of the surgeons during all the "skirmishes, fatigues, and privations" of that midsummer march. The Commission had made extensive preparations to meet the wants of the impending crisis, "the inevitable and perhaps final conflict of two equal armies—100,000 men on either side," Henry Bellows hoped. Experienced officers were sent to Frederick, Baltimore, Philadelphia, and Harrisburg. A systematic communication was maintained between them and the agents who were with the Army, while supplies were accumulated and concealed at different points near the expected field of battle. In the early conflicts of the two armies on July 1 and 2 many of the Union troops were wounded, and the surgeon received prompt assistance from two wagonloads of Sanitary Commission stores that had reached

Cemetery Hill the night before. The hospitals of the 1st, 2nd, 3rd, 5th, 11th, and 12th Corps were materially aided from these stores on the first day of "the general engagement." Empty wagons were immediately sent back to Fredericksburg and reloaded, "one to return via Westminster, the other by the direct route."

Agents of the Sanitary Commission, both women and men, were at work while the battle was raging, helping men off the field when they were injured, caring for them from the moment they fell, working constantly under fire. Two experienced agents were captured by the cavalry of the retreating Rebels, taken to Richmond, and confined for several months in Libby prison. "At this very hour," Henry Bellows wrote, "the Sanitary Commission was taking care of men from the Rebel side with just as much tenderness as of its own troops, and this it did always when the enemy's wounded fell into our hands." The Rebels had left their dead and dying at Gettysburg. Seven thousand of them were buried on the field at once.

Before railroad communication between Gettysburg and the North was restored, the first and most pressing needs of the wounded had been materially relieved by the rapidity with which the Sanitary Commission forced its supplies forward by independent transportation. When communication by rail was fully established the Commission poured its stores into Gettysburg in immense amounts. Large quantities of fresh provisions were sent every day from Philadelphia in refrigerating cars. All buildings on the hillsides and in the little town, both private houses and shops, were full of wounded men.

During the ten days that followed the battle, an enormous amount of relief was sent to Gettysburg by aid societies and independent people through the facilities of the Sanitary Commission. Each morning the supply wagons of the division and corps hospitals were at the doors of the Sanitary Commission storehouse, and departed loaded with everything that was needed. If the stores asked for were not on hand, they were telegraphed for and arrived by the next train, and were delivered. Great indispensable personal services were given in the hospitals to sick and dying men, to men who were awaiting amputations and to men sent off by train and fed on the way by Sanitary Commission agents and nurses.

A second call for nurses went out in every city, hamlet, and town in the North, and once again the women responded to the call. The people felt that an everlasting tribute should be paid to the men who fell at Gettysburg. Governor Curtin of Pennsylvania ordered seventeen acres to be purchased on Cemetery Hill, "where the Union center stood its colors on the second and third of July" and plots of soil were allotted each state for its graves.

On Thursday, November 19, 1863, a consecration ceremony was held at the National Soldiers' Cemetery at Gettysburg. All those who were able to attend traveled to the former battlefield to witness the dedication. More than fifteen thousand people assembled there heard President Lincoln deliver his address: "in a larger sense, . . . we cannot consecrate, we cannot hallow this ground. The brave men, living and dead, who struggled here have consecrated it far above our poor power to add or detract. . . ."

THE UNION LEAGUE MARCHED TO INDEPENDENCE HALL

Emily Bliss Souder

Maine-born Emily Bliss Souder, who had taken part in war work thus far on the home front alone, was to become later in November of 1863 a "lady manager of the Cooper Shop Soldiers' Home in Philadelphia." Meanwhile, she was so shocked by the

*war news after the Battle of Gettysburg that she canceled her
usual trip to her summer home at Cape May, New Jersey, with
her husband, Edmund, and her children, and went instead to
nurse the sick and wounded men at Gettysburg. Her descriptions of the effects of the war on Philadelphia and of her stay
at the front are contained in letters and diary entries written
throughout this period.*

The dark days of the end of June and the beginning of July,
1863, are too recent to be forgotten by any Pennsylvanian. All
hearts were heavy with anxiety as each hour brought reports of
fresh outrages committed by the Rebel invaders. From morning
till midnight the drum was heard in our streets, which were filled
with soldiers drilling and recruiting and two hundred clergymen
walked in procession to the mayor to offer their services. . . .

The Fourth of July was a day of great solemnity. Religious
services were held in nearly all of our churches. . . . Tidings were
received the day previous of a battle in progress at Gettysburg;
that Gen. Reynolds was killed and the corps driven from its
position. The anxiety was intense. . . . On Sunday rumors came
of success to our arms and defeat to the Rebels and, as rumor
deepened into certainty and the pall lifted from the hearts of
the people, the first impulse was to prepare and forward, with
all possible rapidity, supplies of every kind. In several churches
the regular services were omitted and sewing machines were
put in requisition in making up shirts and drawers while from
almost every house, jellies, stimulants, and old linen were sent
to some point to be packed immediately for the battlefield.
Many clergymen and citizens as well as surgeons and physicians
of every grade hastened to the relief of the wounded and dying
and many ladies made speedy arrangements to go to the field.
On Tuesday came the glorious news of the surrender of Vicksburg. It was felt that there should be a public demonstration

of feeling; a public thanksgiving to the God of Battle. . . . The Reverend Dr. Brainerd, whose warm-hearted loyalty has made his name a tower of strength, was invited to officiate and the Union League, preceded by a fine band playing the National airs, marched in procession to Independence Hall where a prayer of thanksgiving for victory at Gettysburg and Vicksburg was offered to the Almighty Deliverer in the presence of assembled thousands who stood reverently and near the consecrated spot. At its close, the solemn notes of Old Hundred were heard from the State House steeple where the band had gone and the vast multitude sang in chorus the words:

Praise God from Whom all blessings flow.

It was an occasion to be remembered forever. . . . As the days passed on, we received continued accounts of the suffering and distress among our noble soldiers. With three other ladies, the writer decided to visit Gettysburg to aid in the great work. . . . We left Baltimore at half past seven this morning and have been waiting here until we are almost *cooked*—the only word that gives an idea of our discomfort. We understand we are to leave at six o'clock. The immense amount of government supplies and hospital stores which are being sent forward and the trains of wounded soldiers coming from Gettysburg make the transportation of passengers inconvenient and uncomfortable to the last degree; two or three days ago an open freight car was the only accommodation and in this the ladies slept with the sky above them. A train of wounded soldiers passed down about an hour ago. A car is stationed here close to the railroad track where four ladies from Baltimore prepare lemonade and bread and butter to refresh the men besides pies, farina, etc.—the Christian Commission car. They have three stations on the way. We made a visit to this car and saw the ladies at work. Presently a young man, a member of the Commission, came in with a market basket full with loaves of bread which he had procured from farmhouses not very far distant. I bought a barrel of bread from a baker in Baltimore and could hardly refrain from adding this to their store; but the accounts which we had received of the great necessity for bread in Gettysburg induced me to retain it as the distance at this point is more easily passed over.

A kind-hearted woman by the wayside has been baking sixty pies per day. . . . Not a trifling service with the thermometer at ninety degrees or more.

A gentleman belonging to the Sanitary Commission came next with an anxious face to inquire if the ladies had any way to cook some meat. The ice in the provision car had melted and he feared the fresh meat would spoil. The heat was so great and there was so much delay on the road. . . .

Persons coming and going all agreed there was a great deal to be done. . . . Adams Express seems the only reliable way of sending. If you could come yourself you must keep your eye on what you have in charge. R. Campion will go back to Baltimore tomorrow if our boxes are not forthcoming. It is, in a manner, impossible to get anyone to handle these things and on this account, ladies who are alone have much trouble. I have a supply of paper and envelopes and can write letters without boxes. This also is much needed. A surgeon from Ohio who is waiting for the Harrisburg trains says he "can take a man's leg off if necessary and not mind it but when a man says 'Can't you write to my wife and tell her how I died and tell her to kiss Mary'; that I cannot do!" . . .

We are all well and have heard of good quarters. . . . Mrs. Rowe's, Baltimore Street. The Doctor offers to take letters and mail them in Harrisburg, of which kind offer we gladly avail ourselves. Sitting on the steps of the platform with a satchel in lieu of a desk, we are giving our friends the earliest information. . . .

Gettysburg,
July 5, 1863.

On the way to the hospital, we saw the rifle pits, the dead horses, the shattered windows and the stone walls all scattered and many soldiers' graves. . . . Chloride of lime has been freely used in the board streets of the town and the state of the hospitals was much improved by the same means but it is needful to close the eyes at the sights of horror and to shut the ears against sounds of anguish and to extinguish as far as possible the sense of smelling. . . . The inmates of many homes hid themselves in their cellars. The Rebels lay all about the streets and in the yards. . . . A young woman near at hand spent five days in a cellar with her four little children sitting on barrelheads with two feet of water in the cellar, eating only crackers and crying for water. At last she ventured to the door to go for it when a Rebel took the bucket from her hand and brought the water as he said it would be certain death for her, the bullets were flying so fast. This poor thing had a baby four weeks old in her arms.

A constant procession of corpses meets the eye; groups of men standing in the fields searching for the name of some friend or brother. . . .

HELL SEEMED TO HAVE VOMITED UP ITS LEGIONS

Sophronia E. Bucklin

During the Battle of Gettysburg, Sophronia Bucklin and other nurses pleaded with Dorothea Dix for permission to go to the front where the conditions were said to be too appalling to describe.

In barns and under sheltering trees, where the shells and cannon balls and deadly bullets were at times flying, the surgeons plied their keen-edged saws, while the horrid rasps grated on ears which would feign have shut out the dread sounds. Men were shot dead as they crawled away to seek a shelter from the storm, where they might have died more peacefully from their fatal wounds. Hell seemed to have vomited up its legions, with its own lurid flames, and to have influenced many desperate souls to seek out their mangled victims.

Days passed, and we knew they needed help. We knew they needed more than could be gathered from the surrounding country, and we besought Miss Dix to allow us to go. . . .

But, "No, you are too young for field duty," was the constant reply, and I chafed under the command which I dared not openly disobey. . . . One day, Mr. Knapp, of the Sanitary Commission, said to me, "Miss Bucklin, will you go to Gettysburg, and help distribute stores? I will stand between you and all blame."

"I will go," I said, and twenty minutes remained in which to gather up a little bundle of clothes, and roll them in a newspaper, to eat my supper, and go on board the train.

Friday afternoon we left Washington, and arrived at Baltimore in the evening, when the first person who met me in the hotel parlor where I stopped was Miss Dix, on her return from Gettysburg.

"Where are you going, child?" she said, looking into my face with keen searching glances.

"To Gettysburg, madam," I replied.

"And did I not forbid you—why do you disobey my orders?"

Mrs. Caldwell (the woman Sophronia had been sent with) related the persuasion which had been brought to bear upon me, and the kind superintendent, with no chiding, forgave me, and said, "Report to the Sanitary Hospital for duty."

On Saturday we entered the battle town. Everywhere were evidences of mortal combat, everywhere wounded men were lying in the streets on heaps of blood-stained straw, everywhere there was hurry and confusion, while soldiers were groaning and suffering. . . . They lay on the bloody ground, sick with the pains of wounds, grim with the dust of long marches and the smoke and powder of battle, looking up with wild haggard faces imploringly for succor. . . . their lives slowly ebbing away, the blood drops still oozing from deep wounds. . . .

A carriage took us out from Gettysburg to the tent, which had partially been fitted up for Dr. Caldwell's wife, but neither bed nor seat of any kind had been put in—only the rough-boarded floor lay under us, soaked through and through with the falling rain.

It was impossible to remain there in comfort—we were weary with travel, and needed rest to recruit ourselves for labor, so back to the town we were driven, where we found shelter in the house of a citizen whose wife had been cooking for the Sanitary Commission. . . .

I was told, when asking to be directed to the Sanitary Hospital, that I was not needed there, but that urgent necessity for woman's work existed in the field, and I must consent to go there for duty. Also that the patients from the Seminary were soon to be brought to the field and that the hospital was to be broken up. So on the following morning we took our way up to the hospital ground, where five hundred tents had already been erected.

It was the field on which the first guns were fired in that memorable battle. . . . I shall never forget that morning or that scene. . . . A line of stretchers a mile and a half in length told us where lay our work, and we commenced it at once. I washed agonized faces, combed out matted hair, bandaged slight wounds, and administered drinks of raspberry vinegar and lemon syrup, while Mrs. Caldwell wrote letters to those who were waiting in dread suspense for news of their soldier. . . .

The Sanitary Commission here did its work of mercy. Without its generous supplies, untold suffering would have visited us, for Government stores could not be obtained, and in view of the host of wounded the ordinary hospital supplies were as a drop of water in the depths of the cool, silent well.

The hospital lay in the rear of a deep wood, in a large open field, a mile and a half from Gettysburg, and overlooking it, the single line of rail which connected the battle town with the outer world sweeping it on one side, and winding through the woods. In this open field our supplies were landed from Washington. Whole carloads of bread were moulded through and through, while for a time we were sorely pinched for the necessaries of life.

It needed only time to right this pressing want. We soon had a Government kitchen, a low diet and an extra diet kitchen, with several large stoves, and large caldrons in which to make the soup which was always served for dinner.

We were the first women on the ground, but the number soon increased to forty, including seven Government nurses. One woman superintended the extra diet, having several under her charge to do the cooking.

The hospital tents were set in rows, five hundred of them. . . . Walks were thrown up between these rows, in order that they might dry quickly after the summer rains. The ground was the only floor in the wards or in our quarters. The latter with those of the surgeons were set at the edge of the woods. . . .

My tent contained an iron bedstead, on which for a while I slept with the bare slats beneath, and covered with sheets and blanket. I afterwards obtained a tick and pillow from the Sanitary Commission, and filled them with straw, sleeping in comparative comfort. I soon found, however, that the wounded

Interior of a hospital train. *(Culver Service)*

The United States Hospital at Georgetown (formerly the Union Hotel) where Louisa May Alcott served as a nurse in December, 1862. *(Brown Brothers)*

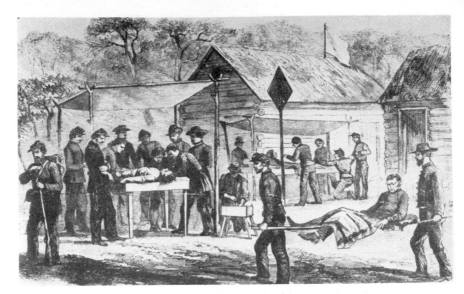

Surgery in the field after the Battle of Bristoe Station.

Field hospital, Savage Station, Virginia.

An artist's conception of the United States General Hospital at Chestnut Hill, 1862. (*Courtesy New York State Historical Association*)

Administering to the wounded at White House, Virginia, March 19, 1864. (*Brown Brothers*)

needed these more than I, and back I went to the hard slats again, this time without the sheets, which were given for the purpose of changing a patient's blood-saturated bed. . . .

THE AIR WAS QUICK WITH PAIN

Anna Holstein

Anna's husband was threatened with an attack of malarial fever and the couple went home to Merion, Pennsylvania, so that he could rest. They remained there only long enough for Mr. Holstein to recuperate sufficiently to bear the fatigues of travel. While he was still unfit for the journey, the great Battle of Gettysburg was fought and within one week after it, the Holsteins were on their way back. They reached the town of Gettysburg late in the evening and spent the night upon the parlor floor of one of the hotels, with a satchel for a pillow. In the morning they were welcomed at the Field Hospital by their old friends of the 2nd Corps. The wounded, at that time, lay just where they had been placed when carried from the battle— "friend and foe resting together."

The scenes around Gettysburg were horrible in the extreme: the green sod everywhere stained with the lifeblood of dying men who had sternly fought and bravely fallen . . . heaps of blood-stained clothing . . . shattered muskets . . . discarded knapsacks, disabled cannon and caissons, and the innumerable heaps of slain horses which literally cover the hard-fought field.

For a few weeks, the events daily occurring in the hospitals were most painful—fearfully wounded men—nurses watching for the hour when suffering would cease—parents and friends crowding to the hospital, hoping for the best, yet fearing the

worst—strong men praying that they might live just long enough
to see, but once more, wife, or child, or mother.

After this battle, relief came promptly; it was upon our soil,
and the "great heart of the people" was stirred to its very
depths. . . .

A nephew of President Johnson, named Burchett, was also
a Union man among Rebels; with a number of others, they
were attempting to come into our lines when captured. The
Rebels told them they would be put in the front ranks, and
when they came to Gettysburg, carrying out their threat, they
were made breastworks of. None of the sixty escaped unhurt;
many were killed. Burchett lost a leg, and one arm permanently
disabled. He was a free-spoken Union man among them, and
seemed to be no favorite with the Rebs on that account. He
remained a prisoner, hoping in the exchange to be sent to Richmond, that he might save some property belonging to his
father, who had lost everything in Kentucky.

In the "Union tent," as it was called, standing alone in a
Rebel row, I found a boy of seventeen, wounded and sick unto
death, whose wan, emaciated face and cheerful endurance of
suffering at once enlisted my sympathy. He was the son of a
clergyman in Maine; and in answer to inquiries about his wound,
told me, with a feeling of evident pride, that early in the day
his right leg was shattered and left upon Seminary Hill, and
he carried to the rear; that the stump was doing badly; he had
enlisted simply because it was his duty to do so; now he had no
regret or fear, let the result be as it might. . . . One week after
his burial his father came; with a heart saddened with his great
loss, said that his eldest had fallen at Malvern Hill, the second
was with the army at Fernandina, and Albert, his youngest born,
slept with the heroes who had made a world-wide fame at
Gettysburg. . . .

Our long residence in the hospital gave us the opportunity

of understanding fully all the prominent points of interest in the battlefield, which was constantly before us; if we but raised our eyes, they rested upon Culp's Hill, Cemetery or Seminary Hill, and in the distance Round Top, made forever memorable by the heroic conduct of the brave men of the Fifth Corps, who, by order of Gen. Meade to Gen. Sykes, directed it to be held at all hazards.

MOTHER AND I WERE AT GETTYSBURG

Georgeanna M. Woolsey

Georgeanna Woolsey wrote to Dr. Francis Bacon, whom she married after the war, of the things she and her mother saw and did at Gettysburg. The battle had been raging for three days. The family knew that Charley was in the thick of it and were anxious and prepared to believe the worst, when Georgeanna received a telegram from Frederick L. Olmsted, head of the United States Sanitary Commission: "If you are going to Gettysburg, let me know." The Woolseys immediately concluded that Mr. Olmsted knew of bad news concerning Charley Woolsey and Georgeanna and her mother started at once to go to him. In Baltimore they learned the boy was safe and the Rebels repulsed.

Fishkill, Aug. 6, '63.

Mother and I were in Gettysburg when your letter came, having hurried on immediately after the battle, under the impression, due to a mistake in telegraphing, that Charley was hurt; and, being on hand, were fastened upon by Mr. Olmsted, to take charge of a feeding station and lodge for the wounded men. So there we were, looking after other people's boys, since our own was safe, for three weeks, coming as near the actual battle fields as I should ever wish to. You know all about that fighting, how desperate it was on both sides; what loss, and what misery; the communications cut, no supplies on hand, no surgeons, or so few that they were driven to despair from the sight of wretchedness they could not help—twenty thousand badly wounded soldiers and only one miserable, unsafe line of railroad to bring supplies and carry men away. We were twenty-four hours in getting from Baltimore to Gettysburg, when in ordinary times we should have been four. This was the only excuse I could think of to give the wretched Rebels who, two weeks after the battle, lay in the mud under shelter tents, and had their food handed them in newspapers: "I am sorry, my man; we are all distressed at it; but *you* have cut our communications and nothing arrives."

Never say anything against the Army of the Potomac again, when so few of our men, after their marching and fasting, overtook and overcame Lee's fatted twice-their-number. I saw but very few who were *slightly* hurt among the wounded, and we fed all the sixteen thousand who went away from Gettysburg. So brave they were too, and so pleased with all that was done for them—even the Rebels. We had our station with tents for a hundred, with kitchen, surgeon, and delegation right on the railroad line between Gettysburg and Baltimore, and twice a day the trains left with soldiers—long trains of ambulances always arriving just too late for the cars, and no provision being made to shelter and feed them except by the Sanitary Commission. We had the full storehouse of the Commission to draw upon, and took real satisfaction in dressing and comforting all our men. No man of the sixteen thousand went away without a good hot meal, and none from our tents without the fresh clothes they needed. Mother put great spirit into it all, listened to all their stories, petted them, fed them, and distributed clothes, including handkerchiefs with cologne, and got herself called "Mother"—"This way, Mother," "Here's the bucket, Mother," and "Isn't she a glorious old woman?"—while the most that *I* ever heard was, "*She* knows how; why, it would have taken our steward two hours to get round; but then she's used to it, you see"; which, when you consider that I was distributing hot grog, and must have been taken for a barmaid, was not so complimentary! Then those Rebels, too, miserable fellows; we hated them so much when they were away from us, and couldn't help being so good to them when they were in our hands. I am, or should be, angry with myself in that I felt worse when Lieutenant Rhout of the 14th South Carolina died on my hands, singing the Lutheran chants he had sung in his father's church before they made a soldier of him, than when E. C. writes me that Amos was their oldest son, and that she and his father were over sixty . . . I am glad we helped those Rebels. They had just as much good hot soup, when our procession of cans and cups and soft bread and general refreshment went round from car to car, as they wanted; and I even filled the silver pap-cup that a pretty boy from North Carolina had around his neck, though he was an officer and showed no intention to become a Unionist. Yes, it was his baby cup, and his mother gave it to him; and he lay on the floor of the baggage car, wounded, with this most domestic and peaceful of all little relics tied round his neck. . . .

It was a satisfaction to be in Gettysburg, though I confess to a longing to shut out the sight of it all, sometimes. The dear fellows were so badly hurt, and it was so hard to bear their perfect patience; men with a right arm gone, and children at home, and no word or look of discontent.

The authorities want us to go back again, and look after the special diet in the new and fine General Hospital for three thousand men, too sick to be moved. We can't do so, though, as

Jane and I have promised to spend the winter at Point Lookout in the Hammond Hospital. Look with respect upon your correspondent; she is at the head of the Protestant half of the women's department of that hospital. The Sisters run half the wards, and I except to have fun with their Lady Superior and to wheedle her out of all her secrets, and get myself invited out to tea. Why shouldn't she and I compare notes on the proper way to make soup? I will call her "Sister," and agree to eat oysters on Friday—(they are particularly fine on the Maryland shore.)

It will be rather jolly down there, particularly as the surgeon in charge is delighted to have us come, and we shall ride over him just as much as your dear old women, black and white, do over their particular conquest. As for gardens of oranges, and flowers—well, we shall have beds of oysters, and, as it is a military station, there will be a band there to keep up our spirits; which reminds me to give the Baltimore fireman his due, who, being one of our friends at Gettysburg, secured two bands before we came away and marched them down to camp to serenade us, which they did standing at the mouth of the long tent and refreshing themselves afterwards with gingerbread and punch, unmindful of the fact that the jolly Canandaigua "delegation," finding its fingers inconvenienced by the sugar on them, just dipped their hands in the claret and water without saying anything! It will be a long time before Gettysburg will forget the Army of the Potomac. Their houses are battered, some of them with great holes through and through them. Their streets are filled with old caps, pieces of muskets, haversacks, scraps of war everywhere, and even the children fling stones across the streets, and call to each other, "Here, you Rebel, don't you hear that shell?" and one babe of four years I found sitting on the pavement with a hammer peacefully cracking percussion caps from the little cupful he had. . . .

JUST IMAGINE MOTHER IN HEAVY GETTYSBURG BOOTS

Abby Howland Woolsey

Georgeanna was urged to write a pamphlet giving her experiences at the front. It was called Three weeks at Gettysburg. *It was meant to fire the hearts of the sewing circles which all over the country were keeping up the Sanitary Commission supplies. The Commission ordered ten thousand copies for distribution and Georgy went off to Point Lookout Hospital leaving Abby all the work of getting it printed. Abby wrote:*

It took so long for letters to come from Gettysburg, and Mother and Georgy had so little time to write, that we didn't hear often. They have come *themselves* at last; arrived Tuesday, midnight. . . . Georgy came up here this noon, and we have been sitting together talking over all the strange scenes in those tents by the railroad, where sixteen thousand men have been fed and comforted in the last three weeks. Just imagine Mother in a straw flat and heavy *Gettysburg* boots, standing cooking soup for two hundred men at a time, and distributing it in tin cups; or giving clean shirts to ragged Rebels; or sitting on a pile of grocer's boxes, under the shadow of a string of codfish, scribbling her notes to us.

She has many a memento of that strange battle—one, of a Rebel lieutenant who died in her care; and a score of palmetto buttons from Rebel coats—dirty but grateful, poor wretches; etc. . . . They say that the *women* of Gettysburg have done all they can, given the wounded all that the Rebels had not taken, and have boarded the Sanitary and Christian Commissions for nothing. At one house, where Mother and G. got their dinner one day, the woman could not be induced to take money. "No,

ma'am," she said, "I would not wish to have *that* sin on my
soul when this war is over."

RESISTANCE TO THE DRAFT

Caroline Caisson Woolsey

*Jane Newton Woolsey and Georgy were still at Gettysburg. Hatty
and Carry were alone in the house in Brevoort Place during the
draft riots.*

It has come—resistance to the draft! The city is in a tumult
and Uncle Edward wishes us to go out to Astoria in the 6
o'clock boat. The regulars are all out and the streets are full
of rioters. The gas house on Twenty-third Street is blown up
and Tenth Street full of black ashes—our doorsteps covered.
They say they will blow up the powder mill in Twenty-eighth
Street where the Gilmans live and we have told them (if they
will) to come all here. Hatty G. was in a minute ago, and Mr.
Prentiss. There has been a great noise in town all day. The carriage is waiting, but I was afraid you would feel anxious. We
would like very much to stay, but Uncle E. insists.

Astoria, July 15, 1863.

We left in such a hurry we had no time to leave directions
for the servants, except to close the house early, and be very
particular about fastening the doors and windows. . . . While
driving out here we heard distinctly the cannon at Harlem. We
have had no real trouble here from the mob, but were *threatened*
last night and the night before. About two hundred men and
boys, principally from Harlem and the upper parts of the city,
were careening around the village. They went to Mr. M——'s

and made him come out and speak against the draft, and announced their intention of visiting Messrs. Wolcott, Woolsey, and Howland among others. Groups of them were gathering in the afternoon as we drove through the village. Uncle Edward was a good deal excited as night came on, and had a man placed in the stable with directions to cut the horses loose should any alarm be made. Robert [*Mary Howland's husband*] had his carriage or rather his horses harnessed and ready to pack the children in. Uncle Edward had a pile of firearms loaded and placed conveniently near the window. Aunt Emily put her rings on and her valuables in a safe place, and we pocketed our purses and laid Mother's camel's hair shawls, which we brought with us, where we could easily seize them in case of sudden chill, caused by the draft! . . . But nothing turned up and things have quieted down. The militia regiments are (five of them) coming home; the 7th has already arrived.

Hatty Roosevelt Woolsey had this to add:

One of the Ball and Black firm came the next morning to ask Uncle E. if he could hide some treasure on his place. He lives in 86th Street and his house had been threatened. Uncle E. said he might take his three or four trunks through the woods to the "black lodge," but of course it was at his own risk, as no one was to be trusted on the place. They were all kept safe in Margaret's hands and he came back and got them in a few days. Isn't it shameful that the fiends should have sacked Mrs. Gibbons' * house?—everything destroyed and all her little things carried off. Uncle E. is perfectly indignant and in a state of suppressed rage at the Irish, but he agrees with Aunt E. in not allowing a word said against them at table, or within reach of any of the servants' ears.

* Mrs. Gibbons was well known as a pronounced abolitionist. She had served until now at Point Lookout Hospital as a nurse.

AN AWFUL RIOT COMMENCED TODAY

Julia Lay

Julia Lay was another socialite New Yorker who kept a diary of some war happenings, although she did not serve as a nurse or sanitary agent.

Monday, July 13, 1863, New York. An awful riot commenced today on account of the draft. The Provost Marshal's Office was burned and other buildings adjoining; they tore up the railroad tracks, cut down the telegraph wires and, at stores, robbed everything they could get. Whole blocks were destroyed. Fires were kindled in every direction. A large sum of money was destroyed by fire in Second Avenue, just below us. I saw thousands of men pass our house with guns and carbines and men running, excited, yelling and shouting for men to join them. They entered all the machine shops and made the men quit their work and follow them. They went to the novelty works and compelled fourteen hundred men to leave and shut up the works. They hunted the poor Negroes, tore them from their homes and killed many, hung some, burned their dwellings, destroyed their beds. I saw a pile in the middle of the street burned till I could hear the crackling. . . . Business has been suspended all over the city for four days. Cars have ceased running and stages. The military has been active; before our door a whole regiment halted and then went up three blocks where they were attacked by the mob. Many were killed on both sides. We had cannon placed in the middle of the avenue twice and fired off, which scattered the rioters. Large numbers were killed. I saw them carried past our door, cut down in a moment. What dread times! I never wish to see again men with clubs and stones. I saw them . . . and heard the soldiers fire back a whole volley then the screams and groans. I was almost frightened out of my senses but I had been calm before this for four days here alone in the house with Georgie Wesey and Gracie. The excitement made Georgie sick and he grew so miserable-looking, I determined to send him to Lyme and David was going this afternoon. . . . I have scarcely slept any for four nights. I have been so much excited. The fires raged so near us. The Orphan Asylum for colored children was destroyed and a great number of private dwellings burned. I have written to sisters Maggie and Laura today—do not feel well but sad and apprehensive, fearing evil, but God can take care of us and ours. . . .

July 19, 1863, Sabbath. There seems to be more quiet and perhaps the riot is over, although the soldiers are placed along our street and avenue, as it is likely at any moment to break out like a wild beast. I have tried to feel tranquil but I have not been able. I cannot eat, I am so afraid of every unusual noise. I'll trust in the Lord and be of good courage.

EAGER CALLS WERE MADE FOR THE PRESIDENT

Emily Bliss Souder

Emily Souder describes her impressions of the Consecration ceremonies.

Gettysburg,
November 20, 1863.

We left home on Tuesday morning at eight o'clock. At Columbia, quitting the cars, we crossed the beautiful Susquehanna in a small flat-bottomed boat more picturesque than comfortable. Many boats crossed at the same time with their living freight and, returning, were again speedily filled. The fine bridge between Columbia and Wrightsville was destroyed in June to prevent the Rebels from passing over it. The piers and abutments are still standing. At Wrightsville we waited about an hour before the locomotive was ready; and when we reached York, we were obliged to remain there until the train came from Harrisburg at about four o'clock. It was decidedly tiresome to say the least. When the cars finally arrived, they were already filled to overflowing and we were obliged to squeeze in as best we could.

At Hanover Junction, it was still worse. The Baltimore train had brought a large number of passengers from that city and the scanty provisions of cars, the platforms around the station piled up with baggage, and the shadows of twilight already approaching made us realize that comfort was an item left out of the program. It was two hours or more before we were ready to move. Seats were finally extemporized in some freight cars and we started, crowded, weary, and hungry. . . .

It was eleven o'clock when we reached our place of destination. We found a worthy citizen who had been apprized of our coming waiting for us at the depot with a lantern in hand and we were soon comfortably quartered.

After a very early breakfast the next morning we engaged a vehicle and rode first to Culp's Hill to the left of the Baltimore Turnpike, the Cemetery being on the right. . . . General Meade's headquarters were at first near this point. At Culp's Hill the Rebels fought with great determination and finally succeeded in breaking the line of defenses and entered the breastworks at two points when the 12th Corps came to the rescue and saved the day as did the Pennsylvania Reserves on Round Top on the same day, July 3rd. The ground is still strewn with fragments of clothing, knapsacks, haversacks, etc. We gathered up as many articles as we could conveniently take in the carriage with us. . . .

In the afternoon we rode to Seminary Hill and saw Lee's

headquarters and the spot where General Reynolds fell. Returning, we visited the General Hospital. . . . The last of the
wounded soldiers had within a few days been sent to hospitals
elsewhere. . . .

The tranquility of the little town was, by this time if not before, completely broken up. The President was hourly looked
for and the interest and excitement were great. We waited a
long time, hoping to witness his arrival but in vain. At a later
hour we walked out to take observations. The churches were
lighted and warm for the reception of those who could not find
quarters elsewhere. The streets were filled with crowds of people. A band was playing the National airs in front of the house
where Mr. Lincoln was staying and eager calls were made for
"the President," who finally stood a few minutes on the door-
step; in response to the wishes of the people, he made a few
characteristic remarks, promising to speak at some length the
next day. Mr. Seward was next called upon for a speech and we
were so near that we heard his remarks quite distinctly as well
as those of some other speakers. It was quite a new experience,
you may be sure, and the whole time and circumstances were
unlike anything we had known before. I must not forget to
mention our introduction to John Burns, the heroic old citizen
who seized his flintlock and fought voluntarily with our army
through the great battles until wounded.

Thursday, the 19th of November, dawned dull and cloudy
and a storm seemed threatening, but the shadows passed over
and the day proved fine. Before it was quite light the perpetual
tramp of foot passengers gave token of the anticipated solemni-
ties. The crowd was continually augmented by fresh arrivals,
coming in every direction by every avenue of approach, on foot,
in carriages, and on horseback. We decided to remain where we
were until the procession passed.

As the hour approached, heavy guns were fired at intervals,

pealing like a solemn anthem on the air. The sadness of recent
bereavement seemed to rest on every heart. Soon we heard the
sounds of funeral marches and the long line of military passed
through Baltimore Street to the Cemetery. Then came the
President, easily distinguished from all others. He seemed as
chief mourner. With him were the members of the Cabinet, the
Governor of Pennsylvania, and delegations from nearly all the
loyal states. Marshals with batons and badges on horseback, a
large cavalcade, and then citizens on foot, men, women, and
children—a great multitude. We joined the company and proceeded to the Cemetery. Mr. Everett, the orator of the day, and
the Reverend Mr. Stockton rode in a barouche. A beautiful flag
floated over the platform which was arranged with seats for the
distinguished guests but there was no place allotted for the
ladies. The crowd was excessive. After listening to the dirge, we
withdrew a little to observe the scene. The oration we could
read. The sight was truly imposing. Among the many banners
was one which touched every heart with mute lamentation; a
white flag shrouded with black, bearing the inscription: "We
mourn our former comrades" and on the reverse, "The Army
of the Potomac." I gathered in the Cemetery many sprays and
green leaves to send to friends at a distance who might value
such mementoes of the day and hour. . . .

It was long past noon when the procession returned. It was a
magnificent sight. The long line of infantry with their bayonets
gleaming in the sunlight, the artillery, the distinguished guests,
the great multitude. As the President passed, every head was
uncovered as three hearty cheers were given for him. The same
compliment was paid to our own Governor Curtin. The solemn
pageant was over.

Soon after, we rode over some portion of the battlefield, visiting an old German woman whose house was completely riddled
with cannon balls. She remained in it, attending to her house-

hold duties during the whole battle, with her daughter, now a bride. They were advised to leave but had, she said, no place to go. They showed us a bureau, one side of which was burst through, and a drawer knocked out by a ball which had entered the house, passed through a middle partition, and out of the opposite side. After this, they retreated to the cellar. General Barksdale of the Rebel army fell in front of their house. . . . A wounded Union soldier asked for something to eat. They gave him a piece of bread and he was seen presently, sitting under a tree with the bread still in his hand, dead! One realizes the battle when hearing these things from an eyewitness on the spot where it occurred. We passed by the peach orchard where the 2nd Corps suffered so terribly and rode on toward Round Top. It was worth the journey to Gettysburg to see our flag floating over Round Top so grandly and beautifully.

At five in the afternoon, the citizens were introduced to the President and we did ourselves the honor of paying our respects to him and to the Governor. In the evening various meetings were held and many speeches were made in the open air, some of which were greeted with hearty applause by citizens and soldiers. . . .

12 Fairs Are the Rage

THE NORTH WAS ENTERING THE THIRD YEAR OF THE WAR. SHER-man's famous march, the bloody battles of the Wilderness, and the long siege at Petersburg still belonged to the dim dark future as the generals laid their plans.

Behind the scenes the women of the North laid plans of their own. Work for the soldiers was being continued all over the country but work alone was insufficient. Their visits to the Army had convinced the women not only of the value of Sanitary Commission relief to the sick in hospitals, but the need for large sums of money to pay for supplies to meet the increasing demands of the suffering troops and for the services of more surgeons and nurses. Determined to strike out on a bold and novel course, they decided that a Sanitary Commission Fair would raise an enormous sum of money and at the same time demonstrate the loyalty of the North and encourage the men on the battlefields. Chicago was the first city to undertake such a project. President Lincoln took a keen interest in it from the moment it was announced. Jane Hoge and Mary Livermore wrote him from Chicago asking him for some personal contribution from him for the Fair. Lincoln agreed that he wanted to send something but did not know what. A happy thought came to a friend of his: Why shouldn't the President send the ladies the original manuscript of the Emancipation Proclamation?

Why not indeed! Lincoln wished to keep it himself but finally consented and the famous document reached Chicago the day after the Fair opened. It was sold for $3,000 at the Fair.

272

At first and for a long time, only two women and no men had been interested in the Fair and it remained throughout a woman's effort. Nevertheless, the success of the Great Northwestern Sanitary Commission Fair, which was held on October 28, 1863, inspired other cities to follow suit. Before long fairs became the rage among debutantes and dowagers and even the wives of the military leaders.

On April 14, 1864, the great Manhattan Fair of the United States Sanitary Commission was opened in New York City in a large wooden building at Union Square. This occasion was highlighted by the singing of an original poem by Oliver Wendell Holmes by a union of volunteer church choirs and the vast multitude that attended the opening. During the three weeks of the Fair two million dollars were raised through the joint effort of the very rich, such as Mrs. August Belmont, who held a concert among her friends for the benefit of the Fair, and those of lesser means, who volunteered their time and services.

While the carrying on of relief work became well co-ordinated by the women during the war, the supplying of nurses continued in a state of confusion. The restrictions that Dorothea Dix had imposed at the outset were bound to be broken. If followed they would have cut down considerably on the number of eligible women. The poor handling of her program led women to apply to other sources for permission to serve. As a result there was a constant misunderstanding throughout the war as to who was authorized to supply women nurses. The Sanitary and Christian Commissions, private relief agencies, and even individuals vied with each other in seeking to place nurses of their own in general hospitals.

An ostensible attempt was made late in 1863 to clear up this matter. Order No. 351 of the War Department, Clause 2, stated: "Women nurses will be assigned only on application to the General Superintendent of Nurses, . . . unless," added

Clause 3, "they are especially appointed by the Surgeon General." Of course Surgeons in Charge, wishing to retain or employ nurses without the "Certificate" of the General Superintendent, applied for their "Special Appointment" by the Surgeon General, which was promptly obtained. This, with other provisions of the Order, practically abolished the office of the General Superintendent of Nurses and threw the selection of nurses into the hands of the Surgeons in Charge, and although the title of Superintendent of Nurses remained hers, Dorothea Dix's influence and power grew less and less significant over the years.

MESDAMES GRANT AND MC CLELLAN HEAD SUBSCRIPTION LISTS

Adelaide W. Smith

Born in 1831 in Brooklyn, Adelaide Smith's work for sick soldiers began early in 1862 in the Department of the East, which included Long Island Hospital, Willett's Point, David's Island, Fort Schuyler, and Bedloe's (later Liberty Island). When the Fair was in the planning stage, she became active in the project, and while it was taking place, she was one of the shining lights of Union Square in lower Manhattan. At the suggestion of Colonel Frank Howe, director of the New England Rooms (a Soldiers' Rest on Broadway near Fulton Street), free passes for a number of convalescents were secured and Adelaide Smith consented to take charge of them during the Fair.

One bright day, the New England ambulance was crowded with the following passengers, namely: one man without legs, two men without arms, one blind from a shot passing through his head, a one-legged boy, the famous John Burns of Gettysburg, and a colored woman to assist. I sat on the front seat with the driver. We drove up Broadway to the fair grounds, quite regardless of the curious crowd that followed.

These brave martyrs were received with outstretched hands and cordial sympathy, and given the freedom of every department in the wonderful exhibition. In a splendid restaurant I volunteered to act as waiter, that I might be certain that the Boys had good meals and attention, for which the Sanitary Commission made no charge.

A crowd followed armless Berry who carried on his strong back legless Smith—who in turn dressed and fed Berry. These two had become great friends and, like the Siamese twins, were inseparable. Always cheerful, they seemed to enjoy life. . . . Berry often carried the legless man about the large building to see the wonders, which they greatly enjoyed.

Another armless soldier, a sergeant always in uniform, traveled about alone, and when in cars or boats was rarely asked for fare, or if so, he would say: "Help yourself from my pockets." Few had the heart to do this, so he usually traveled free.

McNulty, a refined young man, who had lost an arm in an early engagement but was now quite well, was also of our party, though he was quite independent and asked no help, having already learned, like General Howard, to use his left arm for writing and to serve double duty.

Famous John Burns was included with those mentioned above in the freedom of the whole building, and at seventy years of age called himself one of my "Boys." . . .

I had obtained permission for the three men, Smith, Berry, and Mudge, to remain in the trophy department, where, each day, many greenbacks were crowded into their pockets. I had asked Mesdames Grant and McClellan to head subscription lists and to solicit money for the three helpless soldiers. Both ladies cheerfully and effectively urged people to subscribe at one dollar each, and at the close of the last evening they were happy to hand over to me, to be divided among these living martyrs of our cruel war, the sum of about five hundred dollars. . . .

The Arms and Trophy Department of the Sanitary Commission Fair was beautifully draped with bunting, Revolutionary, Mexican, and other old war flags, and also a few Confederate flags, captured by regiments still in the field, that had yet many a bloody battle to fight. A number of distinguished, elegantly gowned women toiled here indefatigably, brimming over with excitement and patriotism, quite regardless of the unusual fatigue of standing and working so many hours daily, in their anxiety to allow no one to pass without contributing in some way to the fund, now reaching thousands of dollars.

Here was to be decided the "sword test," that would indicate the most popular general, by the number of votes cast at one dollar each. The sword was to be presented to the winner of the largest number of votes. How these attractive ladies worked for their favorites! A magnetic thrill pervaded this room, where men of fashion and reputation crowded, ostensibly to learn how the vote was going.

Mrs. Grant, a noble-looking woman, accepted graciously, but without solicitation, all who offered votes for General Grant, of whom she invariably spoke as "Mr. Grant." Mrs. McClellan, with elegant society manner, lost no opportunity in gaining a vote for General McClellan; her vivacity, personal charm, and courteous flattery won many a vote for her husband. I think if her son, our ex-mayor, could have seen his mother at the height of her matured beauty, he would have been justly proud.

The polls were to close at midnight on the last day of the fair. Excitement ran high as the hour approached. At ten minutes before the hour the McClellan vote was far ahead, and that party was already exulting, confident of success; but at five minutes before the final closing of the polls, the Union League, of

Philadelphia, telegraphed, ordering "five hundred votes for Grant," and the sword was his.

Indignant Democrats pronounced this an act of treachery; an ominous dissent spread over the restless crowd, and for a time it seemed as if there might be some dangerous demonstration. Only the general refinement and restraint of the surging, self-respecting crowd prevented an outbreak.

Mrs. McClellan was pitifully disappointed, as her vision of the White House grew dim; and after the popular election of Grant, and the defeat of McClellan, she indignantly declared that she would not live in such an ungrateful country. She actually lived abroad for some years but, like all good Americans, she was happy to return to enjoy the freedom of her own native land. . . .

ABBY IS QUITE WARMED UP ABOUT THE FAIR

Jane Newton Woolsey

New York was busily preparing for the great Manhattan Fair and it is not surprising to find at least part of the Woolsey family involved in the plans.

8 Brevoort Place, March 9, 1864.
We are all sitting together at the round table, Abby looking over the old letters from Point Lookout, and reading an incident occasionally aloud; Carry composing an address on her Bloomingdale orphans for their May anniversary. . . . Mary is very much engaged in her arrangements for the floral department at the Fair, and very much interested in it. All the ladies are agog for novelties. They will be charmed by the occasional communi-

cation from the Hospital at Fairfax.* We are to have a daily paper too, which is to beat the "Drum Beat"—*The Fair Champion.* Do send in poetry and prose and as many incidents as you can; get your doctor and the soldiers to send me an article for it, or letters for the Post Office. Send whatever you have to *me,* that I may have the pleasure of handing it to the committee on *literature!* Abby says, "Georgy, may I write out the German soldier-boy's dream, or any other extract from your old letters that is not too stale?" I am sure you will say yes. Abby is getting quite warmed up about the Fair; it is difficult not to feel so when everybody else is full of excitement about it. She is making a beautiful silk flag, a dozen or two of the new style of tidy-covers of muslin or embroidery edged with lace, beside lots of other little matters. Mary's idea of having garden hats of white straw, with broad ribbons, and their ends painted in flowers, is a pretty one, to be hung in her arbor of flowers. She is also painting a lot of little wooden articles. Every thing of hers is to be of the garden style. We find a use now for all our old flower baskets, rustic stands, etc., and a huge pile of them now stands ready to be carried to the flower department. My chair, the cover for which I was obliged to give up working, is under way, also three silk comfortables, all spandy new, one of your old gowns, lined with silk and beautifully quilted in scrolls and medallions by a Fishkill woman, and trimmed with ribbon quillings; also one dozen ladies' dressing-sacks of various styles; also, one India satin sofa cushion, one embroidered worsted do, four elegant toilette cushions, one doll's complete street dress (even to an embroidered pocket-handkerchief), one doll's stuffed chair, and other articles "too tedious to mention," are all under way. I dare say we shall all do our full part, both in making and purchasing.

Mrs. Chauncey has already sold her baby-house, Sarah Coit

---

* Jane Stuart Woolsey was the superintendent of Fairfax Hospital and Georgeanna was working there as a nurse.

tells me, for five hundred dollars! Kate Hunt has received her Parisian purchases for the Fair, for which she expects to realize a very large amount; says she is furnishing things to the amount of a thousand dollars! Eliza is coming down to-morrow. . . .

NEW YORK IS IN A DISGUSTING STATE OF FASHIONABLE EXCITEMENT

Harriet Roosevelt Woolsey

Hatty writes Jane and Georgy about the Fair.

Fishkill, Sunday.

We came up here last Thursday, and you may imagine it was somewhat of a relief to get Mother away from the everlasting Fair business that, for the last few weeks, has completely run her off her feet. . . .

New York is in really a disgusting state of fashionable excitement; nothing is talked of or thought of, or dreamed of but the big Metropolitan Fair! Mrs. Parker has her thousand-dollar tea sets to dispose of; Kate Hunt her two-hundred-dollar curtains; Mrs. Schermerhorn her elegant watches; and Mrs. Somebodyelse the beautiful jewelry sent from Rome for the Sanitary Commission. . . .

Mary [*Mary Woolsey Howland*] and Edward Potter have been very busy with their floral department, and Mary has made some "sweet" things, one very pretty garden hat, a pure white straw with wide ribbon streamers and a bunch of large pansies painted on the end of each, exquisitely painted and to bring in thirty dollars or more. . . .

All the committees are at swords' points, of course; the Restaurant ladies wish flowers in their department to which Mrs. George Betts, chairwoman of the Floral Committee, says "as sure as they do I will have oysters on the shell in mine and call them seaweeds. . . ."

"TAPS," MARY'S ARMY POEM, IS COMING TO SOMETHING

Abby Howland Woolsey

Abby to Jane and Georgy, on the same topic.

Wednesday, March 30.
I came from Fishkill yesterday afternoon with a trunk full of finished elegancies for the Fair. . . .

They have put up a tremendous and expensive building in 17th Street, reaching from Broadway to Fourth Avenue, which we saw yesterday for the first time. It is a long barrack with the end buildings one story higher, truss roof, huge oriel windows and fine planed plank throughout. This is supplementary to the other structures on 14th Street. . . .

"Taps," Mary's army poem, is really coming to something. Robert [*Mary's husband*] sends word that he has an appointment this afternoon to go to see about the illustrations for it with Mr. Potter. If it isn't ready for the FIRST DAY of the Fair it will still be in time. A discharged one-armed soldier, James Nichols, 5th N.H., has offered himself very promptly as salesman. . . .

13 Heading for the Front

MEANWHILE IN MARCH OF 1864 THE PENINSULA CAMPAIGN RE-ceived a fresh impetus when Grant, now a Lieutenant General, took over the personal command of the Armies of the East, and placed Sherman, on his way to Atlanta, in charge of the West and the South. Grant began reorganizing his Army. All non-combatants were ordered to leave. The sick were sent away from the field hospitals as fast as it was possible, and everything pointed to a speedy move for the Army of the Potomac. Even the Superintendent of Nurses sensed there were great plans afoot and uttered the prophetic note to her nurses that there would soon be severe fighting. She prayed earnestly that "the terrible war cloud might be lifted from the nation," and has-tened to gather her girls and bring them to the safety of the hospitals closer to Washington.

Many women left the front but they went right back again where they were needed—on the transports in particular. Trans-ports waited to convey the wounded to the hospitals in Wash-ington, and men were often taken on board in a dying condition. The hard necessity for immediate removal proved the death of many who had to be closely packed in cabins and on deck be-cause of limited space. Georgeanna Woolsey had an understand-ing with the United States Sanitary Commission that they were to call on her at any time for hospital service at the front. On May 12, immediately after the Battles of the Wilderness, a courier arrived at Fairfax Seminary where she was on duty with her sister Jane, to summon her. She left at once by boat down

281

the Potomac for Fredericksburg. Anna Holstein's husband left Philadelphia on May 9 with a number of Sanitary Commission agents to go directly to the front and wait for the wounded who were expected in large numbers after the Army crossed the Rapidan. Heavy rains had made the roads "horrible even for Virginia," and with many discomforts inevitable in addition to having to sleep on the damp earth, Anna thought she would remain at home until the weather got more settled. But as "battles were occurring daily, and soldiers falling by thousands," she could not stand the inaction, and on May 18 left home and set out for Belle Plain.

It seemed that everyone was heading for the front.

On the last day of May, Dorothea Dix called for Sophronia Bucklin and the other nurses at the tented hospital at Camp Stoneman. She brought them each a "cape and shaker" for one dollar a set, and escorted them to the Sixth Street wharf in Washington to take the boat to White House Landing where men lay on the ground "with blood oozing from their torn flesh, and worms literally covering the festering wounds."

The work of the Sanitary Commission was said never to have been as effective in the East as during the spring of 1864. Supplies were on hand to meet each emergency and this was particularly evident in the bloody battles of the Wilderness—Spotsylvania, Cold Harbor, and Petersburg—where resistance on the part of the Confederates was desperate and the Union losses heavy. By means of two steamboats, two barges, and forty-four four-horse wagons of its own, the Sanitary Commission conveyed two hundred tons of stores to advantageous points while it employed two hundred relief agents in personal service to the wounded.

In May also, the United States Sanitary Commission organized an Auxiliary Relief Corps to supplement the Field Relief Corps, and to look after the wounded left behind in hospitals as the Army moved on. Carefully selected agents responsible to a superintendent gave personal care to the wounded by meeting them, as they were brought in ambulances, with proper food and stimulants—"Our precious flasks," Katharine P. Wormeley wrote, "they do good service at every turn." The new Corps saw to it that the wounded were provided comfortable transportation, accompanied them to the hospitals, and looked after them there, meeting "both their physical and moral wants." Sometimes there were as many as one hundred and fifty men and women engaged in this work, "educated" gentlemen and "refined" women who performed outstanding service. This corps established "feeding stations" to meet the long trains of ambulance "full of famishing wounded" en route to hospitals. At Belle Plain and Fredericksburg after the Battles of the Wilderness, the Field Relief Corps "performed the duties of skilled nurses," and had their share of martyrs who were "treacherously shot by Mosby's guerrillas." The casualties were so great that every woman near the front, witnessing their appalling number, felt the urge to do her part. Many wives of the generals offered their services during the crises. Julia Dent Grant wanted to serve as one of Lincoln's daughters of mercy and felt deeply frustrated at being denied this privilege. "I would gladly have joined . . . in all . . . works of devotion; but the General forbade it, saying when I returned from the hospitals laden with petitions and heartbreaking stories: "Julia, cease, cease; I cannot listen; I hear this all day, every day, and must have some rest from all this sorrow and misery. If you insist on going again to the hospitals, I will have to send you home!"

From May 3 to May 12 the Union Army suffered a loss of thirty-three hundred killed and thirty thousand wounded, and the Sanitary Commission was busy aiding Dr. Cuyler, the efficient Medical Director, in relieving their suffering. At Port Royal, White House, and City Point, their work went on with an equal amount of efficiency. A mass meeting was held in New York early in May at which the women pledged to wear nothing imported from abroad during the war.

On June 3, Grant ordered a frontal assault at daybreak on the enemy forces. The assault lasted just ten minutes and "in those six hundred seconds the Army of the Potomac lost five thousand men and went reeling back to its lines, wounded and bleeding." Cold Harbor came next, and proved to be a "racking defeat" for the Federals. The press called the general "Butcher Grant," but that did not stop him. He "kept his power of movement," and on the evening of June 15 ordered his troops to "slam through" to Peterburg and the "long-drawn-out" siege began.

EVERYTHING WAS IN READINESS FOR THE OPENING CAMPAIGN

Julia Susan Wheelock

Julia ruminated at this point that her stay with the Army, notwithstanding the many sad scenes so often witnessed and the lonely hours sometimes experienced, was rather pleasant than otherwise. She was eager to get back to Washington, but remained in Fairfax Seminary Hospital until she had disposed of a new supply of goods, and took in the review of the 2nd Corps.

The review of the Second Corps on the 22nd of April, by General Grant, was a grand sight. It was estimated that there were fifty thousand troops on review that day. Then, in addition to these, were the almost endless lines of ambulances and army wagons, all having been repaired and newly painted; everything was in readiness for the opening campaign. To one unaccustomed to seeing large armies, it would seem that this corps alone was sufficient to meet and successfully resist whatever force could

be brought to oppose it; and yet what a small part of the vast
army of the Union, and only about one third of the Grand Army
of the Potomac!

The morning of the 23rd, I bade "good-by" to the few sick
left in the hospital and returned to Washington. The day was
warm and pleasant; yet my heart was sad, for it took no great
stretch of the imagination to look forward into the midst of the
terrible conflict about to begin, and to see many of the brave
and the noble fall; to see the wounded and slain by thousands,
scattered far and near, with the advancing and retreating armies
marching and countermarching over their mangled bodies, the
bones of multitudes being left to bleach upon the plain and the
earth made red with human gore. Then the thought of the bitter
grief and unavailing tear which would so soon succeed the
long suspense and anxious fears which filled every home, if not
every heart, in our land, left little room for other than sad reflections. But every picture, however dark, has its bright side, and
so had this fearful one. The hope of victory illumined its dark
background.

*A few weeks after her return to Washington, Julia left for Belle
Plain on the steamer* Wenonah *with hospital supplies and food.*

May 12, 1864.

At six o'clock this morning, the *Wenonah*, richly laden with
hospital stores and volunteer laborers, left Alexandria and
steamed down the Potomac; for Washington is soon passed,
Mount Vernon left in the distance, and other places of less importance appear and recede from view.

As we near our place of destination, cannonading is heard,
rapid and heavy. A terrible battle is raging. Oh! how we long for
"the wings of the morning," that we may fly to the relief of the
wounded; but our anxiety does not accelerate our speed. About

one o'clock we anchor a short distance from Belle Plain, where we remain until nearly dark, when we are all taken on board the *Young America,* and carried over to the landing, but we cannot go ashore, as we would be entirely without shelter for the night, and the rain, which has been falling all the afternoon, still continues.

Before leaving the *Wenonah,* it was suggested by someone that we have a prayer-meeting, and that those wishing to attend would assemble in the cabin which in a few moments was filled to its utmost capacity with delegates from both the Sanitary and Christian Commissions, the ladies on board, and officers and soldiers. . . . Among the ladies present was one whose name has become a household word in thousands of homes throughout our land, because of her untiring efforts in behalf of the sick and wounded. I refer to Miss Clara Barton, of ——, Massachusetts. . . .

Nine o'clock next morning we were taken into a barge and carried ashore. The wounded were arriving by hundreds, and I may say thousands, to await transportation to Washington. The two great Commissions and a few State Reliefs were there with abundant supplies of food; so all hands went to work feeding those poor, suffering, half-starved soldiers with crackers, hot coffee, and light bread—which we cut into slices and spread with apple butter. Thus we worked on, wading through mud to the top of our boots until noon, when, in company with Mrs. Johnson, I started with part of our goods for Fredericksburg—transportation being furnished us through the kindness of Lieutenant Chase, of the Ambulance Corps. The mud was deep and the roads badly cut up; but fortunately we did not share the fate of some of the wounded, whose ambulances were overturned on their way to Belle Plain. It was after dark when we reached the Rappahannock, which we crossed on pontoons, and nearly eight o'clock when we arrived at the headquarters of the

Christian Commission in the "bloody city" of Fredericksburg. On our way we met several thousand prisoners captured by the Second Corps the day previous. Among these were Generals Edward Johnson and George H. Stewart. It was said that General Johnson was so affected as to shed tears when General Hancock extended to him his hand after he was taken, declaring that he preferred death to captivity. But the other, with an air of haughtiness, replied: "I am General Stewart, of the Confederate army, and under present circumstances I decline to take your hand." General Hancock's dignified reply was: "And under any other circumstances, General, I should not have offered it."

We, with three other ladies who were on a similar mission, found quarters for the night in the parlor of the worthy (?) ex-Mayor Slaughter's fine residence, upon whose carpet we had the honor of sleeping! Being very tired, we slept soundly, in spite of our hard bed. Part of the building was used for a hospital. Mrs. Slaughter was still there, but her husband, not caring to fall into the hands of the "hated Yankees," had left for parts unknown.

I TOSSED ROSES AND SNOWBALLS OVER THE MEN

Georgeanna M. Woolsey

Georgeanna reports to her sister Jane from Belle Plain on the Potomac, May 13, 1864, about her experiences during part of the Battles of the Wilderness.

On the Sanitary Commission boat pulling up to the shore. . . . the Government flatboat of horses and cavalry recruits. . . . There are no docks and the supplies are landed by pontoons—a constant stream of contrabands passing with bags of grain and barrels of pork on their shoulders. Doctors Agnew, Douglas, and

Cuyler are here. We have a feeding station on shore and another two miles away where ambulance trains halt sometimes for hours. The mud is frightful and the rain coming on. We are to take the return ambulance train for Fredericksburg. . . .

Just as I finished, the train of ambulances arrived *from* Fredericksburg. Nothing I have ever seen equals the condition of these men; they have been two or three days on the train and no food. We have been at work with them from morning until night without ceasing, filling one boat, feeding the men; filling another and feeding them. There's no sort of use in trying to tell you the story. I can scarcely bear to think of it.

All the "Invalid Corps" from our hospital who marched off that day are down here guarding prisoners: Generals Stuart and Bradley Johnson among them. The wounded arrived in ambulances, one train a day, but the trains are miles long, plunged in quagmires, jolted over corduroys, without food, fainting, filthy, frightfully wounded; arms gone to the shoulder, horrible wounds in face and head. I would rather a thousand times have a friend killed on the field than suffer in this way; it is worse than White House, Harrison's, or Gettysburg. We found thirty-five dead in the ambulances yesterday, and five more died on the stretchers while being put on the boat. Mules, stretchers, army wagons, prisoners, dead men, and officials all tumbled and jumbled on the wretched dock, which falls in every little while and keeps the ambulances waiting for hours. We fed all the five boats that got off yesterday. There is no *government* provision for this beyond bread: no coffee, soup, cups, pails, or vessels of any kind for holding food. The men eat as if they were starving. We are ordered to Fredericksburg, where there is more misery than here. . . .

All right. Hard work, dirt and death everywhere. . . .

Men are brought in and stowed away in filthy places called distributing stations. I have good men as assistants and can have more. We go about and feed them; I have a room of special cases, besides the station; three of these died last night. They had been several days on the field after being shot, in and out of the Rebels' hands, taken and retaken. The townspeople refuse to sell or give, and we steal everything we can lay our hands on, for the patients; more straw-stealing, plank-stealing, corn-shuck-stealing; more grateful suffering patient men. . . .

May 22 (1864).
No confusion was ever greater. Tent hospitals have been put up and the surgeons ordered *not to fill them*. Orders came from Washington that the railroad should be repaired, then orders came withdrawing the guard from the road. Medical officers refuse to send wounded over an unguarded road. Telegram from Washington that wounded should go by boat. Telegram back that wounded were already over the pontoons, ready to go by rail if *protected*. Telegram again that they should go by boat. Trains came back to boat, river falling. One boat got painfully off; second boat off; ambulance trains at many hospital doors; got on train and fed some poor fellows with egg nog; moved on with the slow-moving procession; at every moment a jolt and a "God have mercy on me," through the darkness over the pontoons to the *railroad* again! I cooked and served today 926 rations of farina, tea, coffee, and good rich soup, chicken, turkey, and beef out of those blessed cans.

The government rations are drawn this way: The contract surgeon in charge of a little shop or room full of wounded reports to the surgeon in charge of a *group* of such; this officer reports to the surgeon of the division, the surgeon of the division to the corps surgeon; the corps surgeon draws on the commissary for the number of rations he needs for the day. It has often been ten o'clock at night before dinner was ready.

You may easily see how important the *irregular* supplies of the Sanitary Commission and other organizations have been.

We are lodged with a fine old lady, mild and good, in a garden of roses. We board ourselves. We have crackers, sometimes soft bread, sometimes beef. Last night we had a slice of ham all around. The town will be deserted in a few days. We are sweeping and cleaning Mrs. ——'s rooms to leave the old lady as well off as we can, for all her slaves have packed their feather beds and frying pans and declare they will go with us. . . .

Augur's reinforcements have passed through; as the troops went forward they were met by the ambulances from the front full of wounded men who thrust out their hands and waved and weakly cheered them.

Mrs. ——'s house has a large oldtime garden full of roses. . . . We begged and received permission to take all we could gather and filled the baskets and trays and skirts of our gowns with snowballs, lemon blossoms, roses yellow, white, and red. The 8th New York Heavy Artillery was in the advancing column. In the headstall of Colonel Porter's horse I fastened a knot of roses and tossed roses and snowballs over the men. They were delighted. "In FREDERICKSBURG!" they said; "O! give me one," "Pray give me one," "I will carry it into the fight for you," and another "I will bring it back again."

Three days afterwards the ambulances came, and in them came some of the same men, shattered, dying, and dead. We went out, but this time it was with pails of soup and milk punch; one and another recognized us—all were cheery enough. "A different coming back, Ma'am, no roses today"; and one said, pointing over his shoulder, "The Lieutenant is there on the stretcher, and he's brought the flowers back as he promised." I went to his side, hoping to help a wounded man. The Lieutenant lay dead, with a bunch of roses in the breast of his coat.

THE SANITARY COMMISSION WAS HERE BEFORE THE WOUNDED

Anna Holstein

The wharf was crowded with wounded, waiting transportation to Washington; in twenty-four hours all were removed; and we left on a Sanitary Commission steamboat, in company with other vessels—all convoyed by a United States gunboat. The shores of the bay and rivers were at that time infested by guerrillas, and as the Rebels had a wholesome dread of these *boats*, in their armed defense was our only safety. At 7 P.M., May 26, anchored at Port Royal; during the night, a barge loaded with government hay was fired by the Rebels—it was supposed with the intention of its drifting out among the vessels, and thus destroying much valuable property; fortunately the others could be kept away from it, and no further damage was done. Very early in the morning went on shore, and here had the pleasure of finding Mr. H., who had preceded us by a few hours, with others, was already busily at work.

The Sanitary Commission, with its admirably arranged system of "relief," was here *before* any wounded were brought in; and when the long trains began to arrive, hot coffee, farina, crackers, etc., were in readiness to hand to the exhausted, famished sufferers before they were lifted from the ambulances. *Two thousand* were now here awaiting transportation; the first food and care *all* had upon their arrival was due to them. Night and day—taking turns to sleep—the work of preparing and distributing food among them was continued. Within a few moments after we landed, a long train of ambulances came in sight; and finding they were moving toward a little Methodist church, we wended our way thither, taking as much as we could carry for their present relief. By the time the first man was lifted out, the little building was in readiness to receive them; benches and stove removed, it was soon crowded to its utmost capacity. Very grateful were they for the trifling relief we gave them; no straw, few blankets, and no pillows used in this hasty transfer arrangement, yet no murmuring word escaped them.

A fine-looking Massachusetts man, with a bone crushed from the knee down—where mortification was just commencing—asked in a whisper, as they were placing him within the little chancel: Could I give him some kind of stimulant to keep from fainting? The pain was agonizing. The little tin cup was soon filled, and as quickly drained; with the momentary strength it gave, he could better endure the rearranging of splints and bandages. The surgeon shook his head as he looked at the discolored limb, and to the soldier's urgent entreaties that it might be taken off without a moment's delay, replied "it could be done better on the boat"; but added, when beyond his hearing, "the morning would find him out of the reach of pain."

Noticing a neat-looking church that was not a hospital, with a guard in front, we entered and found it to be the Episcopal church. Upon opening the prayerbook on the desk at the "Prayer for all in Authority," found that the words "the President of the United States" were *cut out*. By it laid a manuscript copy of prayers for the Rebel government. Telling the guard he might look or not, as he chose, that I intended to take that manuscript, and send to the Sanitary Fair, then open in Philadelphia—first reading it aloud for the *benefit* of those present and putting in its place a leaf upon which were the prayers set forth by our beloved Bishop Potter, for the army. That they might not be mistaken in what it was, wrote upon the margin, "Prayers for the Union Armies of the United States, by Bishop Potter, of Pennsylvania." The exchange was a fair one—the Rebels, it is hoped, profiting by the sound doctrine which was given—for their erring prayers.

The burial of the wounded who died at this transfer post was intrusted to the Sanitary Commission. Every soldier was carefully interred, the burial service used for all, the grave marked and numbered, and all money, valuables, and other articles found upon his person forwarded to Washington, to await the orders of relatives and friends. A plan of the ground was left with an old colored man living near, and the care of the graves given to him—for the purpose of aiding friends who came for their remains, and knew nothing of any other direction they might have. The same plan, with the numbered graves, was retained by the Sanitary Commission so that, in case the marks were removed, they could *positively* and certainly be identified.

Last March, Mr. H. went to Port Royal, for the purpose of pointing out the resting place of a Rhode Island soldier, and found that three days after our troops left the town, Rebel cavalry entered it—trampling down every headboard, destroying the graves as much as possible, and threatening to hang old George, if he put them in order. With the numbered plan in Mr. H.'s possession, all marks having been removed, by counting and measurement the spot was readily found; the skeleton remaining as it had been placed, with his knapsack at his feet.

On the 29th of May, left Port Royal with a fleet of seventy-five vessels bound for White House, on the Pamunkey, where the wounded were now to be sent. Vessels loaded with troops for the front were continually meeting us, far outnumbering those who had been sent home weighted down with the wounded "soldiers of the Republic." As they passed, all were cheering heartily; no note of despondency, as they came within sound of the conflict.

The evening of the 30th, landed at White House; found Gen. Butler's command here, on their way to the front; within twelve hours, some of his wounded were brought back; and from that date, much more rapidly than tents could be erected to shelter them, they were sent on. Day and night the interminable trains continued, bringing thousands of wounded men, with the dust and smoke of battle yet upon them. *Acres* of ground were soon covered with bleeding, mangled men, who had so lately stood unflinching mid the storm of Rebel shot and shell; now as bravely they endured suffering, while needing every comfort—thousands not even shielded from the burning sun.

The work of waiting upon them continued uninterruptedly, all resting in turn; sleep was almost impossible, as every spot of ground was covered, close up to the canvas, with soldiers who had crept there for shelter. Our duties were many and various: the preparation of food and drinks, directing and overseeing our diet kitchen, occasionally busy for hours among the wounded.

One morning as I came out of our tent very early, before the bustle of the day had commenced, a soldier came walking fœbly, leaning upon a comrade's shoulder, and inquired: Would I dress his arm? it was untouched since first bandaged upon the field, and he knew was in offensive, bad condition, *filled with creeping life!*

The man said truly, it looked *bad*; and I shrank from the task, but persevered until it was nicely cleansed and dressed. Then with a clean "Sanitary shirt," the sufferer was delighted and happy, and overwhelming in his thanks. The sincere, heartfelt gratitude of those for whom such trifling services were rendered was ample recompense. Their earnest words of thanks were often more than could be borne—destroying, for the moment, the composure which was all-important. As the work of attending to that soldier went on, hundreds of others, reclining upon the ground, were intently watching the process.

Eager for *their* turn, one after another came slowly up, with the same query from all: Would the lady dress their wound?

A rough-looking Irishman among the number, having a fearful-looking wound in his head, said he could bear any pain I gave him, if the doctors did not dress it;—while in the midst of it, one of our best and most experienced surgeons made his appearance; observing what was going on, came to my relief, and to the utter dismay of the poor fellow, took the sponge out of my hand to show me how much too tenderly and carefully the work was done; at every movement of the sponge in his hand, the soldier's head bent and shrank beneath the touch, but not one word of complaint escaped him; as the doctor moved away, his thanks were *not* for the kindness shown him, but that he was *gone*, and that my unskillful hands would now finish. At this hour the regular dressers commenced their work, and the one who had usurped their office gladly disappeared among the heaps of edibles which filled the shelter nearest us. . . .

THE PETERSBURG EXPRESS SENT ITS COMPLIMENTS

Anna Holstein

On June 15, Mr. and Mrs. Holstein walked the mile from what had been the camp, to the wharf. Surgeons, nurses, attendants, and corps officers crowded the Montauk, *a Government vessel. On Anna's boat and on the canal boats which were lashed to its sides there were six hundred people. The fleet was hardly out of sight when Rebels attacked the small force left behind to guard the trains. Fortunately, a portion of Sheridan's cavalry appeared in time to rout the enemy.*

The boats steamed down the Pamunkey, anchored at West Point and the York River overnight, and at daybreak moved on down the York. They were short of rations, a mistake having

been made about the supplies bing placed on the wrong boat—
a load of iron bedsteads sent in their place.

The morning of the 17th [*June*], the men still short of rations, and trouble threatening, the Sanitary Commission gave them the pork and "hard tack" with coffee which had been provided in case of need. This restored peace and order again. Soon after we came up with the rest of the fleet anchored below Fort Powhatan; an order was sent to the supply boat for rations and no further difficulty occurred. Here we were detained while General Grant was crossing with his army to the south side of the James River. The pontoon bridges upon which they passed were the objects on which all eyes were fastened. The roads leading to the river could be traced by the clouds of dust which hung heavily over them. This was the *second* time we had seen that grand army moving in "battle array." In the evening signal lights were seen flashing upon the hilltops and from their camping grounds; the shipping was beautifully illuminated with various colored lanterns; and though in the midst of war, the river with its numerous lights had a gay, holiday look.

On the 18th of June the pontoons were removed, and we passed on up the James; at 1 P.M. landed at City Point; the town filled with wounded. In the evening walked through the dust two miles to the site selected for the hospital, which is a wheat field on the Appomattox. The continued heavy firing near Petersburg plainly heard. A few tents were arranged for the surgeons, nurses, etc., and in refreshing sleep all else was soon forgotten.

In the morning *our* rations were very scanty—we had but the remains of what we brought with us from White House. Before a stove could be had, or caldrons in readiness, those who were slightly wounded came straggling in; soon the number increased; and then trains came in sight and were unloaded upon the ground. Battle-smoked and scarred, dusty, weary, and hungry the poor fellows came—looking longingly at anything to eat; from early morning until late at night the scene was the same as at White House—thronged with wounded. . . . It was impossible with the few conveniences at hand to prepare food for all that number. The night was far advanced before we were ready for the rest we so much needed, and then retire, with wounded and dying men lying upon the ground close to our tent. How heartless it sounds, at *home*, to sleep under *such* circumstances!

The next day commenced at 5 A.M. Nothing before us all the day but wounded; wounded men at every step you take. Three times that day we fed *six hundred men* (when the number is given we know it to be accurate as it is taken from the morning report at headquarters). . . .

The first boatload sent off today, June 20th; but others directly fill their places. All that makes endurable this voluntary life of toil and saddening scenes is the simple fact that we know some lives are brightened by the care we strangers give to sick or wounded men. . . . The weather is now intensely warm, June 24th. . . .

The contrabands have been coming to the hospital in large numbers, for protection . . . in their hasty flight they pick up the very articles we would think they did not need—probably leaving what would be useful. A group of fifty just passed, well loaded: one with a bed upon his shoulders; another a box as large as he was; many of the women carrying cooking utensils; a little fellow of six or eight, wearing a gentleman's coat, the the skirts sweeping the ground, a stovepipe hat upon his head— the style of twenty years ago—and, above all, a huge cotton umbrella! Many of the young girls wore flounced silk dresses evidently "confiscated" from *Missus's* wardrobe. Their arrival quite enlivened the hospital; they were in every direction greeted with continued shouts, which mark of attention seemed gratifying to them. Rations are furnished them by government, and tents supplied for their use; all who wish to remain are employed in some way; the rest are sent to Washington.

July 4th, all the North expecting some great battle or success. . . . Salutes are heard from every quarter in honor of the day; and at the front, the *Petersburg Express* sent its compliments into the town, at intervals of fifteen minutes, to remind them of the day we celebrate.

A steam fire engine has been furnished to force water from the river to the hospital, for sprinkling the streets and to cool the heated tents. Gen. Grant was walking through the hospital a few days since, and observing how much they suffered from dust, said his wounded men must be better cared for; the streets must be watered, if it took a regiment of men each day to do it. As his word is law, the engine came: a large force of Negroes have it in charge, and already the good results are seen. Water tanks were afterward built, more engines and hose obtained, and all day long the street sprinklers are at work. The dust continues fearfully deep; it is the only thing that moves about freely.

The third division of the Sixth Corps marched by today, to embark on transports; going North, it is said, to look after Ewell's Corps—that, we hear, is destined for another raid upon Pennsylvania. Numbers of "volunteer aids" have been obliged to give up their work here; many ill with fever; Mr. H. obliged to go home for a few days' rest, thoroughly worn out with the arduous labors which have occupied him since early in the spring. Each Corps hospital has its share of the colored population: our settlement for them is on the river bank; from there we hear their voices as they join in their evening worship; going into their meeting, we found them kneeling upon the earth, praying earnestly that "God would bless good President Lincoln, and all de great Union armies; that He would take care of de

breddern and sisters, now they be in a foreign land"; then, in-
terrupting the prayers, a voice commenced:

> O, praise an' tanks! De Lord he come
> To set de people free!

Prayers and their simple music were strangely blended, but
all in the most devout manner.

On the 14th of July, a floor was put in our tent; previous to
this, the deep dust was the only carpet we had; an arbor of ever-
green branches was also placed at the two entrances; now sheltered from the scorching sun, we are very comfortable—quite
luxurious living, and certainly we should never complain while
sick and wounded lie upon the ground.

July 30th. Rebel fort blown up at seven this morning; the
cannonading and firing during the night which preceded the
explosion were fearfully distinct, so much so as to prevent sleeping. Large numbers of wounded were brought in today, principally to the Ninth Corps and the colored hospital. Among
the colored troops, four out of every five of their officers were
either killed or wounded; yet the men behaved bravely.

The streets of this city of tents are gradually assuming a much
more cheerful appearance: arbors are erected at the front and
rear of the tents, thus forming a continuous shelter and pleasant walk for the patients.

August 4th was the national fast-day; the camp unexpectedly
short of rations, so many fasted who would not otherwise have
obeyed the President's proclamation; a sermon at headquarters,
in the evening, by the First Division chaplain. A party composed of the ladies in the hospital were invited, with the surgeons, to take a trip up the James in the Sanitary Commission
boat; through the dilatoriness of one of the ladies, all were detained; when we at length reached the wharf, it was only in
time to see the boat slowly steaming on its way with not more

than eight or ten of the invited party on board. Disappointed and sadly vexed, we retraced our steps; but when, a few hours after, they returned with the mournful tidings that, near Turkey Bend, they were fired upon by guerrillas—the engineer instantly killed, two Sanitary Commission agents wounded, one mortally —we saw how providential was our detention; had all gone, the conspicuous dress of the officers would have made them a fair mark for the Rebels; with a larger company, the loss of life would probably have been greater. The boat was obliged to put on more steam, and proceed on her way until they came to the gunboat which brought them in safety beyond the reach of Rebel bullets. The large Sanitary Commission flags were floating from the mast, conclusive evidence to the guerrillas that the vessel belonged to that noble organization whose field of labor embraced all the wounded within our lines; Union and Rebel alike kindly care for.

August 9th, a terrible explosion occurred on board the ordnance barge at City Point; at the moment, I was occupied in the arbor in front of our tent, and so had an unobstructed view; with the first shock stooped to the earth, as though struck upon the head; the tent quivered as though it must fall; it seemed so very near that the first thought was, the Rebels are shelling the hospital; finding that not correct, the next surmise was, General Grant's headquarters have been blown up. There now rose to a great height a dense column of smoke, spreading out at the top in form of an umbrella, and from it fell a shower of death-dealing missiles; it literally rained muskets; shells flew in all directions; some passing over us, exploded beyond the hospital. The scene upon the bluff near the landing was sickening: dismembered bodies were strewn about the ground, the dead and dying side by side; the wounded were soon gathered up and brought to the hospital.

The cause of the accident could not be accounted for, until

the trial of the villain Wirz. A Rebel witness related how he had done it: making some excuse to see the captain, was told he was not on board, insisting the package that he had for him could be given to no one else, asked permission to place it upon his table; as he did so, arranged the fuse, and withdrew to a place of safety. The explosion soon occurred, as he anticipated, destroying many lives, principally among the colored laborers, the others having gone to dinner. A large amount of government property was destroyed, and many buildings.

The fight at Deep Bottom sent to us many wounded, the most serious cases taken without delay to Washington. The day before the battle, as the men marched wearily by the hospital, covered with dust, ignorant of their destination, all were exulting in the prospect of going to Pennsylvania; still further to confirm them in the belief, they were embarked at City Point and the transports started down the river; proceeding on their way until darkness concealed them from view, they silently turned about, and moved up again, to be taken into the battle. While it was raging, a company of the 57th New York was commanded by a sergeant; unwilling to occupy the position, as his comrades told me, he was lagging behind; a corporal near him could bear it no longer, and stepped out to lead the men as though he had always been accustomed to command. Gen. Barlow sat upon his horse, quietly observing the whole manoeuvre; and when the fight was over, sent for the corporal, telling him at such an hour to report to Gen. Hancock's headquarters. The man left, wondering what had been done; and when he returned according to orders, the two generals consulted together for a few moments, the corporal was called in— and when he left the tent, it was with the rank of captain, as a reward for his gallant conduct. He again entered the battle, filling the position he so well merited; but within an hour fell dead, shot through the heart. . . .

GOD HELP US ALL

Harriet Foote Hawley

On May 31, 1864, Hatty wrote of her stay at Armory Square Hospital, where the wounded were brought from the bloody battles of the Wilderness.

I have not had one minute I could call my own except a very little time when I went and laid down and washed and rested. I find that I *must* have that rest during the day or be sick. First I worked straight through, from six in the morning till ten at night, but, of course, I couldn't do that long. But you've no idea of the terrible need of it—I thought I knew something about it before but I didn't know *anything*. I know no words to describe the amount and intensity of this suffering I see around me every moment. . . . I stopped to look at the peaceful face of a poor fellow who had just died eight feet from my chair. One leg had been amputated above the knee ten days ago, and he had suffered terribly and was much wasted. Thank God at least this poor body can suffer no more. . . .

Wednesday morning I came back only to find that another of my poor boys had died just at daylight. I felt hope for him, though I knew he was very low. . . .

Oh, if this baptism of blood does not purify this country and cleanse it of greed and selfish ambitions as well as of slavery, then the nation will deserve to become extinct—for pity's sake, help on this association of the ladies against dress.* The pledge to buy no more imported articles is none too strong. The movement ought to have been commenced three years ago. People give and give generously to the soldiers but I do not know of

* At a mass meeting of women early in May the women pledged to wear nothing during the war that was of foreign import.

one single family to retrench their expenses since this war broke
out. I do not know ten women who have really *denied* themselves of any comfort for the sake of giving to the soldiers. I
don't say it is because they are so selfish—but they don't realize
what this war is. I was shocked and pained at the insensibility I
saw everywhere when I came from the South in April. I am even
more grieved now that I have seen so much more of the un-
utterable misery that is slowly swelling up to flood all the country by and by. Don't think that I don't appreciate what is done.
But I am not so grateful for what is given. Not a day passes that
I am not filled with wonder and delight to see how generous
[*On the side of the letter Mrs. Hawley wrote here in parentheses:*
"Thursday morning: that stupid boy of mine has upset a bottle
of cologne all over my letters and papers."] people are, but they
can't give enough or fear enough just as it's impossible to keep
a hospital supply.

I find I'm in need of a strong calico dress. . . . Now, would
you be good enough to buy me a dark calico. . . . for I don't
want to frighten my boys with any pale thin face and couldn't
some dressmaker there make it up *by guess*, and so send it on by
express? I don't want to be pinched and I don't care what sort
of a waist is made. . . . I can't possibly leave my ward to hunt
up anything and all the ladies advise me to send East as there's
nothing to be bought here and no decent dressmaker. Kate is
too sick to send it (she doesn't gain very fast) and mother and
Mary have all they can do to live. So here I am, sorry to bother
you with all your cares, yet scribbling to do it rather than go
ragged and dirty. . . .

I don't think there's the least chance of Joe's coming on to
the Baltimore convention and, of course, I shall stay here if he
does not. . . . Mrs. Gideon Welles calls often to see me and
has twice brought strawberries enough for all my patients. She
is well known here, I find, for her constant visits and gifts to

the hospital. . . . There goes a stretcher upstairs into the upper
ward by which I know there has been another death up there.
God help us all.

MISS DIX KEPT UP THE FICTION OF APPOINTING
ALL THE ARMY NURSES

Georgeanna M. Woolsey

*In August, 1864, Georgy had been home in New York for a
while, when she and her sister Caroline were asked to go to
Beverly Hospital, fifteen miles from Philadelphia, to help put
in running order Dr. Wagner's new hospital for two thousand
men. Carry had not done any real hospital nursing until now,
but the family didn't feel they had the right to keep her home
when there were hundreds of badly wounded and few nurses to
be had.*

This set of regulations was promulgated this morning regarding "female nurses":

"All deliberations, discussions, and remarks having the object of expressing comparative praise, or censure, of the medical
officers of this hospital, or their individual course or conduct,
are positively prohibited." The provision against our "praise"
is truly judicious. C. and I have one hundred men in our wards,
all in bed. It is grimly amusing to hear the ward surgeon say
day after day, "Milk and eggs for thirty-eight." For two days
there have been no eggs at all, and the milk rations are always
short. The ladies are not allowed in the kitchen, or to have
anything to do with the food for the patients. No steak or po-
tatoes or milk punch come into this ward. We have opened a

private account for bread, and milk and butter and eggs, enough for this ward, with the village store. Our ward surgeon has gone to a horse race, which seems a pretty long one! The surgeon in charge is kind in manner and draws rations strictly according to army regulations; and seems to think that the stewards are the best persons to manage the food business. The object of the minor officer seems to be to subsist the men on nothing and avoid making a row. We cannot keep our men alive; eleven of them have died in three days. . . .

Rocking chairs were still our craze. The government furnished absolutely nothing for a sick man to sit on.

[*Hugh Lenox Hodge, who married Harriet Woolsey after the war, saw to it that the rockers were sent to Georgy and Carry.*] . . .

We had a good-natured laugh over a visit from Miss Dix, who, poor old lady, kept up the fiction of appointing all the army nurses. She descended upon Beverly for this purpose, when finding us already established without consultation with her, she served this printed assignment to duty—not only on me, but on Carry, whom she had never spoken to and knew nothing about!

Office of Superintendent of Women Nurses
Washington, D.C. August 30, 1864
Miss Woolsey (Carry) having furnished satisfactory evidence of her qualifications for the position of a "Nurse" in the employment of the Medical Department, U.S.A., is approved.
D. L. Dix, Superintendent
Assigned to duty at U.S. General Hospital, Beverly, New Jersey, 1864, upon application of Surgeon in Charge.

Caroline writes about the visit of a Christian Commission delegate to their hospital and the gloomy sermons on death he preached to the convalescents till her hair "stands on end."

He [the preacher] haunts the wards early and late when no one is on the lookout for visitors, loaded with pocket-handkerchiefs and *pickled quinces,* demanding all around who has the diarrhea, and quite pleased to find out that *no one* has and all glad to get the sour fruit, though in truth eleven of the men had died in three days of that chronic complaint. . . . If I owned a hospital no philanthropist should ever enter. I could have pounded two benevolent old ladies yesterday on a tour of "inspection" through my ward. One of my poor little boys, feverish and restless, tired of lying in bed for days and days, had crawled to the stove and been tucked up in one of our rocking chairs in his blanket. I had given him a hot drink and he had fallen into a doze when these elderly philanthropists arrived, shook him by the arm, yelling, "Poor fellow, what's the matter, fever? O! my! you're too near the stove; get right back to bed. There now, that's it, you're too weak to sit up." And so, having saved one life as they thought, passed on to the next.

Jane writes from her hospital on the Beverly situation:

I should think Beverly must be one of the worst conducted in the service except Willett's Point Government Hospital, Long Island, where in August I saw them handing about pieces of fat pork on newspapers, to wounded men for their dinners. . . .

SENT TO TAKE THE PLACE OF CLARA BARTON

Adelaide W. Smith

Young Ada felt she was missing something by not being at the front, and made many futile attempts to get a pass. Finally, through the Masonic Mission, she obtained one for herself and three assistants, from General Ben Butler. This pass gave her the eagerly desired "privilege and authority of going to the front." She remembered, in between attacks of mal de mer, that members of the medical profession were not always gentlemen. Eager to ascertain the virtues of her future boss, she managed to blunder into more than one embarrassing situation en route to General Butler's Hospital Department of the James, the tented Point of Rocks. Point of Rocks was located on a large plantation in Virginia, overlooking the Appomattox River. It is said to have been deserted by its owner when he first saw the advancing lines of the boys in blue "with glistening guns and bayonets." He had ordered up the mules, helped his family into the wagon, and driven off at once toward Petersburg.

We sailed (July 24, 1864) on the *Patapsco*, a government transport that had carried sick soldiers to New York, and was returning to City Point for orders, and were the only passengers on board.

Fatigue and the odor of bilge water induced intense "mal de mer," which, added to insubordination on the part of two of my assistants, caused the usual distress and despair.

The atmosphere of my stateroom was intolerable, and the captain kindly ordered a mattress placed on deck for me, where I was comparatively comfortable until I was obliged to stagger below on hearing of unseemly conduct on the part of the two nurses. I threatened, with good effect, to have the captain put them ashore at the first island we came to. Fortunately they did not know that we would sight no island on that short voyage. The third assistant, good Mrs. Dunbar, in her kindly motherly way, was my only comfort.

The captain had tried, in vain, to arouse me by an alarm that the *Alabama* was chasing us. But sea-sickness knows not even the law of self-preservation, and I replied, "I'd as lief as not go down by the *Alabama* or in any other way."

At night I refused to go below to my stateroom and bilge-water odor, quite regardless of the captain's perplexity. After some hesitancy, however, he gave me the only stateroom on deck. This was filled with the accoutrements of a Confederate officer whom, as a prisoner of war, the captain had just delivered over to the government prison at Fort Lafayette, in the narrows of New York Bay. I awoke at night in such perfect peace and comfort that for a time I imagined the *Alabama* had really run us down, and that I was now happy in heaven.

My staterom door had been left open for air, and stepping out on deck, I found there was no motion or sound, save a soft ripple of water against the bow. A full perfect moon cast a broad silvery path across the quiet waters, so intense that it seemed quite possible that Jesus had indeed walked upon the Sea of Galilee. There was no one in sight, nor was there a sound of anything living or moving, though the "watch" probably saw me leaning over the railing. We had anchored in the mouth of the James River, waiting for the pilot.

On the morning of July 29 we again anchored, this time before City Point, Virginia, at the junction of the James and Appomattox Rivers, headquarters of the United States armies in the field under command of General Grant.

I went ashore in a little boat with the captain, and reported to the Provost Marshal at headquarters, to show my pass from General Butler. The camp appeared rather shabby. There were only a few wooden buildings, used by army officers, a number of large tents and Negro cabins, with guards and officers running from one tent to another. City Point was a barren, almost treeless country of untilled land. The United States flag floated over a small house used by General Grant as headquarters.

A small, narrow, cigar-shaped, back-wheel boat, the *Gazelle*, returned with me to the *Patapsco*, and taking on board the three nurses, we steamed up the narrow Appomattox River, a monotonous sail of six miles between low bluffs and sparse foliage, to the hospital tents at Point of Rocks, which were pitched on the very brink of this malarious stream. This was General Butler's Hospital Department of the James.

For the first time I realized my strange position, and felt, when the *Patapsco* was out of sight, as if I had burned my bridges behind me. There were only a half dozen men and officers aboard. Feeling impelled to speak to a refined-looking man, wearing Major's shoulder straps, I found him very courteous. I remarked on my apprehension of the strangeness of the situation and said if I could feel assured that the surgeon in charge of Point of Rocks Hospital was a gentleman, I should have nothing to fear. I asked the Major if he knew that officer; he replied that he did, and thought I would find him a gentleman.

On reaching Point of Rocks Hospital, the Major offered to go ashore and send an ambulance for us, and this took us a short distance to the hospital tent wards, and to a small frame house near the Hospital Headquarters.

I called a passing orderly and reported at once with my Butler pass to the officer in charge, and found, to my consternation, while the color rose to the roots of my hair, that this man was the very Major to whom I had spoken on the boat. Rising and bowing politely, he said, "Miss Smith, I trust you will always find me a gentleman."

It was well for me that he was a gentleman, for I found myself in a very anomalous position, having been sent by the Masonic Mission to take the place of Clara Barton, who was already in charge of this work, but away at the time. I soon discovered that the Masonic Mission had taken advantage of Miss Barton's absence and—quite without authority—had sent me to take her place. The Major, Surgeon Porter, however, courteously invited me to remain until her return. . . .

14 At Last Men Dare to Hope

IN SEPTEMBER, GENERAL PHIL SHERIDAN DROVE THE CONFEDERATE
Army from Winchester, Virginia, and up the Shenandoah Valley. Lincoln wired "God bless you," and one hundred guns
were fired in his honor by the Army of the Potomac. Little Phil
went to Washington for a consultation with Secretary Stanton.
On his return he spent the night of the 18th in Winchester before rejoining his men and did not learn until morning of Confederate General Jubal Early's surprise attack on the Union
Army at Cedar Creek. From Winchester, "twenty miles away,"
he rode past retreating troops with ambulances and provision
wagons rolling North. Galloping along to the front, he called
out to his men along the way to turn back and fight some more.
At the sight of their beloved general the soldiers threw their
hats in the air, cheered in joy, and returned to battle. The victory was complete. The campaigns of the Shenandoah Valley
ended and the Army of the Shenandoah encamped at Winchester for the winter. Congress voted Sheridan a gold sword
and the thanks of a grateful nation. A hospital in Winchester
was named in his honor and the nurses hurried southward to
look after the wounded.

In the South, Atlanta had fallen and victory lay in Sherman's
path. An air of hope swept the country and Abraham Lincoln
was returned to office in the election on November 8.

HOW PRESIDENT LINCOLN RECEIVED THE NEWS
OF SHERIDAN'S VICTORY

Annie T. Wittemyer

Annie T. Wittemyer was born on August 26, 1827, in Sandy Springs, Adams County, Ohio. Her father, John C. Turner, was originally from Kentucky and her mother claimed to be a descendant of John Smith, a Virginia soldier of fortune.

At the age of twenty, Annie Turner became the bride of William Wittemyer, a merchant of Jacksonville, Ohio, and a man many years her senior. In 1850 the Wittemyers moved to Keokuk, Iowa where they had four children. Only one lived beyond infancy, their son Charles Albert.

In Keokuk, Annie found that many children were on the streets because their parents could not afford the school tuition. Quick to remedy the situation, she converted into a schoolroom one of the large upstairs rooms in the home she and her husband had built, hired a teacher, and collected the children into this free private school, which was continued until public schools were opened. The first bill for books was paid for by a wealthy Chicago man.

When the Civil War began, Annie was a widow. Her husband had left her very well provided for but this determined woman with snow-white hair and sparkling blue eyes, inherited perhaps from her Irish or Flemish ancestors, had no intention of staying on the home front. She lost no time in going to work in camps and hospitals set up near Keokuk and took an active part in bringing supplies to the battlefront.

Annie was loyally and generously sustained in her work by the women of Iowa, and was elected a Sanitary Commission Agent of the state by the Iowa legislature. Annie was responsible for the Special Diet Kitchen. She acted as unofficial field

worker for the Keokuk, Iowa, Soldiers' Aid Society. Calm, sensi-
ble, accustomed to leadership, she became a friend of many im-
portant officials, including General and Mrs. Grant, while
working in hospitals in both the West and East. When the
news of Sheridan's great victory was brought to President
Lincoln, Mrs. Wittemyer was sitting with him before an open
fireplace in the White House on a cool October evening. As an
illustration of his deep meditative mood, she said the orderly
bearing the message could not gain his attention for several mo-
ments although he kept repeating that he had a very important
message.

I was personally acquainted with President Lincoln and sat
talking with him in his public office when the telegram was
brought in, announcing General Sheridan's second victory in the
Shenandoah Valley which resulted in the defeat of General
Early.

When the messenger came in, Mr. Lincoln was talking very
earnestly; and although he laid down the telegram with the announcement, "An important telegram, Mr. President," Mr.
Lincoln took no notice of it.

The messenger went as far as the door of the room and, seeing that Mr. Lincoln had not taken up the telegram, he returned, and laying it a little nearer to him on the desk, repeated,
"An important telegram, Mr. President."

But as the President kept on talking and took no notice of it,
the messenger retired.

He was at that time talking of the sanitary condition of the
army; the relation of food to health and the influence of the
special diet kitchen system in restoring the soldiers to health and
its effects in lessening the number of furloughs.

I, too, talked earnestly; as, while pushing the work of the
special diet kitchens, I believed most heartily in furloughs. But,

earnest as I was, I was exceedingly anxious to know the contents of that telegram.

There was, during that interview, that faraway look in his eyes that those seeing could never forget. At last, he paused and took up the dispatch; and, after looking it over, read it aloud.

"This is good news, indeed," he said and a smile lit up his rugged features as he went on with his comments. "This Sheridan," he said, "is a little Irishman but he is a big fighter."

Soon after, I arose to take my leave. He, too, arose and stood like a giant before me as he extended his hand and said, "Well, success to you. Come in again."

I did not realize his greatness at that time but all the world knows that Abraham Lincoln will stand out a colossal figure as long as American history is read. A thousand years will not dim the luster of his name or fame.

WE ARRIVED IN WINCHESTER AFTER MIDNIGHT

Matilda E. Morris

In order to get to the front, Matilda Morris had to enlist with Dorothea Dix. In October, 1864, after going through considerable red tape, she and another nurse were given passes and transportation to Harper's Ferry, where they felt their services might be needed for Sheridan's Army in the Shenandoah Valley.

The passes were made out to take us to Winchester, Va., but we could not go for several days, as General Sheridan was there with his cavalry. We all remember the battle, and the victories he achieved in the Valley of the Shenandoah. In October, when things became a little more quiet, we started for Martinsburg. We had not gone more than half way when we had quite a thrilling adventure. Suddenly our train came to a standstill. The Rebels had been there the night before and torn up the tracks for miles, and wrecked and burned the train ahead of ours. There we were in a barren country, not a house in sight, and with the enemy all around us. The Rebels had made a mistake, and they were wild with disappointment. It was our train that had the pay car attached, and that was why we had so many soldiers aboard.

Report said that a lady had been burned; and as Miss Evans and myself were walking along the track, I found a piece of partly burned hair that surely had come from some woman's head. There was melted glass and iron all around, ruins everywhere; and we were glad when the road was repaired and we could leave that awful place, the sight of which made us nearly sick. We reached Martinsville late at night, very tired and hungry. The next day we started for Winchester, and oh, how it did rain!

But we never stopped for rain in war times. At the station was an ambulance train to take us the remainder of the distance. I think there must have been a thousand soldiers to guard the stores, for an officer had said, "The Rebs are thick as flies in August along that route." General Custer was with us, and several other officers whose names I did not learn. It was a dreadful march. The boys waded through mud and water the livelong day, but not a murmur could we hear. At noon we halted at a place called Bunker Hill. There was wood on one side and an open field on the other. It was a dreary-looking place. Soon after the train stopped we saw two men riding into the woods, and supposed they had gone as scouts. In a few minutes we heard a shot at no great distance, and soon saw the same men returning with a pig across the back of one of the horses. I never saw anything prepared to cook as soon as that pig. They did not stop to scald it, as the farmers do, but pulled off the whole skin, and in a short time the animal was in slices. In the meantime a fire had been started, and soon the coffee kettles and frying pans were on. I told Miss Evans I was going to have some of that meat for our dinner. She skeptically inquired how I should get it. I took a can of condensed milk and some salt, and soon made a trade. The boys seemed to enjoy the fun, and some of them carried us some coffee.

It was a cold, dreary ride, but after a great many halts and skirmishes we arrived at Winchester about midnight. The next day we reported to Dr. Hayden, at Sheridan Hospital, which was composed entirely of tents, some so low that we had to stoop to enter; but they were all full of badly wounded men. If the scene at Armory Square was dreadful, this was a thousand times more so. Here the men lay on the bare ground, with knapsacks, boots, or anything for a pillow that would raise the head. Passing along, I saw things that made me sick at heart. A young man not more than eighteen had both legs shot off. He could not live, yet he seemed cheerful. We did what we could for them with our limited means; but finally our supplies gave out, and even hard tack became a luxury. We were told to care for the Confederates as we did for our own, and we obeyed orders; but deep in my heart I could not feel the same.

We remained there until it was safe to move the men to Baltimore. We had hospital cars, which are a little wider than ordinary ones, and are placed on springs. They have on each side three tiers of berths or cots, suspended by rubber bands, and so arranged as to yield to the motion. I made two trips with this train, and the men said it went like a cradle. It was a pleasure to take care of so cheerful a company. My journey lasted two days and nights, and I think I never passed forty-eight hours so fraught with both sad and pleasant memories. . . .

15 The Darkest, Saddest Page of All

WHILE THE NORTH WAS REJOICING OVER ITS RECENT VICTORIES, Henry W. Bellows struck a somber note in a letter to General Grant on October 25, 1864. The letter was sent with five copies of the report of a Commission of Inquiry appointed by the United States Sanitary Commission "to look into the manner and motive of the treatment of our prisoners of war by the Rebel authorities." The sworn testimony on which the report rested was given in the Appendix. The Commission was applying to the government for permission to get in contact with the authorities at Richmond in order to send relief agents to the prisoners in Rebel hands. "They will doubtless refuse," Bellows wrote, "but it is all that is left to complete the record of their cruelty and neglect. . . . If you think any good can be done by sending copies of this report to General Lee, will you use your discretion in forwarding them and so add to the other favors for which the United States Sanitary Commission is already indebted to you. . . ."

When the released prisoners were sent to Annapolis, the women went there to look after them.

YOU WILL NEVER BE ABLE TO BELIEVE THE TRUE CONDITION
OF OUR PRISONERS

Harriet Foote Hawley

After the capture of Wilmington, North Carolina, Joseph Hawley, promoted to the rank of Brigadier General, was assigned to

the southwest portion of North Carolina with headquarters in
that city. When Harriet Hawley joined her husband, nine thou-
sand Union prisoners had just been sent there, released from
Andersonville and Florence. All of them were in need of food
and clothing, and three thousand required hospital treatment.
"A motley crowd of refugees—old men, women, and children,
white and black, ragged, helpless, and hungry"—followed in the
wake of the prisoners. Hospitals had to be set up in dwellings
and churches as disease increased and deaths multiplied. The
chief of the medical staff died and "of five professional lady
nurses from the North, three took sick and two died."

Surrounded by such sickness and suffering, the former Harriet
W. Foote rose to the emergency with the fortitude of Mary
Bickerdyke, and soon this frail creature had organized all the
women who wanted to help, superintended the making of
clothes, visited all the hospitals including those with the dread
smallpox cases, and, in her spare moments, did what she could
to help the refugees.

You know that over nine thousand of our prisoners were delivered to us here; and no human tongue or pen can describe
the horrible condition which they were in. *Starving to death,*
covered with vermin, with no clothing but the filthy rags they
had worn during their whole imprisonment—a period of from
five to twenty months; cramped by long sitting in one position,
so that they could not straighten their limbs; their feet rotted
off! O God! I cannot even now endure to speak of it.

Of course they brought the jail fever with them—it could not
be otherwise; yet they must be fed, and cleansed, and clothed,
and cared for. There were no hospital accommodations here
worth mentioning. There were not doctors enough, and those
here overworked themselves, and caught the fever and died.
Buildings of all sorts were converted into temporary hospitals,

and the nurses (enlisted men) fell sick at the rate of fifty a day. The chaplains worked as only Christian men can work; and they sickened too. Chaplain Eaton (Seventh Connecticut Volunteers) died, a real martyr. Mr. Tiffany (Sixth Connecticut) has barely struggled through a most terrible attack of the fever, and is slowly recovering. Another, whose name I cannot recall, is still very low, and can hardly be expected to live. Three out of the five lady nurses sent by Mrs. Dix have been very ill and one, Miss Kimball, died this morning, resigned and happy, as such a woman could not fail to be, yet leaving many friends to mourn for her, and a place here that no one can fill.

Dr. Buzzell, the general medical officer, and one who cannot be too highly spoken of, both as a man and a physician, died of the fever last week. Dr. Palmer has since followed him; but the terrible list of those dead and still sick of the fever is too long for me to try to write it. It is only within the last five days that they have received any hospital supplies: previous to that time many of the sick men were lying on straw spread on the floor, although the Union citizens have given and done all in their power. What could a few families do, from their private supplies, towards furnishing three thousand nine hundred men with beds and bedding? Besides these, there were the convalescent ones to be clothed. Thank God! the vessel that the Sanitary Commission sent came soon, with nine thousand shirts and drawers, so that when I first saw them, they had at least so much in the way of clothing.

We got possession of twelve hundred yards of cotton cloth and a bale of cotton. I called a meeting of the benevolent ladies of the place. The Sanitary Commission gave us thread, and in a week's time the materials were made up: one hundred and thirty-eight pillow-cases, one hundred and fifty-three pillows, eighty-four bed sacks, and as many sheets. And now the hospitals are all tolerably well supplied.

Of course many have been sent North—all who were able to go—and many have died on the road; yet there are still many here. And, as if this were not misery enough for one poor little city, Sherman sent here six thousand refugees—black and white, old men, women, children, and babies, with nothing but what they could carry on their backs, or, as in a few cases, drag in a little old mule cart.

And these poor wretches must be housed and fed, with the city already crowded, and the fever spreading among the citizens. It is impossible for you to imagine the misery which has stared me in the face at every step since I have been here. I can find no words to describe it. Why, this very afternoon I carried food and wine to a woman who had been lying sick, for *three days*, on a little straw in an old wagon, in an open shed, discovered accidentally by one of our officers. Of course this is not an everyday case, but it is a wonder that it is not. Many of these refugees have been sent North, and many more will be; but the mere fact of their being thus transported involves a vast amount of labor, which must mostly fall upon the soldiers; and the garrison here is small, as small as it can be kept, and do the necessary work and guard duty. And, besides all this, the city has been shamefully neglected for many months, and it is fearfully dirty, and there is but a small number of teams and wagons to do so great an amount of scavenger work.

It did, and still does, sometimes, look very hopeless here, on all sides. You at the North will never be able to conceive or believe the true condition of our prisoners. You may see all the pictures, and read all the accounts, and believe, or think you believe, every word of them, and then you will have but a faint idea. Men have lain on the ground here dying, with the vermin literally swarming, steady paths, up and down their bodies, as ants go, in lines about their ant hills. One poor fellow, a sergeant, died in the house of a kind lady here, whose limbs were so cramped by long sitting, through weakness, that they could not be straightened, even when he died, so that his coffin had to be made with the cover shaped like a tent, or house roof, to accommodate his knees. Women were afraid to walk over the plank sidewalks where some of the prisoners had been congregated for a little time, through fear of vermin. Men who had once been educated and cultivated, with fine minds, were reduced to idiocy—to utter and hopeless imbecility.

More than forty men, whose feet, or portions of them, had rotted off, left on the steamer yesterday. I do not know how many more such cases there had been among them; but these men I saw. Think of it! feet so rotted away that the surgeons cut them off with the *scissors* above the ankle! Has God any retribution for those who inflicted such suffering? Has their country any rewards for the men who suffered thus, month after month, rather than turn traitor—rather than deny the old flag?

THEIR APPEARANCE REMINDED ME OF SKELETONS

Anna Holstein

To a sensitive woman like Anna Holstein the time spent with the released prisoners in Annapolis was an unforgettable period of horror.

In this closing period of the war comes the darkest, saddest page of all. . . . The inhuman, fiendish treatment of our soldiers in Southern prisons has now become a matter of history, the truthfulness of which cannot be doubted. Would that it could be!

By the bedsides of dying skeletons, as they shudderingly recalled their prison life, I have written their sad stories, which often ended with: "We can never tell the half of all we have endured; it would not be credited, if we did." All of the horrors that I have seen and known during these memorable years faded into insignificance when contrasted with this heinous crime—a systematic course of starvation to brave men made captives by the chances of war! Our first visit to Annapolis was with the object of seeing and knowing more of them; that by a recital of their condition, I might interest still more those who were devoting themselves to the preparation of hospital comforts. . . . In one of the wards at Camp Parole, a man belonging to the 5th Indiana Cavalry was reclining in a large rocking chair near the stove; his features sharpened by suffering, the eyes sunken, skin tightly drawn over the lips, as though they could never smile again; the whole face had an unearthly, smoke-dried parchment look. Upon asking him where he was from, he answered plainly: "Anderson." His age was almost eighteen; I should have said at least forty. There was no appearance of flesh upon the attenuated hands and arms; he died within an hour. . . .

Their mode of burial (in the prison) was this: every morning a wagon was driven through the camp, to pick up those who had died during the night; the poor, emaciated bodies were caught up by an arm and foot; and pitched into the wagon as a stick of cordwood would be thrown; this was continued until no more could be piled in, then taken to the shallow trenches which were to receive them; they were packed in, lying upon the side, the head of one over the shoulder of the man in front of him; a slight covering of earth concealed the victims from sight, relieving them of that much care by lessening the number in their vile prisons—but adding another to the list of martyrs from the North. They crept, at night, in holes burrowed in the ground; those too feeble to prepare such shelter crowded together in rows for warmth; during the winter, the outside sleepers were almost invariably found stiff and cold, in the morning light.

The appearance of those with whom I have been conversing reminded me of the skeletons I had seen washed out, upon Antietam, Gettysburg, and other battlefields, only they had ceased from suffering, and were at rest; these were still living, breathing, helpless, starved men.

In one arrival of four hundred and sixty, only sixty were able to walk ashore; the four hundred were carried; half of these died within a few days; one third of the whole number imbecile. They appeared like a wretched bundle of bones, covered with a few filthy rags. . . .

Though coming from different prisons, all agree in this one fact: they were starved, without shelter, and wearing only the scantiest clothing—the rags which remained from the time they were captured—when their coats, blankets, and valuables were all taken from them. Many, after conversing about it, will say: "You never could imagine such horrors."

In one room, I singled out the two most skeleton-like, and asked the least emaciated one: "What prison did you come from?" He looked at me with a vacant stare, and answered: "Prison? ah—yes, I'm Anderson!" I gave him up, and his friend replied: "He thought they had been shown through all the prisons, though last from Anderson." Another, that I asked the same question, replied that he was from Florence; had been at Charleston once; didn't know how long since; they were all bad alike. . . .

When the prisoners were moved from Andersonville to Florence, they left behind them all their cooking utensils, as they were told they were to be exchanged, not sent to prison; but finding they had been deceived, asked permission of a Rebel, Major Brown (it is humiliating to add that he was formerly from Pennsylvania), to use the tin roofing of the cars which stood near; he consented, and they took off the entire roof of one. The only tools they had were a cold chisel, a railroad spike, and an old table knife; in a marvelously short time, cooking pans and buckets were cut out and hammered together; and when the variety was shown to the Rebel major, he remarked: "They might turn a Yank into the woods with nothing, and he would soon have all he needed." Buckets, plates, and spoons were made of wood. For the buckets, they split staves of wood, the Negroes furnishing poles for hoops and handles. As far as ingenuity could go, they made the best they could of their wretched surroundings. The men were divided by thousands, then hundreds, for convenience in distributing rations: while at Florence, Newman entered his name three times in one thousand, giving, of course, two feigned names—that he might draw sufficient food to sustain life; fortunately, he was not found out; if he had been, the penalty of one hundred lashes, in his enfeebled health, would have killed him.

Staunton, Pete Obrey, and Hoover were the men of infamous notoriety who did more lashing of our soldiers at Andersonville than any others. Staunton was chief of police: the few picks and spades within the stockade were under his control; Newman asked permission to use one, to repair his sleeping-pit; instead of a reply, was felled with it to the earth; when consciousness returned, he dared not complain; suffering with the blow, and ill as he was, could only crawl away to his ditch, thankful to escape with life. The two first named were at Annapolis while we were there; their lives had been so often threatened, if found outside the hospital, that they were glad to keep within its walls for safety. Pete disappeared one night, no one knew where. These men all wore the Federal uniform; while doing so, possessed the entire confidence of the Rebels in command—proving that, though wearing the army blue, they were Rebels in disguise. . . .

April 29. A boat, with three hundred, just arrived: the drum calls the stretcher-bearers to fall in line; and all who can rush to the landing. Following the crowd, we come to the wharf just in time to see the unsteady column begin to move. On board the vessel the hospital band is playing cheerful strains of welcome, and they come ashore to the music of familiar tunes:

> Back to the North, where the air is free;
> Back from the land of pain.

Tottering and feeble, bronzed and smoke-blackened, tangled hair and matted beards, some in Rebel garb, many barefooted and bareheaded, the majority clothed in shirt and drawers furnished by the Sanitary Commission in Wilmington, a few fortunate possessors of a blanket—such is the walking party. It was more than some of them could do to walk, so they gave it up, and, as the line of stretcher-bearers followed in their wake, were added to the number. Sorry plight for three hundred brave men to come from Southern care! Martyrs for the nation, patient and uncomplaining, they do not blame the government—they censure no one! . . .

There had been terrible suffering during all the winter months, among our soldiers in prison, for want of clothing, food, fire, and shelter. Five sticks of wood were given to one hundred men once in three days! That amounted to none at all, for, as they have shown me the size, it could all be burned in an hour.

A man who has been a prisoner since the Battle of the Wilderness now lies entirely stiffened, helpless, and unable to move, from exposure and sleeping upon the cold ground; he says that at one time Sanitary Commission clothing was pretended to be distributed by the Rebels—six pieces to one thousand men! the Rebel guard wore the caps, clothing, and blankets, while our men died by scores for the want of them.

A German named Neabal, 54th New York, Eleventh Corps, who was captured at Gettysburg, July, 1863, stayed in that horrid Belle Island eight months; from there to Andersonville, thence to Savannah, where they had good rations; then taken

to Macon and Charleston; for three weeks they were kept moving, for fear General Sherman would find and release them; the
corn which the cavalry horses dropped upon the ground, when
they were fed, was all they had to eat for several days; he was
paroled in Wilmington the last of February, and soon after sent
North.

Wm. Neely, Company B, 83rd Pennsylvania Volunteers, enlisted in Philadelphia. He was captured the 11th of October,
1863, and taken to Richmond, Va. After having made desperate
efforts to escape with his comrades, on the 24th of December
he was put in the dark, condemned cell of Castle Thunder; an
iron bar, fifteen inches long, was riveted upon his wrists and
ankles; the other end of the same bar fastened in like manner
to Captain Avery, of Kentucky. They were kept in that dungeon
four months and six days; the only clothing they were permitted
to keep was pantaloons and blouse; no covering of any kind
was allowed them; no chair, bench, or bed; nothing to sit or lie
down upon but the filthy floor. Sometimes six men were kept in
the same cell with them; at night, a light was placed near the
bars; during the day, total darkness. He concealed in the roof
of his mouth, for six weeks, a fine steel saw, such as is used about
gun barrels: at the time they were sent away, had one bar cut
through, ready to make another effort to escape. The iron bar
upon his wrist cut into the bone, making an offensive wound;
the scar it made he carried to his grave. When taken out, they
were covered with filth and vermin, so enfeebled that they could
with difficulty stand alone, and looking like nothing human.
The captain was started for Tennessee to be tried for treason;
but on the way escaped, and reached his command at Knoxville
in safety. Neely was sent to Salisbury, from there to Columbia,
thence to Macon, and hurried back again to Columbia, dodging
Sherman.

He finally escaped, by tunneling out under his prison walls, from the Asylum in Columbia, eight days before General Sherman entered the town; a Union lady concealed him, a lieutenant, and a sergeant until they could rejoin our forces; he came to Fayetteville with the Second Division hospital of the Fifteenth Army Corps, from there to Wilmington with the refugees, where they were kndly fed and cared for until able to bear the journey, when he was sent with others to Annapolis. He lingered two months, and died in St. John's Hospital. Continued efforts have been made to find his family: this statement has been published in city and country papers without avail: information of importance to them is still in my possession. . . .

A daily occurrence is the number of those who come searching for friends: all they know is, they were prisoners; and so hope to find them, or hear tidings of them. Many, alas! have filled an unmarked grave at Andersonville, Florence, or Millen, or perhaps may have been among those who, unable to tell their names when landed, died and were buried as unknown!

The Sanitary Commission Home at this place, Annapolis, has been to hundreds a place of shelter when the town was crowded to overflowing, and a home at all times to those who were received beneath its roof: here relatives and friends of those in the hospitals were provided for, meals and lodgings furnished gratuitously, and all made comfortable. . . .

VERMIN ARE OVER THEM IN ABUNDANCE

Lydia G. Parrish

Lydia Parrish had lost three children of her own before the Civil War. Her husband was a doctor and the superintendent of a hospital for feeble-minded children in Media, Pennsylvania. Dr. Parrish became associated with the United States Sanitary

Commission as soon as it was organized and worked actively for the Philadelphia branch. Lydia went to Washington with him and offered to serve in the hospitals there. For a time she was at Falmouth with Mrs. John Harris of Philadelphia during Mc-Clellan's Peninsula Campaign. In December 1863 she accompanied her husband and the Medical Director of the Department of Virginia and North Carolina on a tour of inspection of various hospitals. While at Old Point she learned that there was to be an exchange of prisoners and obtained permission from General Ben Butler to go with a friend on the flag-of-truce boat to City Point to witness the exchange, and give whatever aid she could on the return passage. . . . In the early winter of 1864, she inspected the hospitals of Annapolis with her husband and gladly consented to remain in that city for as long as her services would be needed.

What Lydia Parrish saw and what she did in Annapolis is set forth in these excerpts from two of her letters which appeared in the Bulletin of the United States Sanitary Commission.

December 8, 1864.

No human tongue or pen can ever describe the horrible suffering we have witnessed this day.

I was early at the landing, eight and a half o'clock in the morning before the boat threw out her ropes for security. The first one brought two hundred bad cases which the Naval surgeon told me should properly go to the hospital nearby, were it not that others were coming, every one of whom was in the most wretched condition imaginable. They were therefore sent in an ambulance to Camp Parole Hospital. . . .

In a short time another boatload drew near and oh! such a scene of suffering humanity I never desire to behold again. The whole deck was a bed of straw for our exhausted, starved, emaciated, dying fellow creatures. Of the five hundred and fifty that left Savannah, the surgeon informed me not two hundred would survive. . . . I saw five men dying as they were carried on stretchers from the boat to the Naval Hospital. . . . The stretcher-bearers were ordered to pause a moment by Surgeon D. Vanderkieft, that the names of the dying might be obtained. To the credit of the officers and their assistants it should be known that everything was done in the most systematic and careful manner. . . . There was no confusion, no noise. . . .

Some had become insane . . . others were idiotic . . . a few lying in spasms. . . . When blankets were thrown over them no one would have supposed that a human form lay beneath, save for the small prominence which the bony head and feet indicated.

The hair of some was matted together like beasts of the stall which lie down in their own filth. Vermin are over them in abundance. Nearly every man was darkened by scurvy or black with rough scales, and with scorbutic sores. One in particular was reduced to the merest skeleton, his face, neck, and feet covered with thick green mold. A number who had Government clothes given them on the boat were too feeble to put them on, and were carried ashore partially dressed, hugging their clothing with a death grasp that they could not be persuaded to yield. It was not infrequent to hear a man feebly call as he was laid on a stretcher, "Don't take my clothes"; "Oh, save my new shoes"; "Don't let my socks go back to Andersonville." In their wild death struggle, with bony arms and hands extended, they would hold up their new socks that could not be put on because of their swollen limbs, saying, "Save 'em till I get home. . . ."

16 Fires Along the Potomac and James

IN THE WINTER OF 1864-65, THE UNION FORCES WERE CONCEN-
trated in front of Petersburg and Richmond and the watchfires
along the Appomattox and James lighted the faces of the watch-
ful sentinels who trod their endless beat. Skirmishing and fighting were to continue all the while between the Blue and the
Gray until Grant faced Lee for the last desperate struggle.

As Abraham Lincoln assumed the office of the Presidency for
the second time, the cares of the world rested too heavily on his
weary shoulders; there seemed to be no limit to his grief and
anguish when he read the lengthening casualty lists and the
death of each soldier came as a personal loss. Overwhelmed as
he was with public responsibilities, he still concerned himself
with the condition of the hospitals, and continued to seek new
ways of brightening the quarters of the sick and the wounded.
At his suggestion and with his practical assistance, flowerbeds
were arranged between the long barracks of Armory Square,
Lincoln's favorite hospital.

At this time, when City Point, Virginia, was the center of
activity and Sanitary Commission agents and Army nurses were
arriving in ever-increasing numbers to serve in the overcrowded
wards, Lincoln's somber black-coated figure could often be seen
standing at the bedside of a severely wounded soldier, tears of
sorrow coursing down his cheeks, suffering anew as he had that
time after Fredericksburg, when he is said to have cried out,
"Oh, if there is a man out of Hell that suffers more than I do,
I pity him."

329

Perhaps these visits to the hospitals, more than anything else, made Lincoln recognize the important role that women were playing in the war effort. No small detail of their work seemed to escape the attention of this great man and he was always ready to be of assistance. During this period when it appeared that the war would soon be over, people were less enthusiastic about supporting the various aid societies and Lincoln managed to find the time to appear at a Sanitary Commission Fair to help arouse a more or less lethargic public. All over the North the need for supplies and money was as great as if not greater than during the early years. In the West, the Soldiers' Home in Chicago needed funds for the erection of a permanent dwelling for the disabled soldiers. Hospitals required supplies after the bloody battles in Georgia; and the fierce fighting at Nashville between Generals Hood and Thomas had exhausted the funds of the Northwestern Sanitary Commission. It was absolutely vital to meet these demands. Once again Jane Hoge and Mary Livermore, the two indefatigable managers of the Northwestern Branch of the Sanitary Commission, came east to seek the co-operation of the Eastern branches of the Commission in their proposed new mammoth Fair planned for the following June. They stopped off at Washington personally to invite the President and Mrs. Lincoln and several distinguished statesmen to attend.

Then came a day when attention was riveted on the battle-field once more and for the moment all other problems were set aside. Early on the morning of March 25, General Lee struck.

While the Union campfires were still burning low and red, he seized Fort Stedman, east of Petersburg. The attack came without warning and the graycoats sped on to take secondary Union positions in the rear. But the surprise attack failed. Forts both to the right and left of Fort Stedman were held fast by the Yankees and Grant's troops launched a counterattack. Remnants of the Rebel forces retreated to their own line and the Union recaptured Fort Stedman.

Heavy rains in the days that followed prevented further activity. Fields became like beds of quicksand and the Army could not move. Behind the battle scenes, however, all troops and gunboats were withdrawn from City Point, which had been the base of operations for nine months. An order was issued that all noncombatants from the armies of the James and Potomac should be sent to the rear. Ambulances and supply wagons thundered into the hospital camp at Point of Rocks and stood in long lines closely packed and ready to move at a moment's warning.

At last the skies cleared and the Union troops made ready to charge the Confederate ranks. Grant shortened his lines. Gibbon and Parke began to "force Petersburg" and the entrenchments at Richmond glistened with artillery. The fateful month was at hand!

On the morning of April 1 Sheridan struck the Confederates at Five Forks and overran their earthworks, cutting off the possibility of a final retreat south by Lee's starving Army, opening the way to the capture of Petersburg and the fall of Richmond.

On the following day Grant ordered a grand attack along the whole line from Appomattox to Hatcher's Run. Petersburg was evacuated and the capital of the Confederacy was abandoned.

While Confederate veterans wept, Lee surrendered at Appomattox Court House and the years of useless sacrifice came to an end.

THE SECOND INAUGURAL

Adelaide W. Smith

During the last year of the war Adelaide Smith was still working for the "Boys" at City Point Depot Field Hospital, Virginia,

half a mile from the headquarters of the United States armies
in the field, at the junction of the Appomattox and James rivers.
When the day of the Second Inaugural drew near, "a welcome
ripple of excitement" spread through the camp and she herself
was excited at the prospect of attending the ceremony.

I was fortunate in being able to go to Washington quite in-
dependently, without fear of detention, having a pass from General Grant that ordered all guards, pickets, steamboats, and
government roads to pass "Miss Ada W. Smith," and which
practically would have allowed me to travel free without question over the entire Northern States, as all roads were then
under government control. Thus was I enabled to accept the
invitation of Dr. Hattie K. Painter, Pennsylvania State Agent,
and her husband to join their party going to Washington. On
arriving in that city we went to a small hotel, where we met
some Western friends, and found there also a former patient
from City Point, Lieutenant Gosper, who had lost a leg in the
skirmish before Petersburg, and was no convalescent. He manifested the usual cheerfulness of wounded men, while waiting to
have an artificial limb adjusted—a free gift from the government.

We had secured tickets and good places to see the official
ceremony; but the surging mass of humanity crowded us quite
beyond hearing. On this eventful morning a raw, threatening
gale blew dust and lose debris into our eyes and faces, nearly
blinding us.

"And men looked up with mad disquietude upon the dull
sky," as we awaited the signal of the President's coming. At last
the tall, gaunt form of Mr. Lincoln came forward onto the
portico of the Capitol, surrounded by officials and attendants.
Chief Justice Chase opened the great Bible, and President Lincoln stepped forward, placing his hand upon the book to take,
for the second time, his oath of office. At this moment the

leaden sky, that had not lifted during the day, suddenly opened a small rift, while a strong bright ray of sunshine shot through and rested upon the noble head of the soon-to-be-glorified martyr. A silence of awe seemed for a moment to overspread the startled multitude, and then the darkening gloom closed down again as with an ominous foreboding; but not a word of that memorable address could we hear above the soughing, cold gusty wind.

At the appointed hour we started for the evening reception. Soon, however, we found ourselves in a frightful crush of people, crowding up the White House steps, and we quickly closed around the lieutenant, fearing he might get under foot. Our party was carried up bodily to the landing, where I found that my arm was quite badly bruised by the crutch.

After getting breath and composing ourselves, we fell into the long procession of couples approaching the President, where the ushers went through the form of taking our names and introducing us. In passing we saw a group of cabinet officers and a number of ladies with Mrs. Lincoln, who was gowned in white satin with a deep black thread lace flounce over an expansive skirt, in the style of that day; and she wore her favorite head-dress, a wreath of natural pink roses, entirely around her plainly dressed hair.

The President's band played stirring airs in an adjoining room, while crowds of every grade passed on, some in dashing uniforms, some in evidently fresh "store clothes," others in gorgeous costumes, and the good women from the country in sensible black —with ill-fitting gloves. It was a motley democratic crowd, such as could be seen in no royal country, and of which we are justly proud. Following the almost endless procession we saw the unmistakable form of Mr. Lincoln, his long arm and white-gloved hand reaching out to shake hands, and bowing in a mechanical manner, plainly showing that he wished this demand of the people was well over.

Suddenly straightening up his tall form, while continuing the handshaking, he looked eagerly down the line, and, to my surprise, as the lieutenant and I approached, he stepped out before us and, grasping the hand of the crippled soldier, he said in an unforgettable tone of deep sympathy: "God bless you, my boy! God bless you!" Owing to the lieutenant's crutch I was obliged to take his left arm which brought me on the outside away from the President. I attempted to pass with a bow, but he stood in my way, still holding out his large hand, until I released mine and gave it to him, receiving a warm, sympathetic grasp. Then I saw that wonderful lighting of his kindly beneficent gray eyes, that for a moment often beautified as with a halo that otherwise plain, sad face. As we moved on, the lieutenant exclaimed in happy exultation, "Oh, I'd lose another leg for a man like that!"

Such was the magnetic tone and touch of that rare spirit that carried hope and trust to the hopeless sorrowing, the great heart that could with truth and sincerity enfold not only his own country but the whole human brotherhood of the world, and caused him to reply in effect to those who wished him to subscribe to some special creed: "When I can find a church broad enough to take in the whole human race, then I will join it."

GO TO A FAIR TO REST?

Jane C. Hoge

In the spring of 1865, Jane Hoge and Mary Livermore came East to get the co-operation of the Eastern branches of the Sanitary Commission in their proposed new mammoth Sanitary

Commission Fair. They stopped in Washington to extend a personal invitation to President Lincoln and some other distinguished citizens.

Accompanied by the Honorable Jesse O. Norton and the Honorable I. N. Arnold, by appointment we called upon the President one . . . morning . . . and presented the invitation. The anteroom was filled with an anxious crowd, each one having a petition to offer and doubtful of its issue.

On entering the private room of the President we were deeply touched with the pleasant smile of cordial recognition with which he greeted us. Throwing aside care, he conversed cheerfully and with his quaint simplicity and humor. When the invitation was delivered in due form he gave us the assurance that, unless prevented by state reasons, he would attend the Fair, and twenty-four hours before his assassination he stated his intention to do so.

The interview of that day is recalled with tender interest. . . . We urged as a reason for his attendance at the Fair that the Northwest was longing for his appearance, and that he needed a change and rest. The nation felt he must have them.

"Rest!" he exclaimed humorously, "Go to a Fair to rest? I tried that once in Philadelphia and I will give you my experience. Crowds awaited us at every station on our journey, all expecting a speech from the President; and then they cheered until we were out of hearing. As there were many stations, there was not much rest. I *could not refuse to see and speak to the people. They were so loyal: and I knew it was because I represented the country for which they had suffered so much and so willingly that they wished to see and hear me.* At Philadelphia the people formed a solid phalanx. We could see nothing but masses of heads. The deafening shouts and cheers never ceased. Arrived at the Fair, *we were promised haven and rest.* 'Twas worse than ever. Oh, oh, the shaking of hands! During the collation for half an hour was the only quiet we enjoyed. The good people followed us to the hotel and serenaded us till near daybreak and the next day I came home, pleased and gratified, but worn out worse than before I went."

"Mr. President," said Mrs. Livermore, "I feel constrained to tell you that the enthusiasm of Philadelphia would be far exceeded in the West. Crowds will increase just in proportion as you reach your old home. The whole Northwest is ablaze to see you."

Was it a foreshadowing of coming events that dictated my words?

"Mr. President, myriads of friends will greet you but if you will consent to come, we will shield you from persecution. We will put you on a steamer on the boarder of Lake Michigan where *the people can look at you but can't touch you. Your hands shall be protected and then we shall send you to a quiet place of rest where none can follow you.* You shall go to Mackinaw, that invigorating and lovely island, and *none shall be permitted to trouble you."*

He laughed as gleefully as a child, and, rubbing his long hands, said, "That's capital! That will do."

At the President's request, we repaired to the White House half an hour earlier than the opening of the reception; saw Mrs. Lincoln and presented our invitation. She accepted it courteously and expressed a determination to accompany the President if he should be able to leave Washington.

After what proved to be the *last hearty grasp* of Abraham Lincoln's warm, broad hand, we retreated to a sheltered nook in his vicinity where we could observe the people as they came to pay their respects to him. We had seen and heard him speak in public, had met him in private several times, and had attended the previous levees but had never been so impressed with

the simple grandeur of the man as on this memorable occasion.
His toilet was simple but studiously neat. He was becomingly
attired in a full suit of black. His swarthy and furrowed visage,
that usually looked as though his soul was aching for the nation's
woes, was gilded by his smile, as cheering as a sudden burst of
sunlight scattering portentous clouds. The heavy burden was
loosening; the shoulders were unbent. He stood six feet, two
inches in height, looking fearlessly and hopefully in the face of
the people. . . .

The multitude that thronged the levee was such as may be
found at a republican court and no where else. All the people
had a right to come and come as they chose and as best they
might. Some rolled over the smooth carriageway to the White
House in dazzling equipages with liveried attendants and clad
in velvet and royal ermine. Some wore badges and decorations
which signified rank and honorable service. Some went on foot
wearing sober but comely garments and some with well-kept,
threadbare clothes, the mark of decent poverty. We noticed as
we stood apart, unseen, that the President greeted all courteously but his special and confident attentions were bestowed on
the meek and lowly and the battered veterans of the rank and
file. He stood erect in his place as glitter and pomp, youth and
beauty, approached him with an extended hand and smile of
welcome; but when a pale-faced little woman with black shawl
and gloves and rusty bonnet drew near timidly, scarcely raising
her eyes, he stepped forward to meet her, bent over her, held
her hand till in a low voice he murmured words unheard of men
but registered in Heaven; that flushed the white face, raised the
bowed head and illumined the sad countenance with a flitting
smile as she passed on with a lighter step.

As each rusty, battered, or maimed veteran approached the
President, he stepped from his place to meet him as though he
were each soldier's debtor. . . .

While in Washington, we met Miss Peabody, a rare and gifted woman who first introduced Kindergarten to the United States. Miss Peabody had visited the President and was completely won from vague dissatisfaction to admiration and love. . . . Miss Peabody was introduced as the sister-in-law of the Honorable Horace Mann. Mr. Lincoln at once received her with marked cordiality and entered into conversation which dissolved every mist of prejudice and revealed such a sincere, discriminating, and magnanimous character that he thoroughly charmed her. The President, when placed in contact with Eastern people, appeared even more a revelation than to his Western constituents who had longer known his work and his simplicity. In speaking of the Honorable Horace Mann, Mr. Lincoln naïvely remarked, "I can never forget his reception of me when I first entered Congress. He was then a leader, a man of much learning and wide reputation. I was an obscure young man from a remote Western state; shy, awkward and unknown to fame. Nevertheless, he took me by the hand, helped me up, and stood behind me when I needed backing." He added in a deeply thoughtful tone, "But for his help, I might not have been here today." On the pinnacle of human fame, Abraham Lincoln did not forget the hand that helped him to mount, though it had long ago become stiff in death. His heart kept the record, his modesty believed it, and his big soul acknowledged and proclaimed it.

ADMIRAL FARRAGUT'S MODESTY CHARMED US

Jane C. Hoge

In the early spring of 1865, when Mary Livermore and Jane C. Hoge went to Washington they carried the official invitation to

the second Northwestern Sanitary Fair Commission to several
distinguished military and naval leaders.

We had the privilege, while in Washington, of making the acquaintance of and presenting an invitation to the Fair to Admiral
Farragut and his charming wife, worthy of her heroic husband.
His modesty and naïveté charmed us. He had the proverbial
frankness of the sailor, and the bearing of a gentleman; looked
like a jovial, easy man, at peace with himself and all the world,
rather than the old hero, braced to the mainyards in a tempest of
iron hail and brimstone, roaring his orders through a trumpet,
and directing the fierce, successive naval battles that reduced the
coast and Gulf forts, and took possession of New Orleans. He
was *the* star at Washington at the time, and was hugely lionized,
dined, tead, and toasted. His humility and childlike simplicity
saved him from the baleful effects of adulation. Like Abraham
Lincoln, he looked upon himself as the mere representative of
the triumph of the old flag, and in her name, and for her behalf, he received a grateful nation's plaudits. In the course of a
free and easy conversation, the Admiral made a remark that
furnished the key to his successful life, and may supply a rule
of action, for the young and enterprising. We spoke of the naval
battles in the Gulf, of the huge obstacles to their success, of the
prodigious valor developed, and the brilliant success of the campaign. He said: "I never undertake impossibilities, though some
may call them so. I always expect to succeed, and always have,
for that very reason. I never ask a man to do what he doubts his
ability to perform. That doubt will entail a failure. If he says,
after a full, calm view of the situation, 'It can be done, and I'll
do it,' his success is pretty sure; but if he will only try, and do
the best he can, and doubts the wisdom of the plan, I say he's
not the man for the place. Confidence is necessary to victory—

enthusiasm and indomitable will may overcome almost super-human obstacles. Such men become magnetic, concentrating and consolidating scattered forces, and, like Napoleon's military squares, present quadruple fronts to the enemy, and bear down all opposition when they charge. The tenderness of the Admiral's heart was written in the lines of his mouth, whose womanly sweetness was redeemed by the firm clasp of lips ready to be com-pressed at a moment's warning. He was a Virginian, and he loved his State well; but the *Union more*. He told us he used every effort to induce Virginia to remain within the Union, and predicted the disaster that secession would produce, but was rewarded for his pains by an order to leave Norfolk within two hours, which he used with his accustomed dispatch, bringing off, as he said, sixteen large trunks, containing all their valuables, and the four persons composing the family. His kindly nature gleamed out, as he said he had taken large numbers of his old friends and neighbors prisoners, but always took good care to be out of the way when they surrendered, not wishing to add to their humiliation, which he had predicted to them, with earnest entreaties to forbear from the madness of secession, till they thought him crazy. Brave, good, honest, man! so full of power, and so wreathed with laurels, yet withal, preserving the modesty and simplicity of genius.

SHARING POOR QUARTERS WITH DOROTHEA L. DIX

Annie T. Wittemyer

In the early spring of 1865, Annie came East to help in the over-crowded hospitals in Virginia.

The hospitals were overcrowded at City Point and Point of Rocks. Every cot was occupied, every tent was crowded, and the thousands of troops coming down quartered wherever they could find a vacant place.

I had not been in the cabin of the steamer bound for City Point very long till Miss Dorothy L. Dix came in. After the usual greeting, she informed me that she, too, was going to City Point.

Miss Dix was the stateliest woman I ever saw and she was very dignified in manner and conversation . . . she was tall, straight as an arrow, and unusually slender. . . . Her dress was plain and neat and her linen collar and cuffs immaculate. She wore no jewel, not even a breastpin. . . .

It was not long after the boat left the dock at Washington until we passed Alexandria and Mount Vernon and were speeding on to Fortress Monroe at the mouth of the Potomac with the ocean in full view. . . . It was about nine o'clock that evening when we reached City Point. We had discussed the question of lodging before we left the boat and Miss Dix had said,

"I have no concern. There are always plenty of cots and I'll find room in some of the nurses' tents"; and she urged me to go with her.

But I was equally confident and assured her that the Christian Commission would take care of me. Mr. Cole of Boston, the chief agent, was standing beside a tent when I approached. . . . He lifted his hand in dismay.

"I have no place for you; every space is occupied . . ."

"How about the little tent where I stayed the last time?"

"It is full of delegates, lying on the ground on their blankets. I have given up my little corner to Dr. —— and I've no place to sleep myself."

"How about the storeroom?"

His face brightened. . . . A candle and some matches were procured, and, accompanied by the agent and his assistant, I went to the storeroom nearby. It was a great, rough, strong plank barracks. Boxes and barrels were piled up nearly to the roof. There was a vacant space where they handled the supplies near the door.

"There is not a cot on the premises; they have all been taken for the sick and the wounded. What will you do?"

"I'll sleep on the floor, of course," I answered cheerfully.

But they turned some of the boxes around and gathered up all the straw and shavings that were in sight and had been used in packing; put them together and I placed my satchel for a pillow. After I assured them that it would be all right, they left and I locked the door after them.

"They had not been gone ten minutes till there was a knock at the door. I went very close to the door and called,

"What is wanted?"

"Mrs. Wittemyer, Miss Dix is here and she had no place to stay. Can she come in?"

"Certainly; of course she can." And I opened the door and that stately woman with all her dignity upon her was glad to find even such a shelter as that. My candle lighted up the building sufficiently to show its unsightliness and the dust and rubbish that were all about us. As Miss Dix was old enough to have been my mother, of course there was but one thing to do and that was to give up my bed of shavings and straw to her and, with the stub of an old broom, to try to clear a place in another part of the floor for myself. She generously offered to divide her bed; but there was not enough to divide, so I spread my blanket shawl down on the rough uneven floor for my bed and I took my satchel for a pillow. . . .

PRESIDENT LINCOLN VISITED OUR HOSPITAL

Harriet M. Scott

One day president Lincoln visited the hospital * bringing grapes (with two men to carry the basket), himself giving to all who were allowed to have fruit—shaking hands, speaking kind words to each one. Noticing the small red flag at the foot of some of the beds, he said, "May I ask, nurse, what those flags mean?" "They mean low diet, sir." "What is low diet?" "Wine whey, milk and water, rice gruel—always something very light." Walking with President Lincoln through the ward to the door, he said, "Well, nurse, we often hear the remark that these are days that try men's souls:—I think they try women's souls too. I shall remember you and all the noble women of the North when this land is at peace."

Matilda E. Morris

While I was at Armory Square Hospital, he visited it several times. And how the boys would rally if we told them "Uncle Abraham" was coming. He would go down one side of the ward and up the other, shaking hands with everyone, and speaking a kind word.

He would then shake hands with me, ask me about my work, and my home, and charge me to be good to "his boys." I have often seen the tears roll down his careworn cheeks while he was talking with some wounded soldier.

PRESIDENT LINCOLN'S COMING

Mary Blackmar Bruson

In this letter Dr. Mary Blackmar Bruson describes one of Abraham Lincoln's many visits to the hospitals during the war. Mary

* Armory Square Hospital in Washington.

Blackmar was a medical student who enlisted as a Civil War nurse in order to spend one year in field work with the wide experience it offered, instead of in some regular city hospital.

I was placed in charge of the Confederate wards, and there saw that grandest of men, President Lincoln. . . . Men horribly wounded and sick, from both armies, were rushed into our camp hospital at City Point. I was given especial care of the private Confederates, and my companion . . . took charge of the Confederate officers. I had only an orderly to assist me—a boy of sixteen—and what with the cleaning and caring for each sick, torn body, our powers were strained to the utmost limit of endurance. Our patients' cots were so close together that we could just squeeze between, and our ward so long that it required from three to four tents.

One day the orderly rushed in and cried out, "President Lincoln's coming!" I was at the extreme end of the hospital tent, but, girllike, started forward that I might see him. At that instant, oh, such a puny, helpless wail, as of sick and dying infants, issued from every throat: "Oh, don't leave us, Miss! He is a beast! He will kill us!"

I replied: "Oh, no! He is a grand good man!" Again and again came forth that puny wail, "Don't leave us, Miss!" till I finally said, "Well, I'll not leave you, don't fear!" but by that time I had got to the front of the tent and the orderly had pulled back a flap on my request so that I peered out. Within about fifteen or twenty feet were General Grant, with the inevitable cigar, and President Lincoln, so tall, so lank, giving evidence of much sorrow, looming over him. I heard General Grant say distinctly, "These are the Confederate quarters." President Lincoln immediately said, "I wish to go in here alone!"

I drew myself up into the corner as close as possible, and he bent under the open flap and came in. He went at once to a bedside, and reverently leaned over almost double, so low were the cots, and stroked the soldier's head, and with tears streaming down his face he said in a sort of sweet anguish, "Oh, my man, why did you do it?" The boy in gray said, or rather stammered weakly, almost in a whisper, "I went because my State went." On that ground floor, so quiet was the whole ward, a pin could almost have been heard to fall. President Lincoln went from one bedside to another and touched each forehead gently, and with tears streaming asked again the question, and again heard the same reply. When he finally passed out from those boys, some gray and grizzled, but many of them children, there came as from one voice, "Oh, we didn't know he was such a good man! We thought he was a beast!"

ABRAHAM LINCOLN CAME TO MEET GRANT

Adelaide W. Smith

Abraham Lincoln had come, in his own boat the *River Queen*, to meet Grant at City Point. He was so secure in the conclusion of peace at last that he had brought Mrs. Lincoln and little Tad to share in the general rejoicing. . . .

During this mighty conclave at City Point, Abraham Lincoln was occasionally seen riding to the front and about camp and hospital, and to visit the tents, in his sombre black suit and high hat towering above many striking uniforms about him. . . .

On one of these occasions Mr. Lincoln had ridden up from the Point to visit our hospital, and was, as usual, accompanied by crowds of devoted friends as he walked through the divisions and avenues of the different camps. There were gathered the sick and wounded of the Ninth, Sixth, Fifth, Second Corps, and the Corps d'Afric, who were frequently visited by their regimental surgeons and officers of regiments that were encamped before Petersburg.

I shall always regret not speaking to Mr. Lincoln at that time. It would have been very easy to do, but I could not see the coming catastrophe, and I hesitated to push forward into the surrounding crowd to be presented. As he passed from tent to tent, with many a cheerful word to the suffering men, a young man connected with the Sanitary Commission, now Doctor Jerome Walker, a successful physician of Brooklyn, said, pointing to some tents nearby, "Mr. President, you do not want to go in there!"

"Why not, my boy?" he asked.

"Why, sir, they are sick Rebel prisoners."

With a hasty movement he said, "That is just were I want to go," and he strode within the tent, shaking hands and speaking such words of comfort as only his magnanimous spirit could prompt, to the grateful surprise and pleasure of the Confederate patients.

THE CONFEDERATE IRONCLADS WERE BLOWN UP

Charlotte E. McKay

At this time Charlotte McKay was at the Cavalry Corps Hospital at City Point, Virginia.

The fourth of April, 1865, unlike many of its predecessors, dawned peacefully and brightly at City Point, Virginia. From the moment when, at early dawn on the 25th of March, we had heard heavy cannonading at Fort Stedman which, though at the time we were ignorant of its meaning, proved to be the reveille of the Spring Campaign, all had been eager curiosity and anxious expectation.

Day by day there had been heavy firing, sometimes near, sometimes more distant. Day by day we had seen but one phase of its results; in exhausted, lacerated forms—many of them friends and old acquaintances—laid along on straw in crowded boxcars as they came in train after train from the battlefield and, thence, borne to the hospitals or the transports lying at the wharf.

The gunboats and all the troops having been, within a few days, withdrawn from City Point which had, for nine months, been the base of army operations, the great hospitals with their long lines of tents and barracks and thousands of wounded men, as well as the vast quantities of government stores—supplies for the grand army—were left without military protection; and, as we were totally ignorant of how things were going at the front, we were not without anxiety lest the Rebels should break through and make a raid on us. There was, indeed, such an attempt on the evening of the 29th of March when, at half-past ten, we were electrified by a sudden outburst of musketry and artillery which continued in a prolonged, deafening roar without a moment's letting down for one hour; then with slight intervals for an hour or two more; while in the direction of Petersburg, shells were continuously flying up and swooping over like rockets and the sky all aglow like those death-dealing pyrotechnics. Then came on a pouring rain, the sound ceased and we could breathe freely again.

Then in the early dawn of April third, we were startled from our beds by terrific explosions in the direction of Richmond; concussion breaking on concussion, roar upon roar, louder than the loudest thunder; the earth trembling as if affrighted and the sky lighted with an angry flare. It was then that the Confederate ironclads and bridges on the James River were blown up and Richmond fired by its defenders. But the end of these fearful catastrophes was at hand. Before another sunset, tidings came for which we had long waited and prayed but scarcely dared hope

—Petersburg and Richmond are evacuated by the Rebel army and occupied by our troops! The rebellion has collapsed!

So, as I have said, the fourth dawned peacefully over City Point and anthems of praise to God went up where many lives were still ebbing away in completion of the great sacrifice.

PETERSBURG FELL AND RICHMOND WAS IN FLAMES

Sophronia E. Bucklin

The long lines of blue crossed the bridge in steady column. We had breakfasted, and were just leaving the dining room when we first saw them. They were cavalry, and, in my eagerness to see if any familiar faces were amongst them, I went down to the landing with several nurses.

The men were ordered to dismount and pass over on foot behind their horses.

First came the straggling scouts, disguised in Rebel uniforms, going out into the country across the river to pick out the way. Next came the cavalry seventeen thousand strong; then sixteen thousand artillery, with ponderous caissons, glittering cannon, and gaily decked horses. They were hours in passing, and when fairly over, the cavalry remounted, and taking the different roads, some wound around the hill, while others passed among the scattering trees.

The battle began that day, and lasted through six more. We distinctly heard the cannonading, and saw the bursting of the shells in the air. In feverish excitement we sought to know the progress of the struggle and awaited the end. At last Petersburg fell. The victorious army, without delay or rest, pushed on to the Rebel capital. Hungry, worn down with incessant fighting, they eagerly marched onward. Through the long, dark night

they moved on until the daylight revealed to them the beleaguered capital in flames. Ninety of its most magnificent buildings, including stores, were enveloped by the devouring element.

With magazines bursting, bricks falling, firebrands whirling
through the air, and women and helpless children flying in terror, the boys in blue began to fight a new foe. The fires were
quenched, and prisons were opened, whilst in the noisesome
dens the Rebel prisoners of war took the places just vacated by
our starved men, to whom deliverance had come.

Through those days of conflict many terrible deeds were done.
In one of the forts, the last to yield, a soldier of the Tenth
Connecticut and a Rebel met, while our men were at one side,
and the grays at the other. Rushing upon each other, with almost unparalleled desperation, each touched the other's heart
with his fixed bayonet, and fell dead, Rebel and loyal blood
mingling.

I saw the body of a soldier in which seven Minié balls were
lodged, and which had been pounded with the butts of guns
till his eyeballs protruded from their sockets. He belonged to a
scouting party of five men which had been sent out, just before
the battle, and been surrounded and surprised—the other four
surrendering to the demand of the Rebels, and he being shot in
his resistance.

Whilst the fiendish work of mutilation was going on over his
murdered body the other four escaped and came to our hospital.
A squad was sent out to find the dead body, and it was brought
in, disfigured as described. . . .

Soon the wounded began to pour in. Rebel and Union, side
by side, were borne in on the stretchers, from the boats, and all
cared for alike. Freshly wounded men lay in the beds from which
former patients had convalesced, and death was a frequent
visitor in the wards. Our supplies were ample, and we frequently
distributed oranges and fine fruit at Point of Rocks.

Joyful faces were now on every hand, even in the midst of suffering. *Lee had surrendered.* The rebellion was virtually dead and the Nation survived the struggle. Soldiers waved their hats and cheered with all the vigor of their lungs. One dying soldier, who had been brought in from the victorious field, and who heard the sound of the cheering, summoned all his energies, and lifting himself upon his elbow, cried out, "Glory to God! Thank God I lived to see this day! I can die satisfied, now!"—and soon after breathed his last.

The Rebel capital, for the possession of which we had struggled for years, had at last fallen into our hands, and Abraham Lincoln walked its streets without a bodyguard. Where Southern women spat upon our boys in blue as they were marched to prison, he walked, followed by a people who from their hearts cheered their deliverer.

THE LAST PARADE OF CONFEDERATE SOLDIERS
Adelaide W. Smith

The paroled and surrendered Confederate prisoners were at once marched forward from Petersburg on the road beside the hospital . . . three thousand strong, officers and men without arms—worn, tired, begrimed figures of despair. They were clothed in every degree of shabbiness, from the dulled tinsel of the uniformed officers to the worn, faded, ragged gray that they had so confidently donned at the beginning of the war. They were on their way to City Point under guard, many to be forwarded to some Northern camp. . . .

There was no sound of exultation over the conquered enemy among the Northern men and women standing quietly near to see them pass. Some even saluted the defeated Confederate officers. None showed the slightest disrespect. . . .

Crowds of barefoot, ragged Negroes, nearly nude, who had been shut up for years in Petersburg, now crowded by hundreds along the road. . . .

It seemed like a funeral procession, without fife or drum, as it wound slowly past the hospital to City Point United States Headquarters, there to take their parole.

At City Point I saw General Custer, who lost his life soon after in the Indian raids. He was a small, spare, nervous man, wearing a scarlet-lined cape thrown over his shoulder, and his long, light hair floated back, making a striking picture of a cavalryman as his spirited horse dashed from one headquarters to another.

17 The North Went Wild with Joy

WHEN THE NEWS CAME THAT GENEFAL LEE HAD SURRENDERED AT Appomattox on April 9, 1865, the North went wild with joy. Bells were madly rung in every town and city. Cannons boomed their salutes, and guns were fired on the squares. Flags waved from housetops and church steeples. Every man had a bell or a horn. Little girls carried red, white, and blue ribbons and small bells. People crowded the churches and sang patriotic hymns. At night the streets were bright with bonfires, illuminations, and transparencies.

It became the rage to visit Petersburg and Richmond. In the days before Thomas Cook had started his travel agencies, civilians and soldiers alike managed to plan their own itineraries, and visited former Rebel defenses, residences where the great had slept, infamous prisons like Libby and the headquarters of General Robert E. Lee.

SHOUTS AND MUSIC FILLED THE AIR

Jane Stuart Woolsey

There was great rejoicing when the news came that Richmond was fallen and the war ended. Thunder and smoke ran at once round all the circle of the forts; an improvised salute without orders, and pistol-snapping, shouts, and music filled the air. The men moved about in little squads, in marching time, singing by snatches "Rally Round the Flag" and

The star-spangled banner in triumph shall wave,
O'er the land of the Free and Jeff Davis his grave.

Certain of the cripples hobbled out of the barracks, turned southward, and long and solemnly waved and brandished their crutches in the air. It seemed to do them good. At night the city was illuminated, and we saw from the tower the long lines of buildings and great dome pricked out in light upon the dark blue distance, and the red glare of the joy fires reflected in the sky.

Presently a large number of wounded men, the men who had taken Richmond, came up on the steamers and kept us very busy for a time. It was delightful to work for these men. Their spirit was magnificent. The tide was at the full. The rush to break all bonds and get home had not yet begun. "You have left one foot for the Rebels?" "Oh, yes, the Rebels have got it, but then you know Richmond's gone up." "It was your right arm?" "Yes, but the war is over and the country is saved; they might have had the other arm if they had wanted it"; and, "So say we all of us!" half sang, half shouted all the maimed men within hearing. The little groups about the doors were always breaking into hurrahs on the slightest occasion or allusion.

WALL STREET ON THE SURRENDER OF GENERAL LEE

Georgeanna M. Woolsey

On the day that the news of Lee's surrender reached New York, the Woolsey family couldn't accept it as a matter of course. The

silence and lack of enthusiasm uptown and the sight of the
women going in and out of the dry goods shops as usual was
unbearable. Georgeanna wrote:

Mother and I said to each other, "Come let us see what Wall
Street is doing."

We took a Fulton Street omnibus, which was entirely empty
but for ourselves and drove down to the neighborhood of the
Custom House. As we came near the streets were more and more
blocked, thousands and thousands of men standing, crowding
upon each other, not a woman's face among them,—all the narrow streets which converge to that point black with men, thousands more, solidly packed. As the omnibus came to a stand,
not able to move a step further, they were singing as if their
hearts would burst:

> Praise God from whom all blessings flow,
> Praise Him, all creatures here below;
> Praise Him above, ye heavenly host,
> Praise Father, Son, and Holy Ghost.

A young man, half fainting with fatigue, threw himself into
the omnibus, saying, "They have been at it for hours."

COME FOR THE GRAND ILLUMINATION

Jane Newton Woolsey

At Joe and Eliza Howland's home in Fishkill, peace was cele-
brated by the building, in the spring and summer of 1865, of
the Tioronda School House. Two little framed photographs—one
of the tattered battle flags of the 16th New York as War, and the
other of the School House as Peace—always hung side by side in

Joseph Howland's dressing room, and traveled with him when-
ever he and Eliza went abroad. On April 13 Mother Woolsey
wrote Eliza from New York:

I want you to come down for the grand illumination on the
20th to celebrate the surrender, which will be next Thursday,
that you may see the city in its glory of thanksgiving display.

We have Abby's pretty silk flag in one of our windows pinned
across the curtains, and Willy G.'s little one on the other, with
our larger one over the front door outside, which has hung
through the rains and sun day and night since Richmond was
taken, and begins to lose its bright color. You can bring your
little silk one with you. The girls have been getting some colored
lanterns to decorate the balcony and street door; and this, with
the gas all lighted and the windows open, will be the extent of
our illumination, but we can drive round and see the city. Oh,
I hope you will come certainly. . . .

I enclose our last from Charley; he is undoubtedly in Richmond before this—probably one of Lee's escort into the city, as
the papers mention General Grant and his staff accompanying
him. Isn't it grand to have all these victories coming so fast, and
the Rebels giving up, in a forlorn hope, their boasted Confederacy. . . .

THERE WERE FEW LADIES IN THE STREETS

Charlotte E. McKay

Mrs. McKay decided to go sightseeing in Petersburg.

By a turn in the road, we were suddenly brought in full sight
of the "Cockade City." There it lay, spread out under the bright

sunshine. . . . The blinds were closed on the windows; there were but few ladies in the streets and these, we noted, wore garments in the styles of four years ago, showing that the blockade runners did not bring them the latest London and Paris fashions. One elderly lady, richly dressed, walked slowly along with her white handkerchief held closely to her eyes as if she could not bear to witness the overthrow of her beloved city, or perhaps her heart was breaking for sons or brothers slain in battle. As often as we stopped, poor women, white and black, gathered around our ambulance, their baskets on their arms; they had been walking about since sunrise in hope of finding something wherewith to satisfy the demands of hunger. . . . It was time the city had surrendered, for it was on the eve of starvation. . . . At the corner of one of the principal streets, we stopped to see the 9th Corps pass. They marched with martial music and waving banners but with no look of exultation through the conquered city, for to them it was no holiday parade. They had fought like giants to obtain this consummation and had left thousands of their comrades dead on the field of honor.

Here, a young cavalryman whom we had known at the hospital rode up and offered to serve as escort. He had been riding hard with dispatches to an officer at the front and was on his way back to City Point. Alighting at a hardware store, we were attracted by rows of English-looking cans in the windows. "They are the cans in which were imported beef and mutton for our army," said the shopkeeper. "The blockade runners brought them in great quantities and our soldiers were glad to sell me empty cans. I sometimes paid as high as five dollars apiece for them. I preferred rather to put my money in these than to keep it, as I knew the Confederacy would soon go *up*. . . ."

Observing a tobacco warehouse open and some of our men bringing out tobacco, we, with the help of the young cavalryman, transferred a generous quantity to our ambulance which we distributed next day to the men in our hospitals, much to their delight. . . . Leaving Petersburg on our return, we took the road leading through the entrenchments. All along the road lay the debris of battle—torn garments, caps, shoes, canteens, haversacks, belts—intermingled with abundant cannon balls, solid shot and exploded shells, as well as many shells not exploded to which, in passing, we gave a wide berth. In the forts we gathered a few relics left by the soldiers in their sudden departure.

Halfway between two lines of Rebel breastworks lay a Rebel officer, unburied; he was shot through the head, fell backwards, and lay with his face to the sky, one delicate hand thrown up just as the surprise so left the body. . . .

Passing through our own inside line of fortifications, we came to the deserted camp of the 9th Corps. The camp looked like a miniature city with the long regular streets and little wooden huts. . . .

Near the camping grounds were three recently prepared cemeteries for the dead of the three divisions; for within the last few days, the 9th Corps had poured out its blood like water. . . . Here in the broad open fields lay the dead who fell, storming the Confederate works on the second. . . . They were laid in rows, side by side, in their blue overcoats which were their only wrappings for the grave, to which were pinned slips of paper bearing their names to be transferred to their headboards. A hundred men had been at this work since daylight and, with the sun near setting, there still remained nearly three hundred to be buried. We alighted and walked reverently and tearfully through the ranks of these slain heroes. . . .

THE FAMILY ENTERS RICHMOND

Harriet Roosevelt Woolsey

*When peace had finally come, the Woolsey girls were all eager
that "Mother," who had seen so much of the dark side of the
war and had known its anxieties so keenly, should see something
also of the victorious Army and "of Washington with the smile
of Peace upon it." Without too much delay they went to see
the former Capital of the Confederacy.*

Richmond, May 14, 1865.

We are *in Richmond!* and glad we are—(knock at the door,
and two bouquets with the "Compliments of Major Scott,
Fourth Massachusetts Cavalry," handed in, for Mrs. Woolsey
and Mrs. Woolsey's daughter, Carry, with whom he rode on
horseback yesterday). We arrived too late for the grand display,
but on Wednesday, all day long, Sherman's troops were passing
through the city as quietly as possible, no display of any kind,
no review by Halleck; grim, fierce-looking men some of them,
marching along splendidly, but giving no sign. . . . Sherman and
Halleck are deadly enemies, since the latter's order to disregard
any orders received from Sherman that he had better not show
himself in the streets, as Sherman could not answer for the
reception he might receive from the soldiers. So they marched
sullenly through, leaving the Fourteenth and Seventeenth Corps
to follow next day. We were all ready to review them, when, to
our horror, at 9:30, as we were finishing breakfast, the announcement came that all troops had gone through. No one was told
of it; General Curtis—our wounded Captain of the old Sixteenth, now Brigadier General of Volunteers, who is here—knew
nothing of it, and they began at 5:30 A.M., and went as quietly

as possible. Saturday there was still left one Corps to pass, and we went up to the State House and watched them, but they broke up, passed through different streets, and took no more notice of our handkerchiefs and the flag than if we were posts— sullen fellows, espousing Sherman's cause, and determined not to show the slightest interest in the place where Halleck was. So this personal fight deprived us and the army of what might have been a splendid sight. General Curtis is doing everything for us. We have our order for as many ambulances as we want as long as we stay; we never drive with less than four horses and eight outriders; have been all over the city and to Cold Harbor, going there yesterday with four officers and General Curtis and his wife, and seeing the field and line of works. To my great pleasure we broke down on this side, and were not obliged to eat our dinner on any battlefield, though we did stop where the Rebel army must have camped, and somewhere in the neighborhood of *Gaines's Mill*, where Joe was wounded. . . .

We came back safely to receive Generals Ord, Turner, and someone else, and Captains and Lieutenants thrown in—Mrs. Ord with them. This morning Mother and I have been at home, the girls at a colored church, where to their great delight the announcement was made of *Jeff Davis' capture*. The whole church was overcome with delight, blessing the Lord, crying and kissing Hatty's and Carry's hands. They were charmed to see the northern ladies, and gave them chief places among them, and a bunch of roses each. Numbers of notices were read; people asking information about lost relations and where to find their own families. Tomorrow (Monday) we have been induced by three Major Generals to go with them to Fort Harrison, and they promise to see that we get off to Petersburg on Tuesday A.M., by General Ord's private boat or special train. What *can* we do against the Union Army? We *have* to stay of course, and shall not get to Washington before Thursday, probably. General

Curtis wants me to urge Joe and Eliza to come on soon; he may be sent off from here, and wants them while he is here. They must be sure to, it is all full of interest.

Georgy collected all the striking editorials from the *Tribune* and *Post* on the abuses of the Belle Isle and Libby prisons by the keepers of those shameful pens, which were in daily sight of Lee's own house, and which he could by one condemnatory order have closed. She left the package so collected at his door in Richmond, first ascertaining that he was in the house, and knowing that in the dearth of Southern news they would surely be read.

Carry is in her glory; goes on horseback with the officers when we are in ambulances, and is delighted with all; Hatty, too. Mother keeps up her interest in all she sees.

And Jane Newton Woolsey, the girls' beloved mother, added her impressions:

The air is filled with the burning brick and mortar smell through the whole city. The entire block through to the next street in front of us is in ruins, and all the way down the long street not a house is standing; banks, churches, private dwellings, and stores without number, all lie in ruins. By moonlight the sight is beautiful. They are putting up slightly built shanties here and there for the sale of different articles, mostly beer and cakes, which spoilt the picturesqueness.

The city is a beautiful one, with its fine old trees and large gardens, now filled with every variety of roses. We average about four large bouquets a day in our room, from military friends, and our mantelpiece is filled all in a row with roses, syringas, honeysuckles, and magnolias. I wish every day you had come with us. I am sure you would enjoy it. Do join Eliza and Joe when they come on. . . .

GENERAL GRANT BADE ME GOOD-BY
Matilda E. Morris

Matilda Morris was another tourist in Richmond, but her big thrill was an expected trip back to Washington on General Grant's boat.

May 18th I started for Washington. I reached the boat in good season, and supposed I was all right, but a colored man soon came to me and said, "How came you on this boat?" I told him and showed my pass. "Oh, you are all right, madam, so far as that goes, but we never carry passengers on General Grant's private boat." I said I was exceedingly sorry for the mistake, and he could put me off at the next landing. During the conversation, a military-looking man seated himself near us, and seemed to be reading; but I knew he had heard every word, and I also knew very well who he was. He soon laid down his paper, saying, "Sam, what is the matter?" "Dis lady is on your private boat, sah." He came to me and said, "Madam, will you please to tell me all about it?" I did so, and he answered: "I don't see anything very serious about this mistake; there is room for us all. Make yourself perfectly at home. We only go to City Point, but you can change boats there." Then turning to the waiter he told him to "make the lady comfortable while she remains on board." This gentleman was our good General Grant.

At City Point we shook hands, he bade me good-by, and I thanked him again for his kindness, then continued my journey. In the meantime my husband had secured his discharge papers, and we bade adieu to our associates.

18 Fell the Dark April Morning

ON APRIL 14, 1865, ABRAHAM LINCOLN WAS SHOT. WHEN WORD OF the great tragedy spread through hospital and camp, city and town, mansion and cottage, heartfelt grief quickly supplanted the earlier displays of happiness throughout the North.

THE CIVILIZED WORLD WAS STARTLED

Georgeanna M. Woolsey

April, 1865.

The great President's second term of office began with such lofty words as these:

"The judgments of the Lord are true and righteous altogether. ... With malice toward none, with charity for all, with firmness in the right, as God gives us to see the right, let us strive to finish the work we are in; to bind up the Nation's wounds; ... to do all which may achieve and cherish a just and lasting peace."

Mr. Lincoln was personally with the army for the last few days of the campaign, entering Richmond immediately after its surrender, riding through the city in a common U.S. ambulance, greeted with the benedictions of the Negroes whom he had set free.

On April 14th the civilized world was startled with the news of his assassination. He was shot in his box at Ford's Theatre in Washington by a Rebel bullet, and died in a small house on the

362

opposite side of the street, without regaining consciousness, at about 7 A.M. on April 15. The joy over the return of peace was eclipsed by the grief of the whole nation.

All that I can remember about the first moments of that awful morning at home is that I rushed to Hatty's and Carry's bedroom door, pounding it, and crying, "Let me in, let me in! Mr. Lincoln is murdered."

Men, women and children went about the streets of New York, crying, and hardly a single poor tenement in the most impoverished quarters of the city was without its little black streamer. Clocks were stopped at the hour of his death; and on the anniversary of it, for years, on some of the principal buildings of New York.

THE PULPIT AND CHANCEL WERE HUNG WITH SOFT, DARK FOLDS

Jane Stuart Woolsey

Very coldly on the thunder and the shouting fell the dark April morning on which a vague rumor of the Tragedy in the city crept through the camp like a deadly, chilling fog. A trivial matter made the rumor known at first. John came to the storeroom to say that the market wagons were turned back from the outer guard, and the special diet supplies had not come; that no milk carts or mail riders had got through; that *something* must have happened. By degrees, no one knew how or whence, the story came; a darker and darker version every hour. We believed nothing, till the Surgeon in Charge passed the guard as a medical officer, went to headquarters in the nearest town, and, after two or three hours' delay, got back with authentic information.

Hard work was a blessing in those cold and heavy hours; all our expedients with reserves of canned meats and soups were called into use; no supplies came out for a day or two; every house and hut in the neighborhood was surrounded and searched, and comers and goers were sharply questioned.

How the sun shone and how loud the birds sang on that Easter Sunday! I remember the keen impression made by little things. I can smell the lilacs now. In intervals of work when we sat down to rest we sat with folded hands, looking at each other in silence. The men came with streaming tears to ask for bits of crepe and ribbon to fasten on their sleeves. "It's with me, night and day," they say, "I can't sleep for thinking," "If it had been my own brother"; and the roughest of all contraband women in the quarters drawing the back of her hand across her eyes, says: "Oh, Missis! I feel like as if my own kin was gone."

On Easter Monday the Chaplain went to a meeting of ministers of the District and the whole body waited on Mr. Johnson at the Treasury Building. The President replied with apparent emotion to the address and resolutions, saying in closing: "The American people need to be educated to see that treason is a crime."

On the Funeral Day, the chapel was crowded for the solemn service. We had, unhappily, black shawls and crepe veils enough among us, and the pulpit and chancel were hung with the soft, dark folds. The men all wore tokens of mourning. There was not a contraband hut in all the fields between the Hospital and the city but had its poor little rag of black above the door. . . .

WHAT A MOMENT FOR AMERICA!

Caroline C. Woolsey

Her feelings on Lincoln's death described in a letter from Caroline C. Woolsey to her sister, Eliza Woolsey Howland.

Saturday morning, April 15, 1865.
What can one do? We are all dumb with grief. The extra has just been cried giving the awful moment of his death. What a moment for America! When you think of his unvarying kindness toward those very men who now rejoice—how his whole career has been one of goodness and mercy, and now at the very first beginning of reward, it is too hard to bear. The papers were brought up while we were in bed this morning. You have hardly heard it now. I suppose you will not come down today, but you must on Monday. Charley is in Washington, in rooms with General Williams, on 15th Street. New York seems dead, the streets are quiet and the flags all covered with black crepe— even the "extra" boys subdue their voices. Work is suspended, and Wall Street is thronged with silent men.

Do come down; we ought to be together in these awful times.

IT WILL BE WEEKS BEFORE THE COUNTRY RECOVERS

Jane Newton Woolsey

A letter from Mrs. Woolsey to her daughter, Eliza Woolsey Howland.

New York, April 25, 1865.
I am sorry you postponed your visit, as you would have seen something of the funeral pageant. It will be weeks before the country recovers from the first great shock of this terrible event, and as long, before the people of New York are quieted down again to their everyday occupations. We all feel unsettled, and can really do little else than read the newspapers. Robert left home on Thursday P.M. for Washington. . . .

Georgy means to deluge Lee with Northern newspapers. Commenced this morning by sending him the Post of last evening, with an editorial marked very strikingly, headed, "General Lee."

THE CHIEF HAD FALLEN

Sophronia E. Bucklin

Sophronia was still at Point of Rocks Hospital when news of the assassination of President Lincoln reached her.

On Sunday morning we received the intelligence of his assassination, in the Friday night previous, in one of the theatres in Washington. Suddenly as though the sun had dropped out of heaven, darkness seemed to come upon our land. The chief had fallen, in the hour of triumph, brutally murdered. Our joy was turned into mourning.

Men whose hearts had beat high with exultation looked gloomily into the faces of their comrades, and took the proffered hand in silence. Would it prolong the struggle? Would the rebellion receive fresh impetus from this blow at the soul of the Republic?

I went up to Washington on personal business during the search for the murderers of the President. Every face on the boat was closely scanned, and when it drew near a landing the little tugs swarmed around us like bees.

The Capital presented a scene long to be remembered. The streets everywhere were draped in mourning. The body of the assassinated President had just been taken from the Capitol. The gloom was universal, and no one dared to whisper an approval of the horrible deed by which the nation was robbed of a loved chief, and the name of Abraham Lincoln was made synonymous with that of "The Noble Martyr."

THE TABAH * WAS COVERED IN BLACK

Josephine Philips

Josephine Philips was a member of a distinguished Jewish family. Her grandfather arrived in America in 1756. Her father, Naphtali, was president of the first Portuguese-Spanish synagogue in New York, Shearith Israel, for about a decade and half, and owner for many years of the National Advocate, *a leading New York newspaper. He was active in the Democratic Party in the city.*

Josephine's letter printed here was addressed to her brother-in-law, Adolphus Simeon Solomons of Washington, D.C. Adolphus Solomons was a member of a firm that did a great deal of contract printing for the Government. The company also sold books and had its own photographic gallery. It was in that gallery that Solomons arranged for what turned out to be the last photograph of President Lincoln. Solomons was also prominent in civic affairs, and was one of the incorporators of the American Red Cross, whose preliminary meetings were held in his home. Solomons was said to have enjoyed the personal friendship of Abraham Lincoln.

Josephine did not enlist as an Army nurse, but is believed to have acted in the capacity of a gray Lady at the Jews' (later Mount Sinai) Hospital. The Board of Directors of the Hospital had volunteered to look after wounded soldiers of all faiths. This care included providing beds, medical care, medical supplies, food, and entertainment. According to one historian, the

* The ark in the synagogue, from Hebrew word meaning *box.*

patients were rarely without visitors. Young ladies like Josephine Philips sat at the bedsides and read to the sick men.

New York, April 20, 1865.

Never in history has *any* event in *any* nation brought forth such real regret, & the loyalty of the people high & low rich & poor is seen mingled with love & veneration for the man "whose heart was warm, whose hands were pure, whose doctrine & whose life coincident exhibit lucid proof that he was honest in the sacred cause & to such are rendered *more* than mere respect." These lines from Cowper are forcibly brought to my recollection as illustrating much of the character of our lamented President. New York is literally clad in black & it is more rare to see a house without it than with it, from the splendid mansion to the smallest shanty, even the gates of the poorest black or white display their emblem of sorrow; full well I can imagine how badly you feel: it was only last week you wrote me about your being at his house seeing him come out & request the band to play "Dixie," & today that he appointed to celebrate our victories, his own funeral takes place. I have not yet recovered from the shock of last Saturday. Yesterday we had shul * & a very large assemblage, the services were very solemn, the Tabah was covered with black, also the pillars & gallery, to-day we have it again at three o'clock, nothing is thought or talked of to-day, *no stores* are opened & the poorest person will not work. I see by the paper the body will be here on Monday, his poor wife & children what a sad change for them! I am truly glad Mr. Seward & son will recover & also that his assassin is arrested, but it seems strange Booth has yet eluded the vigilance of the police, his Mother I hear resides in 19th St. NY & is of course in the greatest affliction. What a villain he is!

People already have changed their opinion regarding the new

* Synagogue or temple.

President & seem to think he will carry out the programme in a great measure of Mr. Lincoln.

I trust this will find you all well. Pa has a cold, Beck [Rebecca] has suffered considerably with Neuralgia. Pa felt very badly about the news, & I dare say all the children from Ida down were grieved. You remember how he noticed them the last visit I was there to see him with you, his likenesses sell like wildfire, the one I bought on the Carte de Visit[e] one that he sat last for I gave to Isaac when I first came on & he now has it in his window. I may as well leave off for I can write about nothing else, the late victories are not spoken of. I see by this morning's paper Mosby & seven hundred guerrillas had surrendered. All send much love to dear Rachel, Mary Jane, yourself & kisses to the dear children as ever yours most aff.

19 Aftermath

IT WAS TIME AT LAST TO THINK OF HOME. THERE WERE SOME WHO left immediately after Lee's surrender and there were many who would not go until the hospitals were emptied of the last soldiers. Early in May the armies of the Potomac and James were ordered to Washington as quickly as proper transportation could be provided for them, there to be mustered out of service.

The headquarters of the United States armies in the field had already been transferred to Washington. General Russell with his colored troops was left in command at City Point to finish whatever had to be done by the Government and Adelaide Smith was the only white woman there.

There still was a great deal to be done. It had been a long war, and memory of the bloody years could not easily be erased. There were the physical things that served as reminders of what had passed between the states: hospitals, stores, and people, too. There were many who had been displaced so long that they had nowhere to go. Nurses and soldiers had to be mustered out; Government passes returned. All the buildings temporarily taken over as hospitals by the Government, hotels, seminaries, mansions, and Government buildings in Washington and Virginia had to be restored to their former owners, and reparations made. Military hospitals were to be closed as soon as possible, and the sick sent to city hospitals in Washington or Northern cities as soon as they were able to board one of the many transports crowding the dock at City Point. Barracks and tents were dismantled, canvas roofs removed and turned in to the Government, leaving only "stockaded walls, much useless camp furniture, and debris of all sorts that were not worth shipping north." The hospitals were stripped, bloody stretchers rolled up and stowed away with the bandages and the lint to gather dust in dim corners of Government warehouses.

There was a great deal to be done. But it required time and organization, of which there was little. Proper provisions had not been made for the returning armies. There was a tragic amount of confusion. After the field hospital at City Point had been stripped and groups of contrabands had settled there, subsisting on abandoned rations and leftover supplies until the Government could plan some way of taking care of them, a regiment of sick soldiers from the 6th Corps arrived. No one had expected them. No one knew why they had come there, but the men had to be looked after until arrangements could be made to move them to a city or military hospital in Washington.

In Armory Square Hospital, after an order had been issued that all the patients were to be discharged, it was found that a number of soldiers had been detained under various pretexts in order that the requisite number might be maintained with their rations (thirty-seven cents a day) to keep this hospital open. Many of the men begged one of the nurses "almost upon their knees" to help them.

Six weeks after the war had ended, the Sanitary Commission issued a new call for help for the men of the Army of the Potomac encamped around Washington, and later for the veterans of Sherman's Grand March. The situation among these men was deplorable. All the tinsel and glamour had been shorn away, and what the war had done to the men and women who participated, and what it had done to the country became revealed in all the ugliness of reality. All these soldiers were in a state of destitution. Many had scurvy or chronic diarrhea. The

Army of the West, after subsisting from Atlanta to the sea on the country through which they had passed, acquired scorbutic diseases in the destitute and barren regions of North Carolina and Virginia. A return to their ordinary marching rations gave the men plenty to eat but not vegetables. Surgeons immediately appealed to the Sanitary Commission and the demand soon became greater than the supply.

The work done by the women in Field Relief during this period should not be forgotten. Theirs was a thankless job without the dramatic impetus of wartime patriotism to activate them. It required humanity, and a sense of responsibility, a love for their fellow men that these brave women had in abundance.

The Sanitary Commission too performed its final if not its greatest service. Stations for Sanitary Commission stores were established in the camps to which the soldiers might come without the trouble of getting passes to Washington. Field Relief agents following the armies from point to point called on the officers to inform them of the Sanitary Commission storehouses with supplies of vegetables and pickles. Food and clothing had to be distributed, for here were men who had not been paid for the last six months and still had to be mustered out of the service in their respective states. Government accounts had been closed; there were no longer any sutlers in the regiments. These men had no credit anywhere, and in the words of one woman who served in Field Relief, "Every market day numbers of these war-torn veterans have been asking for some green vegetables from the tempting piles which were forbidden fruit to them. . . ."

The services of "Hospital Visitors," those Red Cross Gray Ladies of the Civil War, were enlisted now to help make this Field Relief work as thorough, rapid, and effective as possible, and they worked side by side with Army nurses and Sanitary Commission agents.

In the last days of June a circular was sent out by the United

States Sanitary Commission announcing that its Field and Hospital Relief Service was finished. Written across in pencil were the following words:

> But now the whole Round Table is dissolved . . .
> The older order changeth, yielding place to new,
> And God fulfils himself in many ways . . .
> Pray for my soul. More things are wrought by prayer
> Than this world dreams of. . . .
>
> But something ere the end
> Some work of noble note, may yet be done
> Not unbecoming men that strove with Gods.

On July 7, 1865, at three thirty in the afternoon, the Woman's Central Relief Association, which had spearheaded the relief work among women throughout the country in that April four years before, had its last meeting. It was 92 degrees in New York City but no one stayed away, despite the heat. Drs. Elizabeth and Emily Blackwell, Georgeanna Woolsey and her sisters Eliza, Harriet, Caroline, and Abby, and their mother, Jane Newton Woolsey, were among the many who had come from near and far. Dr. Henry Bellows presided over the meeting. After the regular business had been disposed of, he spoke a few sentimental words of farewell, and then moved that the meeting "be adjourned sine die."

SHERMAN WON BACK OUR HEARTS TODAY

Eliza Woolsey Howland

Eliza and Georgeanna Woolsey were at the Ebbit House in Washington again for the first time since they sailed away with the Sanitary Commission in 1862. On May 24, 1865, Eliza wrote to Abby:

I wish you could have been here at least for this second day, and have seen Sherman's splendid army. Far from flagging, the interest greatly increased, and there was much more enthusiasm and life today than yesterday, both among the men themselves and the lookers-on. Nothing ever was more false than the report that Sherman's braves were all "bummers," and beyond his control, or if so, it would be well for all armies to have " 'alf their complaint." They beat the A.P. all to pieces in their marching, which is an easy swinging gait but in perfect time and uniformity; and in physique they seemed half a head taller and broad and straight in proportion—great big, brave, brawny men with faces brown as Indians and a pleased smile on every one. The Army of the Tennessee came first with Logan at its head, though Sherman, of course, preceded him, and both were greeted with roars of delight, as indeed was the case with every general officer, every particularly torn flag, and all the men! Flowers—many more than hung around many of the horses' necks or over the flagstaffs, and one of the prettiest parts of all was to watch Mrs. Sherman, who, with her little boy, sat next to the general all day, cheer and wave and toss flowers to one after another of the color-bearers. When she couldn't toss far enough herself, the general himself would throw them, and they were always caught with great cheers and tossing of caps by the men. Indeed Sherman won back our hearts to-day by his perfect delight in watching the ovation to his soldiers and his zeal in helping it on. Most of the day he and *Stanton* sat at the two extremes of the platform, by design we supposed but it could not have been so, for when it was all over the last thing we noticed before the grandees separated were the two standing with their arms around each other! Perhaps a grand review in Richmond would have had an equally happy effect in Halleck's case.

After Logan's army came old Slocum, for whom we all rose and gave a special cheer, and who was cheered by everyone, and the splendid army of Georgia. The 20th Corps more than any other impressed us with its immense size. Each division seemed an army in itself, and after each came the drollest mule train loaded with blankets and camp kettles and *poultry!* and darkies of all sizes, just as they came through Georgia and South Carolina—"Slocum's baggage," the people shouted, as they laughed and cheered. By this time the crowd of spectators had increased and encroached on the street so much that the infantry guards were unable to keep them back, and a file of cavalry were detailed to ride in advance of each division or brigade to clear the way, and Joe means to laugh at Slocum for his dodge in making a little force appear like a great one, for the company filed around behind the White House, as in a theater, and reappeared on the scene every few minutes like new troops.

ANOTHER EAGER CROWD SURROUNDS THE LADY

Mrs. Stephen Barker

Mrs. Barker had served during the war with her husband as a hospital visitor and had lectured throughout the country about the needs at the front. Now she was doing her bit for Field Relief and in this account, which appeared in the Sanitary Commission Bulletin, tells of some of the post-war work being done.

I remember no scene in camp more picturesque than some of our visits have presented. The great open army wagon stands under some shade tree with the officer who has volunteered to help, or the regular Field Agent, standing in the midst of boxes, bales, and bundles. Wheels, sides, and every protecting point are crowded with eager soldiers to see what "the Sanitary" has brought for them. By the side of the great wagon stands the light wagon of the lady, with its curtains rolled all up while she arranges before and around her the supplies she is to distribute. Another eager crowd surrounds her. . . . Quietly and rapidly the supplies are handed out for companies A, B, C, etc., first from one wagon, then the other, and as soon as a regiment is completed, the men hurry back to their tents to receive their share and write letters on the newly received paper, or apply the long-needed comb. . . .

Every day from the first to the twentieth day of June, our little band of missionaries has repeated a day's work such as I have now described . . . among the many pleasant memories connected with our Sanitary work, the last but not least will be our share in the Field Relief. . . .

PARTING WORDS BY MISS DIX

Sophronia E. Bucklin

Miss Dix sent a nurse to Fortress Monroe under my care, thus affording me a visit to the gigantic fortifications, and a look at those who had been for months under my care at Point of Rocks. The hospital being two miles from the landing, we took the horsecar from the boat, and soon reached the surgeon's office, where the nurse was assigned to duty.

I procured a pass and visited my colored man. As I passed the bars, one of them recognized me and uttered a cry of pleasure. . . . I was soon surrounded by many black faces. Upon asking some of the unfamiliar ones, "Did you ever see me before?" they called my attention to circumstances that transpired when they were in my charge at the hospital.

Everywhere there was joy that the war was over. Black and white shared alike in the promises held forth to them in the sur-

render. I found only a few old friends in the white wards, who
were now convalescent, and were about to be sent to their regiments, to be thence transferred home when the hour should
come. . . .

I took the parting hand of some of the old nurses here, who
had been my comrades at Gettysburg and at Georgetown. I
walked to the Soldiers' Cemetery to visit the grave of old Aunty
Alexander. She had gone from Camp Stoneman on a brief visit
to New York, and on her return was detailed for duty here. She
had been a good nurse and had worked hard until sudden death
overtook her. In compliance with her request she was buried
with military honors amongst the soldiers who died in the hospital. . . .

The cars in which we took passage for Richmond were box
cars, without seats or the ordinary traveling conveniences. A
bench, which would hardly have borne our weight, was standing
on the platform, and some of the boys proposed taking it, when
a man stepped up and said we could have it by paying the sum
of *two dollars*. We of course declined the *moderate* proposition.

As we were not in the line of duty just then, and at liberty to
exercise our judgment in the premises, we preferred to sit on
the four corners of a crockery crate which had been put in. Our
unstable seat swung to and fro with the motion of the cars
which, fortunately for our equilibrium, did not move rapidly.
Several gentlemen were also on board, bound for Richmond,
each bringing in a stick of wood for a seat.

We went, for a few miles, slowly through the lovely wooded
country, and then switched off to allow a train of cars to pass.
A short distance on, and another pause was made, in which the
fireman and the engineer went to a desolate-looking house, away
up in a clearing, bringing us back a cup of water. It was evident
that the demoralization of the country had even driven railroad

companies and their employees into a disregard of systemization.

The road being exceedingly rough, and the train hands corresponding with the road, we did not enter Richmond until about five o'clock. The only vehicle which awaited the convenience of the passengers was a one-horse wagon driven by an Irishman—both considerably dilapidated.

We found a lodgment, and on the following day, while strolling through the city, we met some of the men from our hospital, who had just made the round of Libby Prison and Castle Thunder.

Libby Prison we found to be a gloomy brick building, standing at the foot of the road—its three stories seeming quite low as we descended to it. The rooms were long, low, and narrow, having small grated windows, as indeed nearly every dwelling and barn in the Confederacy seemed to have.

On the cold floor, paved with round stones, which were hurtful to the feet at every step, our martyred men had lain till the bones wore through the flesh and they died from starvation. The lieutenant pointed out to us a hole in the cobblestone floor, large enough for a man to pass through, and told us the story of men who dug through fifteen rods of solid earth, with only their plates and spoons, scooping out the hard clay till they reached a point on the outside. My mind naturally recurred to the details of their long, patient toil; how they had managed to elude the vigilance of the guards, while crawling at a snail's pace with their puny tools; how near they had been to exposure, before the tunnel was finished, and how, in the hope of soon reaching the Union lines, even through swamps, and rivers, and deadly foes, one hundred and fifty men dropped themselves down, one by one, into the mouth of the den, and passed noiselessly out. Some of them were retaken, to suffer over again the horrors of the prison; other received the boon of liberty for the indescribable toil of weary days and nights.

It was dusk when we began our way from this place, made infamous by the torture of hundreds of the nation's best men, and we soon after reached the hospital at which we were favored with accommodations during our brief visit.

In the morning we visited the cupola of the capitol building and took a survey of the devastated city. Ewell had left the evidences of his destructiveness in the black ruins which lay around us. In the distance we distinctly saw Belle Isle, with the demolished bridge over the James River leading to it.

We next entered the office where the "ironclad" oath was being administered. We overheard one person remark, as he passed out, "Wall, now that's about the tallest swearin' I ever done," while others seemed unconscious of the meaning of the act. Some came in unable to tell what they did want. Of one such, the officer asked, "What shall I do for you, sir?" "I want a parole," was the reply. "Are you a soldier?" "No." "Then you do not want a parole." "Don't I want a pass?" asked the Rebel, the happy thought giving just a little ray of light across his stolid face. "Those are done away with now," replied the officer, and the anxious Rebel stepped back. About one hundred or more took the oath, and all were, with one exception, ragged, dirty, barefooted, and bareheaded.

The poverty apparent in these rooms gave rise to many reflections. The Senate Chamber was covered with a rag carpet very much worn. In another room we found a common ingrain, while the stair carpet was so far gone that we were obliged to use care to avoid tripping in its rents.

Our curiosity finally led us in the direction of the buildings that had been temporarily occupied by General Lee and Jefferson Davis. . . .

An order was issued, to take effect on the first day of June, that all hospitals kept open after that date should be at the expense of the surgeons in charge. So few patients remained to be nursed. Officials were suspected of a design to nurse the "good job" a little longer. The order had the desired effect, and the hospitals were broken up without delay.

Home was now the beautiful port in view. It was the first time that I felt a willingness to seek its shelter during three long years. While battles were to be fought, I was ready and truly anxious to endure suffering, to be near the scene of conflict, and to help minister to the bleeding heroes. I have even thought that imprisonment alone would have kept me from my country's service after the way to enter into it had been opened up. . . .

I fully realized the truth of the parting words, "You will have some pleasant as well as sad remembrances of your military life!" spoken by Miss Dix as I left her residence for the depot on my homeward way.

I arrived at Auburn, New York, just in time to meet with an old friend, and hear the salutation, "Well, I suppose you have fought, bled, and died for your country," when, in the wildest excitement, several ladies rushed in and exclaimed, "They have come!" and without giving me time to effect a change of clothing, I was marched off to assist in welcoming the remnant of the warworn One Hundred and Eleventh Regiment back to its native city.

Sick, weary with travel, dusty, and ragged, many were taken into the clean rooms of the hotel, and laid on the white counterpanes, while I, who was supposed to know how, went about at my old work of washing begrimed faces and combing tangled hair. *This time the heroes were not blood-stained.*

EACH WARD SEEMED LIKE A HAUNTED HOUSE
Julia Susan Wheelock

Julia had stayed on in Washington through the early months of the summer.

A certain number of hospitals were assigned to me as my special field of labor; yet I did not confine myself entirely to these, but made several visits to the surrounding camps with supplies, not only for those sick in the regimental hospitals, but also in their quarters. . . . Soon the hospitals in the city began to be broken up, and before the close of the month of June, several were entirely discontinued. . . . I can never efface from memory the feelings of loneliness experienced in passing through those empty hospitals. Each ward seemed like a haunted house, where the spirits of the departed still lingered. How suggestive even the number of these barracks or tents, many of which would bring to mind vivid recollections of painful scenes therein witnessed.

TRANSFERS AND DISCHARGES THINNED THE HOSPITAL RANKS

Jane Stuart Woolsey

Jane, the last of the Woolsey family to enlist in the war, remained on hospital duty longer than her three sisters as Superintendent of Fairfax Seminary Hospital.

Transfers and discharges thinned the Hospital ranks. Two hundred and ninety men went in one day. Wardmasters and cooks, "emergency men" disappeared among them, and it was very difficult to get through the day's work for the sixty to a hundred Special Diet Patients on the routes in July. Volunteer labor was never more needed. The men who remained in the wards required more care, and owing to the general disorganization, got less from the regular sources than ever before. Day by day we dissolved; night by night the camps about us vanished.

The slopes of the near hills, all twinkling and musical one evening, were on the next almost savagely silent and lonely.

The last of July the final order came: "You are directed to
say how soon your Hospital can be emptied, property packed,
and place turned over," etc. The Surgeon in Charge, being a
prodigious worker, answered, "In ten days. . . ."

All the Hospital goods were packed and boxed, and daily
wagon trains went down the hill carrying the "property" to the
city; the last of the sick were taken over—one man in his bed—
to a city hospital, and in the middle of August the quartermaster
made his last inspecting tour, with a paper in his hand in which
the fugitive owners of the place asked that the Secretary of
War would "Restore the buildings, cause thorough repairs to
be made, and pay a proper rent for the time they had been
occupied by the Government."

TRANSPORTATION HOME

Adelaide W. Smith

I was about to start for Washington when we were surprised
by a belated regiment—of the 6th Corps, I think—of sick men
toiling wearily into the deserted hospital camp, now in confusion
as if a raid had torn everything asunder. There was not a furnished bed or bunk for these poor sick discouraged men to lie
upon, nor was there any food for their famished bodies as they
dropped upon the bare ground exhausted, almost fainting.

I still had the use of an ambulance, and in this emergency
hastily ordered the driver to take me to City Point, one-half
mile distant, for help. Fortunately the Sanitary Commission
barge, loaded with surplus supplies, had not started, but was

just about to cut loose, when I informed them of the destitution and helplessness of the sick stranded soldiers.

Mr. J. Yates Peek, formerly of the 147th New York Infantry, at once reversed orders, unpacked supplies, and put his men to work. By night the barracks were covered with canvas roofs; comfortable beds were made of fresh hay, and the men were fed. The "contrabands" cheerfully assisted me in preparing food and caring for the famished men. I think Dr. Pooley was the only surgeon in camp. Contrabands helped, in their rude way, to nurse the helpless, and a little camp sprang up and remained until the men were able to travel and get transportation to Washington. There was probably no better work done by this great organization than that by the belated company of agents of the United States Sanitary Commission in that emergency. Without their help and supplies these men would have suffered keenly, and perhaps have died before relief could have been sent back from Washington on an unprecedented requisition, and the necessary red tape regulations complied with. . . .

Government passes and government roads were of the past, only regular army transportation was now allowed, except to the Medical Department for the purpose of sending home delayed patients. My "Grant Pass," that had made me so independent, became at once only a relic. Therefore, being entitled to transportation to my home, I went to Surgeon-General Barnes, U.S.A., to receive that privilege. After a pleasant conversation with the General, he remarked, "Your name is not on the payroll, and you are entitled to pay for army service. If you will make out your claim I will endorse it."

To this I replied, with more sentiment, as I now see it, than judgment, "General, I thank you, but I do not wish pay for my services in hospital work. If I had been a man I would have enlisted as a soldier. But being only a woman it was all I could do, and I wish to give that service to my country."

Often, since then, I have thought of the quizzical expression of the General's eyes, though he said not a word about an impractical girl who did not think far enough to see what good she might have done with that accumulated wage of several years.

At that time, however, I was receiving (during several months) sixty dollars per month as New York State Agent, the only pay I ever received. But that seemed different. The war was over.

The General then asked how far I wanted transportation. I replied that I lived in Brooklyn, but would take transportation as far as he would give it. . . .

Resting only a few days after my return to my home, I was urged by friends on the Sanitary Commission to assist in dispensing some surplus funds for the Sanitary Commission, with headquarters in New York City. This surplus could not, according to their organization, be used for other purposes than for the benefit of soldiers. After much discussion it seemed that the soldiers' families should be the natural recipients. So during most of that unusually severe winter, 1865-66, I went daily from my home in Brooklyn to New York, and with my companion found many families in need of help, who might otherwise have perished with cold. When spring brought relief, the last dollar of that grand life-saving organization was expended.

This was, of course, before the day of pensions. We continued this work until the funds were exhausted. Then I retired finally from the engrossing activity of hospital life and caring for soldiers' families, in which I was engaged from 1862 through 1866.

TAPS

Mary Woolsey Howland

Mrs. Jane Newton Woolsey's longing for a full family reunion was never satisfied. Frail, beautiful Mary died May 31, 1864, in her Astoria home. In her last days Mary wrote her "Taps," the Army bugle call to sleep, to put out the light.

> Put it out! Put it out! Put it out!
>   The clear notes rising, climb
>   A ladder of sweet sound,
>   And from each golden round
> The ascending angels, nearing heaven, do chime,
> "God's watch begins, put your dim lanterns out!"
>
>   Put out each earthly light;
>   It is God's shadow falls
>   Along the darkening walls,
> Cosing us round, when men say "it is night";
> HE draws so near it shuts the daylight out.
>
> Put it out! Put it out! Put it out!
>   Forbear each scheme of ill;
>   Good angels walk the ward,
>   And heaven is all abroad
> When twilight falls, and earth lies hushed and still;
> Room for the angels! Put the dark deeds out.
>
>   Put out all thoughts of care:
>   Rest gently, aching head;
>   He stands beside the bed
> Who brings in peace and healing, unaware,
> And sends soft-footed sleep to shut pain out.

Put it out! Put it out! Put it out!
    Put out—quite out—the light.
    Hark! as the notes grow faint,
    Was that a new-voiced saint
Who climbed with them, and scaled the starry height?
Has from among us any soul gone out?

    God's love falls as a screen.
    Where lights burn dim and pale
    No flickering flame shall fail,
For with His hand held steadfastly between,
No wind can blow to put these life-lamps out.

    Through earth's long night He waits,
    Till, to the soul's glad eyes
    Filled with divine surprise,
Heaven opens wide her golden morning gates:
Then, day being come, He breathes the candle out.

20 New Freedom and New Horizons

MANY OF THE ARMY NURSES AND SANITARY COMMISSION AGENTS continued their hospital and field relief work through 1866 when the last soldiers were mustered out of service. Some, such as Jane Stuart Woolsey and Charlotte E. McKay, devoted themselves to working among the Freedmen in Virginia. At Poplar Springs, Mrs. McKay received supplies of clothing from various charitable societies in this country and England, which she distributed to the destitute Negroes who were living in makeshift settlements or camps formerly occupied by the Union soldiers. Still other women returned to their homes and obscurity, forgotten too soon by the country they had loyally served. Several years had to pass after the war before official recognition was given the Army nurses and the female social workers by the Government. Not until 1886 did the legislature of New York State dare authorize the Department of New York of the Grand Army of the Republic to erect a monument on the Capitol grounds at Albany in honor of the women of the state for their humane and patriotic acts during the war. And still more time had to elapse before a national pension bill was finally passed.

Between 1865 and 1877 the United States struggled through a period of corruption in Government, economic depression, and Indian wars. The Radical Republicans in power put party and personal interest above reform, devoting their energies to humiliating the South rather than to humanitarianism. They found it convenient and useful at election time to recall the bravery of the boys in blue and wave the bloody flag. These were sure-fire vote-getting tactics. But the politicians were not interested in securing pensions for needy veterans, let alone for sick and needy Army nurses who did not have the right to vote.

Now and again, through the intervention of friends or former military leaders, individual women were granted some compensation. Annie Turner Wittemyer, for example, who was a great friend of Julia Dent Grant, managed to receive fifty dollars a month from a Congress that was otherwise dedicated to graft and greed. But it was not until after President Rutherford B. Hayes brought decent government back to the United States that it was possible to ameliorate the situation. Hayes as a Congressman had fought for pensions for sick and destitute veterans and had won the thanks of the men. As President he put an end to the period of Reconstruction and carpetbagging. Troops were removed for all time from the Southern states. The nation embarked upon a period of reform, which at first did not improve the situation of the women of the war.

The soldiers of the Grand Army of the Republic loyally remembered the women who had looked after them on the battlefields and in the hospitals. They expressed their gratitude in many ways. A report of the Michigan Soldiers' Relief Association stated that the services of "Miss Wheelock . . . and others who have labored in the field and hospitals under the auspices of this Association have all largely earned the thanks of the people of Michigan, and especially of the thousands of soldiers who received their kind ministrations." When the soldiers learned of the financial straits of Mary A. Bickerdyke, they proposed to tax themselves a certain sum yearly to maintain her above want, but broken as she was by the hardships she had endured, "Mother" Bickerdyke refused to allow the men to make any sacrifices for her. At last, through the efforts of Generals Sherman and Grant, and her friend, Mary A. Livermore, Congress allotted Mrs. Bickerdyke in 1886 a pension, not of fifty dollars as had been requested by her supporters, but twenty-five dollars a month. But no provision even then was made to recompense nurses as a group.

In 1892, many of the women who had faithfully served their country were old and destitute. Many had been in poor health since the war. In desperation, they appealed to Annie Wittemyer for help. Annie went at once to Washington to see what she could do. She had always known the right people and exerted a certain amount of influence because of her connections. But it was more likely a reflection of the mood of the times rather than Annie's influence that, after five months of lobbying and debating, brought about the passage of a bill granting twelve dollars a month to those who could prove their title under the law. Those who had been compensated for their work during the war received between six and ten dollars a month. But the record of their services was so incomplete that it was almost impossible to prove a claim. A great number of the women died without reward or recognition and in extreme poverty, despite the fact that the Civil War soldiers were more indebted to these women than to any other class of people.

Meanwhile, the Woman's Suffrage movement, which had faded temporarily from the political scene during the war, returned greatly strengthened by the new freedom women had won for themselves during the years of crisis. Old prejudices and restrictions against them had been swept aside. A need for their labor had been created in new and untried paths, and they had finally been given an opportunity not only to prove their ability but to demonstrate that women could be as courageous as the men. The Treasury Department opened its doors wide to women and many, such as Julia Wheelock, who worked for the Registrar's Office, were offered lifelong jobs as clerks. No women appreciated the advances their sex had made more than the Army nurses and Sanitary Commission agents whose names appear in the annals of the Woman's Suffrage movement. Mary A. Livermore worked for women's rights from the start and kept the columns of her paper "ablaze with demands for the opening to women of college and professional schools . . . and for the enlargement of their industrial opportunities." For thirty years, Jane C. Hoge was the recognized leader among the women of Chicago in Social Service work. In June, 1893, Mary Bickerdyke addressed a letter "To the Heroes of 1861-1865" in a local newspaper in Russell, Kansas, where she was living, requesting the soldiers to assist the women who had stood by them and cared for them in the war "by voting for them to have the right to vote. . . . We ask you to stand by us as we stood by you in all the hard-fought battles." Her letter was read at Memorial Day gatherings everywhere and listened to with loving attention. A committee was appointed to act on the request and a resolution was drawn up in which the soldiers offered to "support and aid the proposition by their vote and influence." Unfortunately, the letter did not succeed in arousing the general public.

Reform movements were particularly popular with the nineteenth-century ladies. The temperance stand of the White House during the Hayes administration helped the cause of the W.C.T.U., which flourished successfully until Prohibition became the law of the land in the twentieth century. Crusading on behalf of the Woman's Temperance Union was Mary Livermore, of course, finding keen competition on the lecture platform in the person of handsome, blue-eyed Annie Wittemyer, who also became prominent in the Anti-Saloon League. Annie found stimulation in noble causes such as the Women's Relief Corps of the Grand Army of the Republic (of which she became president) and home missionary work.

Five of the women connected with the United States Sanitary Commission continued their interest in the field of nursing. In

1870, when the Franco-Prussian War broke out, Mary Phinney
von Olnhausen went overseas to the battlefield. Fifty-two-year-
old Mary nursed her husband's countrymen and received from
the grateful Prussians the Iron Cross and a certificate for her
noble acts of service. In 1872, Louisa Lee Schuyler founded and
was elected the first president of the State Charities Association
of New York, of which Abby Howland Woolsey was a charter
member. Miss Schuyler issued a call to the women who had
worked with her during the Civil War to meet and discuss
the deplorable condition of Bellevue Hospital. Before the meeting ended, the wheels were in motion. A committee was sent
to inspect the Bellevue wards. The ladies of the State Aid
learned of the "ten-day women" in Bellevue who, after being
arrested for drunkenness or disorderly conduct and given ten
days in jail, were permitted to serve their sentences (after being
sobered up) as nurses in the wards. Conditions were particularly
bad at night, when it was the usual practice to leave the care
of the patients to a few night watchmen who made periodic
rounds of the wards.

The wheels moved faster. Bellevue had to have a training
school for nurses. That was Louisa Lee Schuyler's idea and her
friend, Abby Howland Woolsey, willingly drafted the plan. Although Georgeanna had married Francis Bacon and no longer
had time for hospital work, Abby and her sister, Jane Stuart
Woolsey, carried on a private war for a training school for nurses
at Presbyterian Hospital, New York City, where Jane was Resi-
dent Directress and Abby her associate. These Woolsey girls
were given credit for the co-ordination of the various departments, staff, and activities of the Presbyterian Hospital. They
employed middle-aged women as nurses who learned through
serving under the guidance of Abby and Jane, with a little help
from the doctors! The leading nurses of the Civil War set an
example to the nineteenth-century debutantes and influenced

young girls of good families to enter the School of Nursing at Bellevue to replace inmates of the workhouse who were caring for the poor emigrant patients in the hospital wards.

Harriet Foote Hawley, whose husband became first senator and then governor of Connecticut, was made president of the Western Branch of the Indian Rights Association. The Government had been paying six million dollars a year in an effort to solve the Indian problem, but managed to achieve little more than scandals and small wars until Carl Schurz began investigating the Indian Bureau. It is a credit to such women as Harriet Hawley that they saw their role in the field of reform even in this neglected area, and recognized the claim of the Indians to the elemental rights of humanity. At her death in 1886, the G.A.R. Posts at Washington sent a wreath of flowers for Harriet's casket, which members of the Union League Club escorted across New York City. Two posts attended her funeral at Hartford and the 7th Connecticut Regiment, which her husband had formerly commanded, sent an arrangement of flowers to adorn her coffin, in token of her having become a "daughter of the Army and the Country." The votaries of women's rights had indeed come a long way!

Many of the former Civil War nurses took up writing to the extent of recording memoirs of their War experiences. A great number of these books were privately printed, but 175,000 copies were sold of *Unsexed, or The Female Soldier,* by Sarah Emma Edmonds. The entire proceeds of the sale were donated by her to soldiers' aid societies. After returning to her home state of Massachusetts and settling with her family in Melrose, Mary A. Livermore wrote large tomes about her busy life before and during the Civil War as well as numerous biographies, essays, and books of poetry. Katharine P. Wormeley, who took an active part in public affairs and charitable enterprises in Newport, Rhode Island, found time to write not only her own memoirs, but a book dealing with the purposes and work of the United States Sanitary Commission, compiled from documents and private papers. In 1879, Katharine and her two sisters wrote a book about their father, *Recollections of Ralph Randolph Wormeley.* Annie Turner Wittemyer wrote many religious, purposeful books and a number of hymns that people enjoyed singing. For eleven years she edited a monthly paper with a large circulation and for five years a department in *The New York Weekly Tribune.* Eliza Woolsey Howland and Georgeanna Woolsey Bacon collaborated on a history of their family during the Civil War, *Letters of a Family During the War for the Union.* Later Eliza Woolsey Howland came up with a very sentimental family history. In 1893, Abby Howland Woolsey produced a book about nursing.

Perhaps the most recent tribute to a Civil War nurse is a Silverdale limestone bust of Mother Bickerdyke, created in 1956 by F. R. Wentworth, a sculptor in Russell, Kansas, who immortalized the famous nurse, beloved by the boys in blue during the Civil War.

Certainly the most incredible story of the women of the war, particularly to the former comrades of the Second Michigan Volunteer Infantry, Company F, was the revelation that Franklin Thompson, the supposed male nurse and spy in McClellan's Army, had been Sarah Emma Edmonds all the while!

In April, 1863, Emma had suffered again from the severe malarial fever that she had contracted originally in the Chickahominy swamps. All the quinine the doctors gave her "but seemed to increase the vehemence of the malady," and she was advised to apply for leave of absence. She and one or two other hospital attendants did so, and their furlough papers were made out and sent to headquarters for approval. For days they waited for these papers and when they finally did come Emma's alone was marked "Disapproved." Sick as she was, she dared not go to the hospital as her sex would have been discovered, and such discovery seemed to her at the time a fate "far worse than death." She therefore went off AWOL and as of April 22, 1863, was listed as a deserter from the 2nd Michigan. Emma never for a moment considered herself a deserter but felt that her illness left no other course open.

After resting for a few weeks, she set about writing her memoirs, *Nurse and Spy or Unsexed, the Female Soldier,* and then, fully recovered from her chills and fever, returned to the Army "in another costume." As a woman, she served with the Christian Commission at Harper's Ferry, Virginia, until the close of the war, nursing the wounded and distributing with her own hands thousands of dollars from her first literary venture to the poor, suffering men whom she had "learned to love as brothers."

At the close of the war, Sarah Emma went back to St. John's River, New Brunswick, Canada, where she renewed her friendship with Linus H. Seelye, a young mechanic she had known since childhood. Emma remained in her home town until 1866 when, apparently restless once more, she left for Oberlin, Ohio, where she had convalesced during the war. Linus Seelye followed her to Ohio, and the two young Canadians were married April 27, 1867, in the parlors of Wedwell House, Cleveland. They lived a rather nomadic existence for several years, moving from Ohio to Michigan, then to Illinois, and finally to Fort Scott, Kansas.

It was while the Seelyes were living in Kansas that Emma communicated with her former comrades of the 2nd Michigan Infantry. Her friends had continually urged her to try to get a common soldier's bounty and the back pay that legitimately belonged to "Frank" but she refused to do so. Finally her health had deteriorated to such a degree that she decided it would be no more than right if Uncle Sam "should pension one female soldier who has actually served two years, or nearly so, of faithful, hard service, when he has pensioned so many male effeminates who never smelt powder on a battlefield."

As soon as the address of "Frank Thompson" was received, an invitation was forwarded to Emma at Fort Scott, Kansas, by Colonel Frederick Schneider, Post Commander of Charles T. Foster Post, G.A.R., and Past Commander of the 2nd Michigan Volunteer Infantry, to attend a reunion in 1883. Emma was moved by the invitation to be present at the reunion, but unfortunately she was bedridden at the time. She did not even have the strength to write a letter to be read at the reunion, but sent a brief message, that Frank's heart beat just as warm and true to them today as when it beat under a regulation blouse. She requested each of her friends of the 2nd to send her his picture.

After some correspondence, a few comrades of the "Old Second" induced her to attend the next Reunion of their regiment and obtained free passage for her.

What a surprise the veterans had when they found out that Franklin Thompson was now Mrs. Linus Scclyc! After twenty years everyone had changed, of course, but not to a different sex. This may seem unbelievable, but even Sarah Emma's mother had failed to recognize the girl when she visited Canada once before the war. It was not until Emma had revealed a childhood scar that the mother admitted that young Franklin Thompson was her daughter, Emma. The soldiers had known Sarah Emma as a trim, adventurous young man, Franklin Thompson, and here they were exchanging war memories with a "somewhat fleshy" middle-aged matron!

Her old comrades gave Emma a royal reception. Since among all her other duties she had held the position of regimental postmaster and subsequently brigade postmaster, she had become a familiar figure to all the boys, who were always watching her goings and comings for letters from home and friends.

Meanwhile active steps were taken by the regimental association and a committee was appointed to push her claims before Congress, "to restore her to honorable standing on the records of the War Department, to grant her an honorable discharge, a pension, back pay, and bounty." Through the influence of her fellow soldiers, all was forgiven the young matron who was in poor health and equally poor circumstances; the 48th Congress passed an act removing Emma's disabilities as a deserter and granting her a pension of twelve dollars a month.

On November 14, 1884, Sarah Emma appeared before the clerk in the District Court of Records in Kansas to swear that she "was enrolled in or about the 12th day of April, 1861, in Company F, Second Regiment, Michigan Volunteer Infantry, under the name of Franklin Thompson, and that said company . . . was raised at Flint, in the State of Michigan." Emma claimed she was mustered into the United States service on or about May 25, 1861, and that under the name of Franklin Thompson she had served the United States and performed the duties required by a soldier "to the full satisfaction of the officers in command." Emma explained how she had become ill again while in the line of duty near Lebanon, Kentucky with a fever originally contracted in the Chickahominy swamps. She had failed to procure a furlough and on or about April 22, 1863, had been forced to "absent herself without leave from said company and regiment and under the said name of Franklin Thompson was borne on the muster rolls as a deserter." She now requested that her name might be placed on the pension rolls and that "said pension and all back pay and bounty may be allowed as set forth in said Act of Congress which was approved July 5, 1884."

In 1891, Emma's son, Frederick, married and moved to La Porte, Texas. Not long afterward she and her husband joined the young couple there. This was Emma's final move. She was soon in contact with her former comrades who lived in the Lone Star State and was mustered into the George B. McClellan Post in Houston, thereby becoming the only woman member of the Grand Army of the Republic. A year later, on September 5, 1898, Emma Edmonds Seelye died and was buried near La Porte. The funeral was held at La Porte under the direction of a delegation of the G.A.R. Post. Emma was survived by her husband and two sons. One, Charles, decided to be a soldier, "like Mama," and joined the regular Army.

On Memorial Day in 1901, the body of Emma Seelye was removed to Washington Cemetery in Houston, then called German Cemetery. She was re-interred in the G.A.R. burial plot in a grave indicated by a simple metal marker and is said to be the only woman buried there.

The names of many of the women who served their country during and after the War are not included in the histories of the times, but to them as to the unknown soldiers belongs a share in the glory of those whose names have been preserved. To them as to the better known their country owes an eternal debt of gratitude. Their deeds of self-sacrifice and unselfishness, their crusades on behalf of their sex, should not be forgotten. The examples of true courage and patriotism set by the women of the century should be recalled by all the generations to come.

Epilogue

I AM NOT ACCUSTOMED TO USE THE LANGUAGE
OF EULOGY. I HAVE NEVER STUDIED THE ART OF
PAYING COMPLIMENTS TO WOMEN. BUT I MUST
SAY THAT, IF ALL THAT HAS BEEN SAID BY ORA-
TORS AND POETS SINCE THE CREATION OF THE
WORLD IN PRAISE OF WOMEN WAS APPLIED TO
THE WOMEN OF AMERICA, IT WOULD NOT DO
THEM JUSTICE FOR THEIR CONDUCT DURING
THIS WAR. I WILL CLOSE BY SAYING, GOD BLESS
THE WOMEN OF AMERICA!

—ABRAHAM LINCOLN

Bibliography

ADAMS, GEORGE WORTHINGTON. *Doctors in Blue: The Medical History of the Union Army in the Civil War*. New York, 1952.

An Account of Bellevue Hospital with a Catalogue of the Medical and Surgical Staff from 1736-1894. Edited by Robert J. Carlisle.

ALCOTT, LOUISA MAY. *Hospital Sketches*. Boston, 1863.

ANDREWS, MARY SHIPMAN. *A Lost Commander: Florence Nightingale*. New York, 1929.

ANTHONY, KATHARINE. *Louisa May Alcott*. New York, 1938.

ASHBY, THOMAS A. *The Valley Campaigns*. Ch. XXIV: "Military Operations of 1864."

AST, HENRY M., Brevet. Brigadier General, U.S.V., Secretary of the Army of the Cumberland. *The Army of the Cumberland*. New York, 1882.

AVARY, MYRTA L. *A Virginia Girl in the Civil War*. New York, 1903.

BACON, GEORGEANNA WOOLSEY (and Eliza Woolsey Howland). *Letters of a Family During the War for the Union*. New Haven, 1899.

BAKER, NINA BROWN. *Cyclone in Calico*. Boston, 1952.

BAKER, RACHEL. *The First Woman Doctor*. New York, 1944.

BARRINGER, EMILY DUNNING, M.D. *Bowery to Bellevue*. New York, 1950.

BARTON, GEORGE. *The World's Greatest Military Spies and Secret Service Agents*. Boston, 1917.

BLANTON, WYNDHAM B., M.D. *Medicine in Virginia in the 19th Century*. Richmond, 1933.

BENSON, B. K. (Fiction). *Who Goes There: The Story of a Spy in the Civil War*. New York, 1901.

BOYD, BELLE. *Belle Boyd in Camp and Prison*. New York, 1865.

Battles and Leaders of the Civil War. Edited by Ned Bradford. New York, 1956.

BREMNER, FREDERIKA. *America in the Fifties*. New York, 1924.

The British Traveller in America 1836-60. New York, 1943.

BROCKETT, L. P. *Men of the War*. Philadelphia, 1869.

BROCKETT, L. P. and MARY C. VAUGHN. *Woman's Work in the Civil War*. Philadelphia, 1868.

BROCKETT, L. P. *Scouts, Spies, and Heroes of the Great Civil War*. Jersey City, 1892.

BROWN, ESTHER LUCILLE, Ph.D. *The Future of Nursing*. Russell Sage Foundation, 1948.

BRYAN, GEORGE S. *The Spy in America*. Philadelphia, 1943.

BUCKLIN, SOPHRONIA E. *In Hospital and Camp*. Philadelphia, 1869.

BURR, FRANK A., and RICHARD J. HUNTER. *The Life of General Philip Sheridan*. Providence, R.I. 1888.

BURTON, MARGARET DAVIS. *The Woman Who Battled for the Boys in Blue: Mother Bickerdyke*. San Francisco, 1886.

BUSHNELL, HORACE. *Work and Play*. New York, 1864.

CADWALLADER, SYLVANUS. *Three Years With Grant*. New York, 1955.

CARLISLE, ROBERT J., Ed. *An Account of Bellevue Hospital With a Catalogue of the Medical and Surgical Staff from 1736 to 1894*. New York, 1894.

CARPENTER, GEORGE H. *History of the Eighth Regiment Vermont Volunteers*. Boston, 1886, pp. 156-235.

CATTON, BRUCE. *This Hallowed Ground*. New York, 1955, 1956. *Glory Road*. New York, 1952. *Stillness at Appomattox*. New York, 1953.

CHASE, JULIA. *Mary A. Bickerdyke, "Mother."* Published under auspices of the Woman's Relief Corps, Department of Kansas. Lawrence, Kan., 1896.

CHESTNUT, MARY BOYKIN. *A Diary from Dixie*. Edited by Isabella D. Martin and Myra L. Avary. New York, 1905.

CASTLEMAN, ALFRED L., Surgeon, 5th Regiment, Wisconsin Volunteers. *The Army of the Potomac*. Milwaukee, 1863.

CHENEY, EDNAH D. *Louisa May Alcott, Her Life, Letters, and Journals*. Boston, 1928.

CIST, HENRY M. *The Army of the Cumberland*. New York, 1882.

COMMAGER, HENRY STEELE. *The Blue and the Grey*. Indianapolis, 1950. 2 vols.

COOPER, PAGE. *The Bellevue Story*. New York, 1948.

COULTER, E. MERTON. *A History of the South*, VII, *The Confederate States of America 1861-1865*, Ch. XVIII, "Progress and Decay—Women, Hospitals and Relief." Baton Rouge, 1950.

CROOK, GENERAL GEORGE. *Autobiography*. Edited and Annotated by Martin F. Schmitt. Norman, Okla., 1946.

CURTIS, O. B. A. M. *History of the 24th Michigan of the Iron Brigade*. Detroit, 1891.

DANNA, DAVID D. *The Fireman*. Boston, 1858.

DANNETT, SYLVIA G. L., and RACHEL FRANK. *Down Memory Lane—The Picture Story Of Social Dancing*. New York, 1954, pp. 40-65.

DAVIDSON, MARSHALL B. *Life in America*. Boston, 1951. Vol. II.

Deeds of Daring by Both Blue and Gray. Philadelphia, 1883.

DE FOREST, JOHN WILLIAM. *A Volunteer's Adventure*. New Haven, 1946.

DE LEON, T. C. *Belles, Beaux and Brains of the 60's*. New York, 1907.

DENNISON, REV. FREDERIC (Chaplain). *Sabres and Spurs—The First Regiment Rhode Island Cavalry*. 1876, pp. 380-383, 389-435. Providence, 1865.

Dictionary of American Biography. V, p. 4; IX, pp. 291-293; XI, pp. 306-307; XX, pp. 518, 534.

Dictionary of American History. V, p. 146, "Sarah Emma Edmonds."

DOCK, LAVINIA L., R.N., in collaboration with ISABEL MAITLAND STEWART, A.M., R.N. *A Short History of Nursing*. New York, 1920.

DOUGLAS, HENRY KYD. *I Rode With Stonewall*. Chapel Hill, N.C., 1940.

DOUNS, EDWARD C. *Four Years a Scout and Spy*. Zanesville, Ohio, 1866.

DUPONT, HENRY A. (Colonel.) *The Campaign of 1864 in the Valley of Virginia*. New York, 1925.

EDDY, T. M. *The Patriotism of Illinois*. Chicago, 1865.

EDMONDS, SARAH EMMA. *Nurse and Spy or Unsexed, The Female Soldier*. Hartford, 1864; later reprinted in Philadelphia.

ECKENRODE, H. J. *Rutherford B. Hayes, Statesman of Renown*. New York, 1930.

ELLET, MRS. *The Queens of American Society*. Philadelphia, 1867.

Encyclopedia of Quaker Genealogy. Minutes of Burlington Monthly Meeting.

EPLER, PERCY H. *The Life of Clara Barton*. New York, 1915.

Famous Adventures and Prison Escapes of the Civil War. New York, 1885, 1888, 1890, 1891, 1893, 1911.

FEDERAL WRITERS' PROJECT, TEXAS. *Houston: A History and Guide*. 1942, pp. 328-329.

First Fifty Years of Mount Sinai Hospital. Printed privately by Hospital, 1944.

FISKE, JOHN. *The Mississippi Valley in the Civil War*. Boston and New York, 1900.

FAULKER, JOSEPH. *The Life of Philip Sheridan*. New York, 1888.

FORSYTH, GEORGE A. (General, U.S.A.). *Thrilling Days in Army Life*. New York, 1900.

GLAZIER, WILLARD. *The Capture, the Prison Pen, and the Escape*. Hartford, 1868.

GOODMAN, PHILIP. "A Personal Tribute to Lincoln by Josephine Philips." A pamphlet reprinted from publication of the *American Jewish Historical Society*, XLI, No. 2, December 19, 1951.

GRANT, ULYSSES S. *Personal Memoirs.* New York, 1885-86, 2 vols.

GREENHOW, ROSE O'NEAL. *My Imprisonment and the First Year of Abolition Rule at Washington.* London, 1863.

GREENBIE, MARJORIE B. *Lincoln's Daughters of Mercy.* New York, 1944.

GUNN, MRS. MOSES. *Memorial Sketches of Doctor Moses Gunn.* Chicago, 1889.

Harper's Pictorial History of the Great Rebellion. 1866.

HARROLD, JOHN C. *Libby, Andersonville, Florence.* Philadelphia, 1870.

HART, CHARLES S. *George Washington's Sons of Israel and Other Forgotten Heroes of History.* London and Philadelphia, 1937.

HASSLER, WARREN W., JR. *McClellan, Shield of the Union.* Baton Rouge, La., 1957.

HAYNIE, J. HENRY (Ed.). *The Nineteenth Illinois, A Memoir of a Volunteer Infantry Famous in the Civil War.* Chicago, 1912, pp. 166-168.

HENDERSON, G. F. R. (Colonel). *Stonewall Jackson and the American Civil War.* London and New York, 1936.

HIRSH, JOSEPH and BELLA DOHERTY. *The First Hundred Years of the Mount Sinai Hospital of New York.* New York, 1922.

HOLLAND, MARY GARDINER (Compiler). *Our Army Nurses.* Interesting Sketches, Addresses, and Photographs of Nearly One Hundred of the Noble Women Who Served in Hospitals and on Battlefields During Our Civil War. Boston, 1895.

HOLSTEIN, ANNA (Mrs. W. H.). *Three Years in Field Hospitals of the Army of the Potomac.* Philadelphia, 1867.

HOLZMAN, ROBERT S. *Stormy Ben Butler.* New York, 1954.

HOGE, MRS. A. H. *The Boys in Blue, Heroes of the Rank and File.* New York and Chicago, 1867.

HANCOCK, CORNELIA. *South After Gettysburg, Letters of Cornelia Hancock.* Philadelphia, 1937.

HOGE, JANE B. *In Memoriam.* Chicago.

HOOD, EDWIN. *History of Genessee County (Michigan).* Vol. 1, p. 350 gives the date of the reunion of the Second Infantry Company F, to which Mrs. Seelye was invited.

HORAN, JAMES D. *Desperate Women.* New York, 1952.

HORN, STANLEY F. *The Army of Tennessee.* New York, 1941.

Hospital Transports. A Memoir of the Embarkation of the Sick and Wounded From the Peninsula of Virginia in the Summer of 1862. Boston, 1863.

HOWE, JULIA WARD. *Reminiscences, 1819-1899.* Boston, 1899, Ch. XI.

HOWLAND, ELIZA NEWTON WOOLSEY. *Family Records, Being Some Account of the Ancestry of my Father and Mother, Charles William Woolsey and Jane Eliza Newton.* Copyright, 1900. In Thomas Jefferson Room, Library of Congress Annex, Genealogical Section. 1900.

IRWIN, RICHARD B. *History of the Nineteenth Army Corps.* London and New York, 1893.

JAQUETTE, HENRIETTA STRATTON (Ed.). *South After Gettysburg, Letters of Cornelia Hancock from The Army of the Potomac, 1863-1865.* Philadelphia, 1937.

JOHNS, GEORGE S. *Philip Heuson, The Southern Union Spy.* St. Louis, 1887.

JONES, KATHARINE M. *Heroines of Dixie.* Indianapolis, 1955.

KEIFER, J. WARREN. *Slavery and Four Years of War.* New York, 1900, 2 vols.

KELLOGG, FLORENCE SHAW. *Mother Bickerdyke as I Knew Her.* Chicago, 1907.

KIRKLAND, FRAZIER. *The Book of Anecdotes of the War of the Rebellion.* Hartford, 1866, 2 vols.

KIRKLAND, FRAZIER. *The Pictorial Book of Anecdotes and Incidents of the War of the Rebellion.* Hartford, 1885.

KORN, BERTRAM W. *American Jewry and the Civil War.* Philadelphia, 1951.

LANGDON, W. C. *Everyday Things in American Life 1776-1876.* New York, 1941.

LEECH, MARGARET. *Reveille in Washington.* New York, 1941.

LEE, ELEANOR, A.B., R.N. *History of the School of Nursing of the Presbyterian Hospital, 1892.* New York, 1942.

LIVERMORE, MARY ANN. *My Story of the War.* Hartford, 1890.

LIVERMORE, MARY ANN. *The Story of My Life.* Hartford, 1898.

LOMAX, VIRGINIA. *The Old Capitol and Its Inmates.* New York, 1867.

MAGILL, MARY TUCKER. *Women, or Chronicles of the Late War.* Baltimore, 1864.

MARTINEAU, HARRIET. *Society in America.* New York, 1837.

MASON, WHITING TYLER. *Recollections of the Civil War.* New York, 1912.

MAXWELL, W. QUENTIN. *Lincoln's Fifth Wheel.* New York, 1956.

MEADE, GEORGE GORDON. *The Life and Letters of George Gordon Meade.* New York, 1913, Vols. I, II.

Memorial of Margaret E. Breckinridge. Philadelphia, 1865.

MILLER, FRANCIS TREVELYAN. *Photographic History of the Civil War.* New York, 1911.

MONOGHAN, FRANK. *This Was New York, the nation's Capital in 1789.* Garden City, 1943.

MONAGHAN, JAY. *Civil War on the Western Border 1854-1865*. Boston, 1955.

MONTEIRO, ARISTIDES. *War Reminiscences by the Surgeon of Mosby's Command*. Richmond, Virginia, 1890.

MOORE, FRANK. *Women of the War: Their Heroism and Self-Sacrifice*. Hartford, 1866.

MOORE, FRANK. *Anecdotes, Poetry and Incidents of the War*. New York, 1866.

MOORE, FRANK. *The Civil War in Song and Story*. New York, 1865.

MOORE, FRANK, ed. Rebellion Record, 12 vols. 1861-65.

MORTON, FREDERIC. *The Story of Winchester in Virginia*. Strasburg, 1925.

MOSBY, JOHN S., Colonel, C.S.A. *Mosby's War Reminiscences and Stuart's Cavalry Campaigns*. Boston, 1887.

MOSBY, JOHN S. *The Memoirs of Colonel John S. Mosby*. Boston, 1917.

MUNROE, JAMES PHINNEY. *Adventures of an Army Nurse in Two Wars*. Edited from the Diary and Correspondence of Mary Phinney, Baroness von Olnhausen. Boston, 1904.

McCORMICK, HENRY. *The Women of Illinois*. Bloomington, Ill., 1893, 1913.

McDONALD, CORNELIA. *A Diary With Reminiscences of the War and Refugee Life in the Shenandoah Valley 1860-65*. Nashville, 1935.

McGUIRE, MRS. JUDITH W. *Diary of a Southern Refugee*. New York, 1867.

McKAY, CHARLOTTE E. *Stories of Hospital and Camp*. Philadelphia, 1876.

McKAY, CHARLOTTE E. *Testimonial of Army Officers to the Services of Mrs. C. E. McKay*. Cavalry Corps Hospital Near City Point, Virginia. December 22, 1864.

National Cyclopedia of American Biography. New York, 1904. Vol. 12.

NUTTING, M. ADELAIDE, R.N., and LAVINIA L. DOCK, R.N. *A History of Nursing*. New York, 1907, 1935, 4 vols. Vol. II.

OLMSTED, FREDERICK L. *Hospital Transports, A Memoir*. Boston, 1863.

O'CONNOR, RICHARD. *Sheridan, The Inevitable*. Indianapolis, 1953.

PACKARD, FRANCIS R., M.D. *History of Medicine in the United States*. New York, 1932, Vol. I.

PATTON, JAMES WELCH, and FRANCIS BUTLER SIMKINS. *The Women of the Confederacy*. New York and Richmond, 1936.

PEMBER, PHOEBE Y. *A Southern Woman's Story*. New York, 1879.

PHINNEY, MARY, BARONESS VON OLNHAUSEN. *See* Munroe, James Phinney.

PHISTERER, FREDERICK, Captain in U.S. Army. *New York in the War of the Rebellion 1861-1865*. Albany, 1890.

The Photographic History of the Civil War. Edited by Francis Trevelyan
Miller. Robert S. Lanier, Managing Editor. New York, 1911-12.
Vol. 2, "Two Years of Grim War," text by Henry W. Elson, Pro-
fessor of History, Ohio University. Photo. descriptions by James
Barues. Vol. 7, "Prisons and Hospitals," Holland Thompson, Editor.
Vol. 9, "Poetry and Eloquence of Blue and Gray," Dudley H. Miles,
Editor, with an appendix, "Songs of the War Days." Edited by
Jeanne Robert Foster. Vol. 10, "Armies and Leaders."

PINKERTON, ALLAN. *The Spy of the Rebellion.* New York, 1883.

POLLARD, EDWARD. *The Lost Cause.* New York, 1866. Sold by subscription.

POND, GEORGE E. *The Shenandoah Valley in 1864.* New York, 1883.

PORTER, DAVID DIXON, Admiral. *Incidents & Anecdotes of the Civil
War.* New York, 1886.

PORTER, MARY H. *Eliza Chappell Porter: A Memoir.* Chicago, 1892.

POWERS, ELVIRA. *Hospital Pencillings.* Boston, 1886.

PRATT, FLETCHER. *Ordeal by Fire.* New York, 1935.

The Private Journal of a Journey from Boston to New York. Albany,
N. Y., 1863.

REED, WILLIAM HOWELL. *Hospital Life in the Army of the Potomac.*
Boston, 1866.

RHODES, JAMES FORD. *A History of the Civil War.* New York, 1917.

RICHARDS, CAROLINE COWLES. *Village Life in America 1852-1872.* New
York, 1908.

RICHARDSON, ALBERT D. *The Secret Service: The Field, the Dungeon
and Escape.* Philadelphia, 1865.

RIDLEY, B. L. *Battles and Sketches of the Army of the Tennessee.*
Mexico, Mo., 1906.

ROBERTSON, JOHN, Adjutant General. *Michigan and the War.* Lansing,
Mich., 1882.

ROBINSON, VICTOR, M.D. *White Caps.* New York, 1946.

ROSS, ISHBEL. *Angel of the Battlefield, the Life of Clara Barton.* New
York, 1956.

RUSSELL, WILLIAM HOWARD. *My Diary North and South.* New York,
1954.

SANDBURG, CARL. *Storm Over the Land.* New York, 1939, 1942.

SARMIENTO, F. L. *Pauline Cushman, Union Spy and Scout.* New York,
1865.

SCHAPPES, MORRIS U. (Ed.). *Documentary History of the Jews in the
United States.* New York, 1950.

SCOTT, MARY WINGFIELD. *Houses of Old Richmond.* Richmond, 1941.

SELLEW, GLADYS and C. J. NUESSE. *History of Nursing.* St. Louis, Mis-
souri, 1946.

SEGERIST, HENRY E., M.D. *American Medicine.* New York, 1934. Ch. VII, "Hospitals and Nursing," p. 204.

SHERIDAN, P. H. *Personal Memoirs.* New York, 1888, 2 vols.

SIGAUD, LOUIS. *Belle Boyd, Confederate Spy.* Richmond, 1945.

SMITH, ADELAIDE W. *Reminiscences of an Army Nurse During the Civil War.* New York, 1911.

SOUDER, MRS. EDMUND A. *Leaves from the Battlefield of Gettysburg.* Letters from a Field Hospital and National Poems. Philadelphia, 1864.

STEARS, AMANDA AKINS. *The Lady Nurse of Ward E.* New York, 1909.

STERN, MADELEINE, "Civil War Nurse." In *Americana,* XXXVII, pp. 296-325. Somerville, N. J., 1943.

STINE, J. H. *History of the Army of the Potomac.* Washington, 1893.

TIFFANY, FRANCIS. *Life of Dorothea Lynde Dix.* Boston and New York, 1891.

TRENCHARD, C. EDWARD. *The Services and Sacrifices of the Daughters of the Republic During the Civil War.* New York, 1912.

TURNER, GEORGE D. *Victory Rode the Rails: The Strategic Place of the Railroads in the Civil War.* Indianapolis, 1953.

VANDIVER, FRANK. *Mighty Stonewall.* New York, 1957.

WAYLAND, JOHN W. *Twenty-five Chapters on the Shenandoah Valley.* Section: *A Concise History of the Civil War in the Valley.* 1957.

WELCH, SPENCER GLASGOW. *A Confederate Surgeon's Letters to His Wife.* Georgia, 1954.

WELLES, GIDEON. *Diary.* With an Introduction by John T. Morse, Jr. Boston and New York, 1911. Vol. II.

WERTER, DIXON. *The Saga of American Society, 1607-1937.* New York, 1937.

WHEELOCK, JULIA S. *The Boys in White.* New York, 1870.

WHITMAN, WALT. *The Wound Dresser: A Series of Letters Written From the Hospitals in Washington, During the War of the Rebellion.* Edited by R. M. Bucke. Boston, 1898.

WILLIAMS, BLANCHE COLTON. *Clara Barton.* Philadelphia, 1941.

WILSON, JAMES HARRISON, Major General. *Under the Old Flag.* New York, 1912. Vol. II.

WITTEMYER, MRS. ANNIE T. *Under the Guns. A Woman's Reminiscences of the Civil War.* Boston, 1895.

WITTEMYER, ANNIE T. *U.S. Christian Commission: A Collection of Recipes, 1864.* Rare Book Room, Library of Congress, Washington, D.C.

WOLFE, SIMON. *The American Jew as Patriot, Soldier and Citizen.* New York, 1893.

WOOLSEY, ABBY HOWLAND. *Handbook for Hospitals.* New York, 1895, 3d ed. Published originally by State Charities Aid Association, No. 32, 1877. Second ed., revised, 1883.

WOOLSEY, JANE STUART. *Hospital Days.* New York, 1870.

WORMELEY, KATHARINE PRESCOTT. *The Other Side of the War.* Boston, 1889.

WORMELEY, KATHARINE PRESCOTT. *The U.S. Sanitary Commission, A Sketch of Its Purposes and Its Work.* Boston, 1863.

WORTHINGTON, C. G. *The Woman in Battle.* Hartford, 1876.

WRIGHT, RICHARDSON. *Forgotten Ladies.* Philadelphia, 1928.

MAGAZINES, PERIODICALS, PAMPHLETS

Annals of Iowa, IV, No. 1 (April, 1899), 3d Series; IV, No. 6 (July, 1900), 3d Series, pp. 277-288. The Hon. George D. Perkins, *Sioux City Journal,* "Annie T. Wittemyer."

Century Illustrated Monthly Magazine, XXVI (July, 1883), "Washington on the Eve of the War"; LXV, No. 1 (November, 1902), "The New York Police Court."

Davis and Elkins Historical Magazine, II (March, May, 1949). "Pryce Lewis, Spy for the Union."

Demorest's Illustrated New York Monthly, April, 1884. Article by Henry W. Bellows, D.D.

Fort Pillow Massacre. Report No. 65. 38th Congress, First Session. *Harper's Weekly,* 1861-1865.

House Report No. 849, 48th Congress, 1st Session, 1883-84. July 5, 1884. Report of the Committee on Invalid Pensions: Sarah E. E. Seelye, alias Franklin Thompson.

The Iowa Journal of History and Politics, October, 1931.

Keifer, J. Warren, Brevet Major General of Volunteers. *Official Reports While Serving in the Armies of the Potomac and Shenandoah.* Springfield, Ohio, 1866.

"The Last Battle of the War." Pamphlet, N.Y. Public Library, pp. 69-72.

Magazine of American History, XII (July, 1884), "Washington in 1861."

Maryland Historical Magazine, September, 1946. Louis Sigaud, "Mrs. Greenhow and the Rebel Spy Ring."

NATIONAL WOMAN'S RELIEF CORPS. "Activities and Services of the National Woman's Relief Corps." Permanent National Headquarters, Springfield, Ill. Revised, 1943.

New Brunswick Museum, Dept. of Canadian History, St. John, N. B., Canada. George MacBeath, Curator, "Report on Sarah Emma Edmonds," 1956.

Pearson's Magazine, William Gilmore Beymar, "The Woman Who Was a Man." June, 1913.

"Personal Narratives of the Rebellion," No. 2, 2nd Series.

Record of Services of Michigan Volunteers in the Civil War. Vol. E, "Second Infantry," p. 170, by the Adjutant General of Michigan.

"Record of the U.S. Medical Department" (pamphlet). From a preliminary inventory of the Surgeon's Office (Record Group 112) compiled by Elizabeth Bethel, National Archives and Record Service, Washington, 1952.

SCHNEIDER, COLONEL FREDERICK, *The Story of a Remarkable Life.* A Sketch from the Civil War. A paper read June 13, 1900, before a Joint public meeting of Charles T. Foster Post No. 42 and W.R.C. No. 7 of G.A.R., Lansing, Michigan, by Colonel Frederick Schneider, post commander of Charles T. Foster Post and last Commander of the 2nd Michigan Volunteer Infantry, Lansing, Michigan, courtesy of Michigan Historical Commission.

Spies, List of References on, Library of Congress, Division of Bibliography, 1954.

Spirit of the Fair, A Daily Bulletin, N.Y., April 5-23, 1864. April 5, p. 4; April 8, p. 41; April 12, p. 47; April 18, p. 137.

State Charities Aid Association, No. 11, "A Century of Nursing," by member of Hospital Committee (Abby Howland Woolsey). New York, 1876.

Transactions of the American Medical Association, XX (1869), p. 161, "Report of the Committee on the Training of Nurses."

United States Sanitary Commission, Archives of. Mss. Division, New York Public Library.

United States Sanitary Commission, Documents, 1861, No. 31.

1. Report of a committee of associate medical members of the Sanitary Commission on subject of amputations.

2. Pp. 5-67. Condensed essays and handbooks, conclusions of the highest medical authorities on medical and surgical questions likely to present themselves to surgeons in the field.

3. Report on yellow fever.

With Sheridan's Cavalry from the Rapidan to Appomattox. A. D. Rockwell, M.D. A paper read before the New York Commandery of the Loyal Legion. New York, 1907.

United States Sanitary Commission, Pamphlet No. 1, Woman's Relief Association of Brooklyn, N.Y.

United States Sanitary Commission, Pamphlet No. 13, To the Loyal Women of America, New York Public Library, American History Room.

United States Sanitary Commission, report of the Field Relief Service with the Armies of the Potomac, Georgia, and Tennessee in the Department of Washington, May and June, 1865.
United Sanitary Commission Bulletin, Vol. 1, Nos. 1-12, p. 87.
United States Sanitary Commission Bulletin, Vol. 2, Nos. 2, 9, 13-24, pp. 449, 495, 705-9, 724, 741.
United States Sanitary Commission. No. 73, Document 14-83.
United States Sanitary Commission Bulletin, Oct., 1864, pp. 844, 893-99, 901, 930, 983-84.
United States Sanitary Commission Bulletin, No. 35, Philadelphia, April 1, 1865. "The Battle Above the Clouds," pp. 1089-90.
"The United States Sanitary Commission," by Henry Whitney Bellows, D.D. Reprinted from Johnson's Universal Encyclopedia for private distribution. New York, 1878.
War of the Rebellion, Official Records, Union and Confederate Armies. Series I, vols. 3, 4, 7, 10, 23, 31, 52.
Series II, vols. 2, 4, 5.
Series IV, vol. 2.
WOOLSEY, GEORGEANNA M. "Three Weeks at Gettysburg." New York, 1863, 24 pp.

NEWSPAPERS

The Baltimore Sunday Express, April 27, 1884, Henry W. Bellows, D.D., "Lookout Mountain."
The Bangor Whig and Courier, "An American Heroine," Washington, January 20, 1867(?).
The Detroit Free Press, "Annie Etheridge." October 30, 1881, p. 9, col. 7.
The Detroit Tribune, "Annie Etheridge," June 29, 1886, p. 1, col. 5.
Frank Leslie's Illustrated Newspaper, 1861-1865.
The Houston Daily Post, September 7, 1898, June 2, 1901, "Sarah E. E. Seelye." *Harper's Weekly*, 1861-1865.
The Peoria Transcript, April 22, 1862, p. 1. col. 3, "An Unprecedented Military Appointment"; May 19, 1862, p. 1, col. 3, "Major Belle Reynolds"; May 22, 1862, p. 1, col. 3, "Mrs. Major Belle Reynolds Again—An Unexpected Family Difficulty."
[Photostats of articles obtained through the Peoria Public Library of *The Peoria Daily Transcript* for June 19, 1863, p. 3, col. 3, stated that Mrs. Reynolds was a member of the Women's National League of Peoria. The *Transcript* for November 22, 1859, states that she

was on a committee for entertainment for the benefit of the poor. Frank R. Chase, Assistant, Reference Section, Peoria Public Library.]
The Russell Record, Russell, Kansas, Monday, May 28, 1956, "Mother Bickerdyke Immortalized in Stone by Russell Sculptor."
The State Republican, Lansing, Michigan, June 19 and June 26, 1900, "Sarah Emma Edmonds Seelye; the Female Soldier. . . ." Typescript given by Michigan Historical Commission, January 31, 1958, to the author.

MICROFILM

Recl 4. U.S. Sanitary Commission Papers, N.Y. Archives. Standing Comm., 636-641. New York Public Library Mss. Division.
Reel 6. Woman's Central Relief Association, 667-669, 673-675; Letter Press Copies, 667; Woman's Central Relief Association, May 9, 1861-April 10, 1865. Washington Archives, 727, 728, 730. Condensed Historical Material, 990.
Reel 7. U.S. Sanitary Commission Papers, Woman's Central Relief Association, 654-655; N.Y. Archives, Woman's Central Relief Assn., letters, etc.
Reel 9. U.S. Sanitary Commission Papers, Z-160; California Archives; New England; Philadelphia Agency, 570-574, 590-593; New York Archives, 636.

LETTERS AND ORIGINAL MANUSCRIPTS

BARTON, CLARA. *Diary*. Read in manuscript in Mss. Division, Library of Congress, Washington, D.C.
BARTON, CLARA. *Papers*. No. 2-7-A Diaries 1849-68 AC.10,337 containing letters to her father; to B. B. Vassall, Esq., Office, *Worcester Times*, Worcester, Mass.; to B. B. Vassall, 4th Lt., DeWitt Guards; to B. W. Childs, Oxford, Mass.
BUTLER, BENJAMIN F. *Personal Papers*, Box Mar. 21-31, 1864 Mss. Division, Library of Congress, Washington, D.C.
CAMERON, SIMON. *Personal Papers*, Boxes 10, 11, 12, 13. Mss. Division, Library of Congress, Washington, D.C.
DIX, DOROTHEA LYNDE. *Her letters During the War* (unpublished). Mss. Division, New York Historical Society.

DUNN, GERTRUDE. *Diary*. Mss. Division, New York Public Library. "Saw Lincoln shot. . . ."

DUNSTAN, CAROLINE. *Diary*. Mss. Division, New York Public Library.

HAWLEY, HARRIET FOOTE. *Letters* by Mrs. Joseph R. (Harriet Foote) Hawley, 1864. A letter from Mrs. Harriet Foote Hawley to her cousin Belle, Mss. Division, Library of Congress, Washington, D.C.

LAY, JULIA HANNAH HARTNESS. *Diary*. Mss. Division, New York Public Library.

SCHUYLER, LOUISA LEE. *Letters* to Angelina Post, born 1803, daughter of Jotham Wm. Post, M.D., who married in 1869 Caspar Wistar Hodge, D.D. Gift of their daughter, Miss S. Madeline Hodge. New York Historical Society, Mss. Room.

WITTEMYER, ANNIE T. *The War Correspondence of Annie Wittemyer*. State Historical Department, Des Moines, Iowa, 1931.

WOOLSEY, SARAH CHAUNCEY. *Letters*, originals in The Yale University Library.

Index